Chris Turner

Contract Law

Hodder & Stoughton

A MEMBER OF THE HODDER HEADLINE GROUP

Orders: please contact Bookpoint Ltd, 130 Milton Park, Abingdon, Oxon OX14 4SB. Telephone: (44) 01235 827720.
Fax: (44) 01235 400454. Lines are open from 9.00–6.00, Monday to Saturday, with a 24 hour message answering service.
Email address: orders@bookpoint.co.uk

British Library Cataloguing in Publication Data
A catalogue record for this title is available from the British Library

ISBN 0 340 86959 3

First Published 2003
Impression number   10 9 8 7 6 5 4 3 2 1
Year   2008 2007 2006 2005 2004 2003

Typeset by Servis Filmsetting Ltd, Manchester.
Printed in Great Britain for Hodder & Stoughton Educational, a division of Hodder Headline Plc, 338 Euston Road, London NW1 3BH
by Martins the Printers, Berwick upon Tweed.

CONTENTS

Chapter 1 The origins and character of contract law

Chapter 2 Principles of formation: offer and acceptance

Chapter 3 Principles of formation: consideration

Chapter 4 Principles of formation: intention to create legal relations

Chapter 5 Formalities and speciality contracts

Chapter 6 Third-party rights

PREFACE

This book is aimed primarily at students on A Level Law courses, of whatever examining board, but there is no reason why it should not be used by any first-time student of contract law.

The book is obviously a companion to the very successful textbooks on *The English Legal System* by Jacqui Martin and on *Criminal Law* by Diana Roe and to my own *Tort Law*.

The book is in effect the second edition of the tort aspects of 'Contract Law and Tort'. Changes to the structure of A Level courses following Curriculum 2000, and the encouraging increase in the numbers of candidates entering A Level Law courses, make it advisable to introduce a separate text for both the law of contract, and for the law of torts. Sections from the original book have been separated into chapters and sections that more adequately represent a contract law syllabus. It also contains all necessary updates from the first edition.

Contract law is mostly a common law subject although some areas have been subject to some statutory intervention, particularly in areas of consumer protection. As a result, much of the book is devoted to cases and case notes, and these are separated out in the text for easy reference.

Since the book is also intended to be a practical learning resource rather than a prose-heavy text, each section of the book contains 'activities' of different types. These include 'self-assessment questions', some of which are mere comprehension exercises, while others are designed to be more thought-provoking. A variety of other activities, such as quick quizzes, multiple choice tests, case tests etc., are also included to encourage maximum interaction.

Each section of the book also contains a Key Fact chart summarising the most important points contained in the section, and these can also act as a revision aid. Wherever they would meaningfully add to the text and aid learning, I have also included diagrams or flow charts.

Many chapters also contain sections entitled 'Points for discussion' or 'Comment'. These occur where there are controversial points that are often the subject of essay titles in examinations.

Finally, a number of chapters also contain a brief explanation of how to attempt either an essay or a problem question on the area.

One new inclusion is the final chapter dealing with the synoptic element of both OCR and AQA specifications.

Once again, I hope that you will gain as much enjoyment in reading about contract law and answering the various questions in the book as I have had in writing it, and that you gain much enjoyment and interest from your study of the law.

The law is stated as I believe it to be on 1st January 2003.

TABLE OF STATUTES AND OTHER INSTRUMENTS

Acts of Parliament

TABLE OF CASES

LIST OF FIGURES

ACKNOWLEDGEMENTS

AQA examination questions are reproduced by permission of the Assessment and Qualifications Alliance. OCR examination questions are reproduced with the kind permission of the Oxford, Cambridge and RSA awarding body.

Chapter 1

THE ORIGINS AND CHARACTER OF CONTRACT LAW

1.1 The development of a law of contract

Much of the modern law of contract law developed in the 19th century and derives from the *laissez-faire* principles of economics that were the hallmark of the Industrial Revolution.

Nevertheless, the origins of contract law are much more ancient than that and are to be found in the early common law of the Middle Ages. Society at that time was preoccupied with land ownership and interests in land. As a result, the law of that time was also mainly concerned with property rights.

The distinction that the law drew in terms of identifying the enforceability of rights was between formal agreements and informal ones. A formal agreement was one made in writing and which was authenticated by the practice of 'sealing'. This is the origin of the deed which was the method accepted for transfer of land and interests in land up to 1989, when the requirement to complete the document by the process of sealing was relaxed in favour of the already common practice of witnessing the document.

Two principal types of **formal** agreement, required to be under seal to be enforceable, developed during the 12th century.
- A **covenant** – such an agreement was usually to do something, for example an agreement to build a house. The available remedy that developed in relation to such agreements was specific performance.
- A **formal debt** – this was again an agreement under seal, but to pay a sum of money. This agreement was actionable as an 'obligation' and the available remedy was the payment of the debt.

Informal agreements also gradually gained the recognition of the law. These became known as 'parol' agreements following the simple meaning of the word at the time: 'by word of honour'. The clear problem with informal agreements was the availability of proof of their actual existence in order to be able to enforce their provisions.

Two particular actions developed for informal agreements:
- An **action for debt** – this was usually an oral agreement for the sale of the goods, and the remedy sought was usually the price of the goods.
- **Detinue** – this was a claim in respect of a chattel due to the person bringing the action, for instance for delivery of a horse or other livestock.

The more modern law of contract begins with the law of '*assumpsit*' in the 14th century. This had its origins in the tort of trespass, and was an action in respect of the breach of an informal promise. The *assumpsit* was the undertaking to carry out the promise.

Moving even further forward in time, one of the most essential requirements of modern contract law, the doctrine of consideration, was also established. The **consideration** was the reason for the promise being given, and was based on the assumption that nobody does anything for nothing.

1.2 The character of modern contracts

It is common for non-lawyers to assume that a contract is an official agreement of some kind that is written down, and probably prepared by a lawyer. This, of course, is not the case. We all make many contracts every day, even though we rarely put them in writing or contemplate the consequences of making them.

For instance, this morning I had to go to Birmingham. I parked my car in the multi-storey car park at Wolverhampton station, taking the ticket from the machine at the entrance. Inside the station I bought a newspaper. On the train I bought a cup of coffee and a slice of cake.

There is nothing exceptional about any of these events. I gave no thought to contract law in relation to any one of them, but I was making a contract in every case.

What, then, if, on opening the newspaper, I found that only the cover pages were printed on? How about if I bit into my cake to find a piece of finger inside it? Finally, how would I feel on returning from Birmingham if I found my car stolen or crashed into? In all these instances I would want at least my money back, and probably some other form of remedy. At that point I would be very eager to know about the contractual nature of the arrangements I had made.

What distinguishes a contract in the modern day, then, is not whether it is in writing or not (as may have been absolutely critical in former times) but that it is an agreement made between two parties, by which they are both bound, and which if necessary can be enforced in the courts.

It can be in written form, but most often it will be made orally, and can even be made by conduct, as is often the case in auctions. Such contracts are called **simple** contracts.

Some contracts, because of their nature, have to be in writing or evidenced in writing. These contracts we call **speciality** contracts, and the most common is a contract for the transfer of land, but these are beyond the scope of this book.

A contract is essentially a commercial agreement, an agreement between two parties which is enforceable in law. It is based on the promises that two parties make to each other. However, while the law rightly protects many of the promises that we make to one another, not all promises are contractual. For instance, a beneficiary under a will has in effect been promised that inheritance and has a legal right to receive it. The will is not, however, covered by contract law. The heir has promised nothing in return for the inheritance.

A contract can alternatively be called a **bargain**. One party makes a promise in return for the promise of the other and the promises are mutually enforceable because of the price that one party has paid for the promise of the other.

Many of the rules of contract law came about in the 19th century. At that time people believed very much in the idea that there was freedom of contract. This is a nice idea, that we are all free to make whatever contracts we want, on whatever terms we want.

It does not, of course, bear much relationship with reality. Commonly, the two parties to a contract have unequal bargaining strength. A prospective employee at interview is rarely telling the prospective employer what conditions (s)he is prepared to work for, but is trying to impress in order to get the job.

Consumers too, even though they may have the choice where to buy from, will rarely negotiate the terms of the transaction they are making. More often than not, in the present day, contracts with businesses will be done on the latter's 'standard forms'.

As a result of this, Parliament in the 20th century has produced many laws inserting, or implying, terms into contracts which the parties themselves have not chosen but by which they both are bound.

So the notion of freedom of contract is not as straightforward as it seems, and a party to a contract has to be aware of the numerous contractual obligations by which (s)he will be bound other than those which (s)he has personally negotiated.

1.3 The reasons why contracts are enforced

As we have seen, then, a contract is an enforceable agreement between two parties. The rules regarding enforceability of agreements obviously grew out of the need for certainty in relationships, whether between businesses or between private individuals. We can none of us safely conduct ourselves without knowing that we are able to rely on arrangements that we have made.

The enforceability of contracts is based on three significant factors:
- An agreement made between two parties creates legitimate expectations in both that the terms of the arrangement will be carried out and that they will receive whatever benefit that is expected from the agreement.
- Parties will commonly risk expenditure or do work in reliance on a promise that a particular agreement will be carried out.
- It is simply unfair that if one party is ready to perform, or indeed has performed, their part of the bargain, that the other party should escape or avoid his/her obligations without some means of redress for the injured party.

1.4 Contracts compared with other areas of law

Sometimes both the law of contract and the law of torts are seen as a general law of 'obligations'. Certainly, both branches of the law compensate victims for the harm done to them. Both branches of the law are also ultimately based on duties owed by one party to another.

The traditional distinction between the two is the character of the duty owed. In the case of torts, specific duties are imposed by law and apply to everyone. In contract law, the duties are imposed by the parties themselves and only operate to the extent agreed upon before the contract was formed. Similarly, in the case of tort the duty is usually owed generally to all persons likely to be affected by the tort. In contract law, on the other hand, the duty is only to the other party to the contract.

Nevertheless, the distinction is not always so clear and there are many complications and overlaps. In the law of contract, many duties are now imposed on parties by statute and as a result of European law irrespective of the actual wishes of the parties to the contract. This has been particularly the case in the area of consumer contracts. In the law of torts, in those situations where the law does allow recovery for a pure economic loss the distinction between the two again is blurred somewhat.

There can be overlap too in areas such as product liability where there can be a claim for negligence and also for breach of implied statutory conditions under the contract. In such circumstances a choice is sometimes made whether to sue a manufacturer in tort or a supplier under contract law.

Similar complications have arisen in the field of medicine. Normally we would expect actions legal actions to be bought in medical negligence in tort. However, where a patient has taken advantage of private medicine, the rules of contract law can be invoked if they are may have a more satisfactory answer, if, for instance, the contractual duty is higher than the duty in tort.

Difficulties can also arise because of the doctrine of privity in contract law and the exceptions to it, although legislation has removed some of the hardships here. Though the absence of a contractual relationship again may not prevent an action being bought for a breach of a duty in tort if such a duty exists.

Activity

Self-assessment questions

1 How were the courts originally certain that there was an enforceable contract?
2 What was the difference between 'covenants' and 'debts'?
3 What was 'detinue'?
4 What is '*assumpsit*' and what does it have in common with modern contract law?
5 What are the major features of modern contracts?
6 Why are many of the original rules of contract law impractical in modern times?
7 What are the main reasons why contracts are enforced?
8 What features does contract law have in common with tort?
9 What are the major differences?

Chapter 2

PRINCIPLES OF FORMATION: OFFER AND ACCEPTANCE

2.1 The character of agreement

We know from our introduction to the law of contract that the law concerns 'bargains' that are made between parties. The major significance of the word 'bargain' is that it involves an agreement that is binding on both parties. In contract law, then, it is insufficient merely that an agreement exists between two parties but rather that it involves that specific type of agreement which is enforceable by both parties.

A contract is completed when both sides honour an agreement by carrying out their particular side of the bargain. It is a breach of contract when a party fails to do so.

However, because of the special nature of contractual agreements, we cannot identify a breach of contract where we may feel that we have not got what we paid for or 'bargained' for, without first showing that the agreement was indeed a contract.

So our first objective in a contract case may be to prove that there **is** actually a contract in existence. We can tell if it is a contract because to be so it must have been formed according to certain standard rules.

It will only be a contract where there is:

An **agreement** – which is based on mutuality; **consideration** – which means that both sides are bound to give something to each other; and **intention** – to be legally bound by the terms of the agreement. These elements are considered in these next three chapters.

A contractual agreement is said to exist when a valid **offer** is followed by a valid **acceptance**. This seems straightforward enough, and where one person offers to sell something to another party who accepts the price and agrees to buy, then there is no difficulty.

In practice, though, negotiations can be much more complex than this and on the other hand agreements can be identified which appear to have no formal negotiating steps, purchasing goods from a vending machine being a classic example of that.

In **Butler Machine Tool Co. v Ex-Cell-O Corporation (1979)** Lord Denning MR suggested that judges should decide whether a contract existed by examining the evidence in its totality rather than trying to apply a strict test of offer and acceptance. Even if other judges sympathised with the logic of this, they would not publicly admit it, so we still have to return to the traditional test of offer and acceptance.

2.2 The nature of offers

2.2.1 Distinguishing offer from invitation to treat

A person making an offer is called an **offeror**. The person to whom the offer is made, and who thus can accept it is called the **offeree**.

The offer is a statement of intent by the offeror to be legally bound by the terms of the offer if it is accepted, and the contract exists once acceptance has taken place.

If the offer is plainly stated e.g. 'Would you like to buy my car for £8,000?', there is no problem. The question is easily identified as an offer, and you only have to say 'Yes, I will buy your car for £8,000' for there to be an easily identifiable acceptance too.

It is not always the case, however, that the first stage in negotiations is an offer. Often the first step is an entirely passive state and is not therefore open to acceptance, e.g. a tin of beans sitting on a supermarket shelf. This is not an offer and is called an **invitation to treat**, in other words an invitation to the other party to make an offer, usually an offer to buy. The contract is then formed by the agreement to sell which is the acceptance in this case.

It can be illustrated in diagram form:

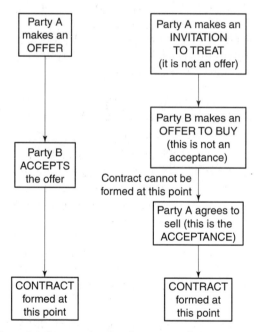

Figure 2.1 Diagram showing the point at which a contract is made in a standard offer and acceptance, and where there is firstly an invitation to treat.

2.2.2 Examples of invitation to treat

a) Goods displayed on shelves in a self-service shop

These are not an offer that is then accepted when the customer picks the goods from the shelves. They are an invitation to treat – an invitation to the buyer to make an offer to buy. This is done by the customer taking them to the cash desk where the contract is formed when the sale is agreed.

> ### Pharmaceutical Society of GB v Boots Cash Chemists Ltd (1953)
>
> Boots altered one of their shops to self-service. Under s18 Pharmacy and Poisons Act 1933 a registered pharmacist was required to be present at the sale of certain drugs and poisons. It was important to know where the contract was formed. CA held that the contract was formed when goods were presented at the cash desk where a pharmacist was present, not when taken from the shelf.

The rule preserves the freedom of contract of the shopkeeper and sensibly allows the shopkeeper to accept or refuse a sale. This might be particularly important where a child selects alcohol from shelves in an off-licence and tries to buy it.

b) Goods on display in a shop window

Again, there is no offer, only a display of the goods that the customer might go into the shop and offer to buy.

> ### Fisher v Bell (1961)
>
> A prosecution under the Offensive Weapons Act 1959 failed due to bad drafting of the Act. The offence was to offer for sale prohibited weapons. The shopkeeper displaying a flick knife in the window was not offering it for sale. It was a mere invitation to treat.

c) Goods or services advertised in a newspaper or magazine

Here, a contract will not be formed until the person seeing the advertisement has made an offer to buy, which has then been accepted.

Partridge v Crittenden (1968)

A prosecution for 'offering for sale' a wild bird under the Protection of Birds Act 1954 failed. The advertisement ('Bramblefinch cocks, bramblefinch hens, 25s each') was not an offer but an invitation to treat.

d) An invitation to council tenants to buy their property

Gibson v Manchester City Council (1979)

Gibson returned his completed application form when receiving an invitation to buy his house from the council. When there was a change of policy by the council, Gibson's action for breach of contract failed. His completed application was an offer to buy, not an acceptance of any offer by the council.

e) A mere statement of price

The mere fact that a party has indicated a price which (s)he would find acceptable does not make it an offer.

Harvey v Facey (1893)

Harvey wanted to buy Facey's farm and sent a telegram saying 'Will you sell me Bumper Hall Penn? Telegraph lowest price'. Facey's telegram replied 'Lowest price acceptable £900'. Harvey tried to accept this but could not. It was merely a statement of price, not an offer.

f) Lots at an auction

The rule in fact derives from auctions. The lot is the invitation to make a bid. Bidding is an offer to buy, and the acceptance is the fall of the auctioneer's hammer at which point the contract is formed. The contract is formed between the highest bidder and the owner of the goods. The auctioneer is merely acting on behalf of the owner of the goods.

British Car Auctions v Wright (1972)

A prosecution for offering to sell an unroadworthy vehicle failed. At the auction there was no offer to sell, only an invitation to bid.

The consequence of this is that there is an absolute entitlement to withdraw any lot prior to the fall of the auctioneer's hammer. This is no more than an example of the rule that an offer can be withdrawn any time prior to acceptance (see section 2.3: The rules of offer)

Harris v Nickerson (1873)

Here, Harris had attended the auction, hoping to buy certain furniture which was advertised as being in the sale in the catalogue of the auction. The auctioneer had withdrawn these items from the sale and Harris sued, arguing a breach of contract. The court held that the advertising of the goods in the catalogue was no more than an invitation to treat. Moreover, any contract could only be formed on the fall of the auctioneer's hammer when a bid was accepted.

The result may be different in an auction that is advertised as being 'without reserve'. This means that there is no minimum sale price that must be reached by the bidders before a sale can be concluded, so that the goods are sold to the highest bidder (see later).

2.2.3 Situations which are not invitation to treat

Sometimes, in situations that we would normally associate with invitation to treat, the circumstances involved or the nature of the words used mean that there has in fact been an offer rather than an invitation to treat. These include:

(i) Advertisements involving a unilateral offer

If the advertisement indicates a course of action in return for which the advertiser makes a promise to pay, then (s)he is bound by this promise.

Carlill v The Carbolic Smoke Ball Co. Ltd (1893)

The company advertised a patent medicine, the smoke ball, with the promise that if a purchaser used it correctly and still got flu, then the company would pay them £100. Mrs Carlill did get flu after using the smoke ball in the correct fashion. The court enforced her claim for the £100. The promise was an offer that could be accepted by anyone who used the smoke ball correctly and still got flu.

(ii) A statement of price where an offer is also intended

A mere statement of price is not binding, but if other factors indicate that an offer is included in the statement then it will be binding if it is accepted.

Biggs v Boyd Gibbins (1971)

In response to the offer of a lower price the claimant wrote 'For a quick sale I will accept £26,000'. The defendant replied 'I accept your offer'. The claimant then wrote 'I thank you for accepting my price of £26,000. My wife and I are both pleased that you are purchasing the property'. His first letter was an offer that the defendant had accepted.

(iii) Competitive tendering

Normally, an invitation to tender for the supply of goods or services is no more than an invitation to treat. For instance, a company wants its office painted. It invites tenders and various decorators will respond with different prices for the work. The company is free to choose any of the decorators, not necessarily the cheapest. If, however, the company has in its advertisement agreed that the work will go to the tender with the lowest price, then it is bound to give the work to the bidder with the lowest price.

Harvela Investments Ltd v Royal Trust Co. of Canada Ltd (1986)

The Trust Company had invited tenders from two interested parties for the purchase of some land. The sale would go to the party making the highest bid. The party making the lowest bid had tendered a price of $2,100,000 or $101,000 in excess of any other offer. When it was accepted and Harvela, the party making the higher bid, found out, they sued successfully. The wording of the invitation to tender made it an offer that could only be accepted by the highest bidder.

There may also be an obligation on the party inviting tenders to consider all tenders regardless of whether a tender is accepted.

Blackpool and Fylde Aero Club Ltd v Blackpool Borough Council (1990)

For many years, the aero club had held the concession to run pleasure flights from the council's airport. When the concession was due for renewal the council put it out to competitive tender, and invited tenders from other parties. All tenders were to be submitted in unmarked envelopes in a particular box by 12 noon on a specific date. The council stated that it would not be bound to accept any bid. The club placed its bid in the box at 11.00 a.m. but by accident the box was not emptied after this time and its bid was not therefore considered.

The concession was given to another group, R.R. Helicopters. When the council later discovered its mistake it at first decided to repeat the exercise but was threatened with legal action by R.R. Helicopters. The club claimed breach of a contract to consider all tenders delivered by the due time. Its claim was upheld. The court felt that there was an implied undertaking to operate by the rules that it had set, even though the invitation to tender for the concession was only an invitation to treat.

(iv) Auctions advertised as 'without reserve'

Traditionally, an auction might take two forms. The first includes a 'reserve price' (a minimum price acceptable to the seller) and in this case no sale can take place, and thus no contract is formed, unless the bidders reach this reserve price. See *McManus v Fortescue* (1907).

In the case of an auction held by reserve then there is only one possible outcome: the goods will become the property of the highest *bona fide* bidder. It has, however, been held *obiter*, that no contract of sale can materialise between the owner of the goods and the highest bidder where the auctioneer refuses the sale or for any reason fails to accept the bid of the highest *bona fide* bidder. In this instance it was said that a collateral contract is created between the highest *bona fide* bidder and the auctioneer himself, so that the auctioneer may then be sued for breach of contract. See *Warlow v Harrison (1859)*. This point has been examined more recently.

Barry v Heathcote Ball & Co. (Commercial Auctions) Ltd (2000)

Here, in an auction advertised as 'without reserve', the auctioneer withdrew two lots, machinery worth £14,251, from the auction. In doing so he refused bids of £200 for each machine made by the claimant and which were the highest bids. The auctioneer then sold them on privately at £750 each. The claimant bidder sued, arguing that the highest bid rule should

apply. The court, approving *Warlow v Harrison*, accepted the existence of a collateral contract between the bidder and the auctioneer and awarded the claimant £27,600 damages.

Activity

Quick quiz

Explain whether the following situations involve offers or mere invitations to treat:

1 A sign in a shop window reading:

> **SPECIAL OFFER**
> BAKED BEANS
> ONLY 6p PER TIN

2 My friend has an old sports car that I particularly like. When I ask him how much he would sell it for he replies: 'You could not buy a car like that for less than £20,000 these days.'

3 An advertisement in a local newspaper which reads:

> YOU MUST NOT MISS SUPERSTORES'
> SPECIAL OPENING BONANZA
> MICROWAVE OVENS RRP £199
> ONLY 99P
> TO OUR FIRST 10 CUSTOMERS

Activity

Quick quiz

Now do the same in a simpler form and suggest whether or not an offer exists in the following examples.

1 I tell you that I have a thousand copies of my new contract law text, the price of which is only £13.99.

2 My new contract law text is advertised in the college handbook at only £13.99.

3 I write you a letter in which I say 'Would you like a copy of my new contract law text book? It is only £13.99'.

2.3 The rules of offer

Once we know whether a party is making an offer, and is then intending to contract, we must be satisfied that the offer conforms to the rules to show whether it is a valid offer or not.

The offer must be communicated to the offeree

It is impossible to accept something of which you have no knowledge.

Taylor v Laird (1856)

Taylor gave up the captaincy of a ship and then worked his passage back to Britain as an ordinary crew member. His claim for wages failed. The ship owner had received no communication of Taylor's offer to work in that capacity.

An offer can be made to one person but it can also be made to the whole world

Anyone can then accept the offer who has had notice of it.

Carlill v The Carbolic Smoke Ball Co. (1893)

The company's claim that it had no contract with Mrs Carlill failed. It had made its offer generally and she had accepted by buying the smoke ball, using it and still getting flu.

So the offeree must have knowledge of the offer in order for it to be valid and enforceable

Inland Revenue Commissioners v Fry (2001)

The IRC claimed that Fry owed it £113,000. She sent a cheque for £10,000 to the IRC with a letter stating that the cheque was 'in full settlement' and that if presented for payment this would be acceptance of her offer. IRC procedure was for cashiers to bank cheques received before accompanying correspondence was then sent on to a caseworker. The caseworker here immediately phoned the defendant' to say that the £10,000 could be treated as part-payment or she could have the money back. Fry insisted that the Revenue was bound to accept the offer, having cashed the cheque. The court held that while an offeree could accept a unilateral offer which prescribed its manner of acceptance by acting in accordance with that manner, there had to be knowledge of the offer when the act was done. The IRC was actually ignorant of the offer here so there was no acceptance.

The terms of the offer must be certain

If the words of the offer are too vague then the parties might not really know what they are contracting for and should not then be bound.

Guthing v Lynn (1831)

When a horse was purchased a promise to pay £5 more 'if the horse is lucky' could not be an offer. It was too vague.

Activity

Quick quiz

In the following examples, consider whether the terms of the offer are certain enough for a contract to be formed if they are accepted.

Sukky agrees to sell an important book on contract law for:

1 a fair price
2 a price which will be fixed by Sukky's friend Dalvinder when he next sees him
3 a price that is half of the normal retail price
4 a price to be agreed between Sukky and myself at a later date.

It is possible to withdraw an offer, at any time before the offer is accepted

Routledge v Grant (1828)

Grant had offered his house for sale on the understanding that the offer would remain open for six weeks. When he took it off the market within the six weeks that was legitimate because there had been no acceptance.

If, however, the offeree paid money to the offeror to keep the offer open, then (s)he would be bound to do so.

The offeror must communicate the withdrawal of the offer to the offeree

Byrne v Van Tienhoven (1880)

On 1st October Van Tienhoven wrote to Byrne, offering to sell certain goods.

On 8th October he changed his mind and sent a letter withdrawing the offer.

On 11th October Byrne accepted the offer in a telegram.

On 15th October he confirmed this in writing.

On 20th October Byrne received Van Tienhoven's letter withdrawing the offer. It was invalid because it had not been received until after Byrne's acceptance.

This shows how important it is to keep a track of dates as well as other information during contractual negotiations.

Communication of withdrawal of the offer can be by a reliable third party

It need not be done personally but the third party must be a reliable source of information

Dickinson v Dodds (1876)

Dodds had offered to sell houses to Dickinson. When Berry notified Dickinson that Dodds had withdrawn the offer this was acceptable. Berry was shown to be a mutual acquaintance on whom both could rely.

A unilateral offer cannot be withdrawn while the offeree is performing

In a unilateral contract the offeree actually accepts by performing his/her side of the bargain (as in *Carlill*). It would clearly be unfair to prevent this once the other party had begun.

Errington v Errington & Woods (1952)

A father bought a house and mortgaged it in his own name. He promised his son and daughter-in-law that it would become theirs when they had paid off the mortgage. When the father died and other members of the family wanted possession of the house, the couple's action failed. The father's promise could not be withdrawn so long as the couple kept up the mortgage repayments, after which the house would be theirs.

2.4 Termination of offer

An offer can be terminated in a number of ways:

- It can be accepted, in which case there is a contract. (or indeed it could be refused or met with a counter-offer, in which case there is no contract).
- It can be properly withdrawn, as we have seen above.
- The time for acceptance can lapse.
- A reasonable time can have lapsed. (It would be rare that an offer could stay open indefinitely.)

Activity

Self-assessment questions

1 What is an offer?
2 What is the major difference between an offer and an invitation to treat?
3 What would happen if a customer in a supermarket took tins of beans from a shelf but changed her mind and discarded them before reaching the cash desk?
4 What would happen if I ordered goods advertised in a magazine and the seller wrote back to say that supplies were exhausted?
5 What makes a unilateral offer different to an invitation to treat?
6 Is it possible for an offer to be made to more than one person?
7 Why is it important to notify an offeree before withdrawing the offer?
8 Is it true to say that it is better for an offeree that negotiations prior to a contract are all carried out by letter, and if so why is that so?
9 What factors would you take into account in determining whether a reasonable time for an offer to stay open had lapsed?
10 If you find my lost dog and return it to me and later see an advertisement in the newspaper offering a reward for return of the dog, can you claim it?

Ramsgate Victoria Hotel Co. Ltd v Montefiore (1866)

Montefiore had offered to buy shares in June but the company only issued the shares in November. It was held that his offer to buy had lapsed.

- When one of the parties dies. Generally, this may operate in different ways depending on which party dies.
  - If the **offeree** dies then this will cause the offer to lapse and his/her representatives will be unable to accept on his/her behalf. See *Reynolds v Atherton* (1921).
  - If an **offeror** dies, however, (s)he may still be bound by an acceptance that is made in ignorance of the offeror's death. See *Bradbury v Morgan* (1862).
  - Although, if the **offeror** dies and the offeree **knows** of this then it is unlikely that (s)he could still claim to accept the offer.

2.5 The rules on acceptance

a) The acceptance must be communicated to the offeror

Just the same as for the offer, communication is required. Otherwise the unscrupulous might hold people to offers of which they were unaware. It goes without saying, then, that the acceptance must be a positive act, and that acceptance cannot be taken from silence.

Felthouse v Bindley (1863)

An uncle and nephew had negotiated over the sale of the nephew's horse. The uncle had said 'If I hear no more from you I shall consider the horse mine at £30:15s'. On sale of the nephew's stock, the auctioneer failed to withdraw the horse from the sale, as instructed by the nephew. The uncle tried to sue the auctioneer in tort but failed. He could not prove that the horse was his. The nephew had not actually accepted his offer to buy.

b) The acceptance can be in any form

It can be in writing, by words, or conduct. Of course, if the offeror requires it to be in a specific form then it must be in that form or it will be invalid.

Yates v Pulleyn (1975)

An option to purchase land was required to be exercised by notice in writing 'sent by registered or recorded delivery post'. When the option was sent by ordinary post only, it was invalid.

c) The 'postal rule'

Where use of the ordinary postal system is the normal, anticipated or agreed means of accepting then the contract is formed at the time the letter of acceptance is posted, not when it is received (the postal rule).

Adams v Lindsell (1818)

The rule began with this case where wool was offered for sale, an acceptance by post was requested and sent, but not received until long after the wool had been sold. The rule developed then from the possible injustices caused by delays in the postal system in its early days.

The rule applies even where the letter is never received, rather than merely delayed.

Household Fire Insurance v Grant (1879)

Grant made a written offer to purchase shares. Notification of acceptance was posted but never received. When the company went into liquidation, Grant's claim that he was not a shareholder and should not be liable for the value of the shares failed. He had become a shareholder, even though unaware of it.

It is possible to avoid the effects of the postal rule by stating in the offer that there will be no contract until the acceptance is actually received, in which case the contract is only complete on communication of the acceptance.

Holwell Securities v Hughes (1974)

An attempt to use the postal rule failed where the acceptance was required to be 'by notice in writing'. The fact that actual notice was required meant that the postal rule did not apply.

d) More modern methods of communication

In the case of more modern methods of communication, the picture is not so clear. The important factor seems to be how instantaneous the method is.

Brinkibon Ltd v Stahag Stahl (1983)

Previous case law had stated that an acceptance by telex, like telephone, was immediate enough communication to be effective straightaway. This case, however, concerned a telex received out of office hours. HL held that this could only be effective once the office was reopened.

Faxes and e-mail are even more modern forms of communication and the same problems and the same principles very often apply.

More recently, as a result of having to implement EU Directive 97/7, the distance selling directive, the Consumer Protection (Distance Selling) Regulations 2000 have been introduced.

- These apply to contracts for the sale of goods and provisions of services made by a variety of modern methods, e.g. telephone, fax, Internet shopping, mail order, e-mail and television shopping.
- The Regulations do not apply to transfers of land, building contracts, financial services, purchases from vending machines and auctions.
- Under Regulation 7, the seller/supplier is bound to provide the purchaser with certain minimum information, including the right to cancel the contract within seven days, description, price, arrangements for payment and delivery (and how long all of these remain open for) and the identity of the supplier.

Written confirmation must also be given, according to Regulation 8.

- Inevitably, if these rules are not complied with then the contract is not formed.

The Electronic Commerce Directive 2000/31 has an impact also on offer and acceptance by electronic means. Article 11 says that

'where [a purchaser] in accepting [a seller's] offer is required to give his consent through technological means, such as clicking on an icon, the contract is concluded when the recipient of the service has received from the service provider, electronically, an acknowledgement of receipt of the recipient's acceptance'.

So this would appear to clear up some of the problems formerly encountered in determining when such agreements are actually complete and a contract formed.

e) The acceptance must be unconditional

This is the so-called 'mirror image rule'. The acceptance must conform exactly with the terms of the offer or it is invalid and no contract will have been formed. It follows that any attempt to vary the terms of the offer is a counter-offer, terminating the original offer, which cannot then be accepted.

Hyde v Wrench (1840)

Wrench offered to sell his farm to Hyde for £1,000. Hyde rejected this and offered to pay £950, which Wrench rejected. When Hyde then tried to accept the original price and Wrench would not sell, Hyde's action failed. The original offer was no longer open for him to accept.

f) Mere enquiries do not count as rejection

A mere enquiry about the contract is not a counter-offer, as it does not reject the terms of the offer. This means that the offer is still open to acceptance by the offeree.

Stevenson v McLean (1880)

In a response to an offer to sell iron, the price and quantity were accepted but the offeree wished to know whether delivery could be staggered. Hearing nothing further, the claimant sent a letter of acceptance. He sued on discovering that the iron had been sold to a third party. The defendant's claim that there had been a counter-offer failed. It was not a rejection of the offer, merely an enquiry about it, and the offer was still open to acceptance.

─Activity─

Self-assessment questions

1 Why is it necessary for acceptance to 'mirror' the offer?
2 What are the different consequences of a counter-offer and a mere enquiry?
3 How does the judge decide whether something is a counter-offer or a mere enquiry?
4 In what way can a counter-offer operate to influence the formation of a contract?
5 In what possible situations might a silent response nevertheless lead on to a contractual relationship?
6 Is there any justification for the postal rule in the modern day?
7 What problems result from modern day rapid or instantaneous forms of communication and how have they been resolved?

2.6 Points for discussion

Problems associated with offer and acceptance

Many contracts in a modern commercial context are not formed as the result of one party straightforwardly accepting the simple offer of the other. This would be too restrictive and rigid. Businesses contract in a variety of ways and may be subject to disagreements, rejections, compromises and even threats before an agreement is ever reached. Sometimes people too will negotiate to try to get something different than what is first offered. We have already seen the effect that a counter-offer can have on the parties. When does a mere enquiry end and a counter-offer begin? That is a question that judges will often be called on to answer.

A further complication is the common use of 'standard forms' by businesses. These are used so that the business can be sure of always dealing on terms advantageous to it. This may not cause any problems in a consumer sale. When two businesses are contracting, however, it can prove a nightmare. This is the so-called 'battle of the forms'. One business makes an offer on its standard forms. The customer accepts on its. The two forms may be entirely contradictory. The question is which terms are taken as being the contractual ones in the case of a conflict between the two businesses.

The general rule in the modern day is to take the last counter-offer as having been accepted, and give effect to its terms in the contract.

Davies & Co. Ltd v William Old (1969)

Shop fitters, following their successful tender, contracted with the architects in a building contract to sub-contract to the builders. The builders, under instruction from the architects, issued an order for work to the shop fitters. They did this on their own standard form that included a clause that they would not pay for work until they themselves had been paid. When the shop fitters later sued for some work that had not been paid for; their action failed. The builders' standard form was a counter-offer that the shop fitters had accepted by carrying on with the work.

The problem is further compounded because often the services or goods are provided before any settled agreement is reached. In a later con-

flict the courts may find a contract does exist, provided there has been no major disagreement between the parties. Sometimes, however, this is impossible.

British Steel Corporation v Cleveland Bridge and Engineering Co. (1984)

Cleveland Bridge were sub-contracted to build the steel framework of a bank in Saudi Arabia. The work required four steel nodes that they asked BSC to manufacture. BSC wanted a disclaimer of liability for any loss caused by late delivery. The parties were never able to agree on this and so no written agreement was ever made. BSC, however, did make and deliver three of the nodes, but the last was delayed because of a strike. Cleveland Bridge refused to pay for the three nodes and claimed that BSC was in breach of contract for late delivery of the fourth. Because there was a total disagreement over a major term, the judge in the case found it impossible to recognise that a contract existed. He did order that BSC be paid for what they had supplied.

Activity

Self-assessment questions

1 Is there a satisfactory method of resolving a 'battle of forms'?
2 Is there any logic to the outcome of *Cleveland Bridge*?

KEY FACTS

- A contract is made where there is an agreement between two parties
- An agreement is a valid offer followed by a valid acceptance
- Offer must be distinguished from:
  - an 'invitation to treat' – *Pharmaceutical Society of GB v Boots*
  - and from a mere statement of price – *Harvey v Facey*
- Competitive tendering is different – *Harvela Investments v Royal Trust Co. of Canada*
- An offer must be communicated – *Taylor v Laird*
- The offeree must be aware of the existence of the offer – *IRC v Fry*
- An offer can be made to the whole world – *Carlill v Carbolic Smoke Ball Co.*
- The terms of the offer must be certain – *Guthing v Lynn*
- An offer can be withdrawn any time up to acceptance – *Routledge v Grant*
- The withdrawal must be communicated to the offeree – *Byrne v van Tienhoven*
- This can be by a reliable third party – *Dickinson v Dodds*
- Unilateral offers do not require acceptance, only performance – *Errington v Errington & Woods*
- An offer ends –
  - on acceptance
  - on proper withdrawal
  - on lapse of time
  - on death of one of the parties
- Acceptance must be communicated – *Felthouse v Bindley*
- If use of the post is the normal, anticipated method of acceptance the contract is formed on posting (the postal rule) – *Adams v Lindsell*
- This applies even if the acceptance is never received – *Household Fire Insurance v Grant*
- Acceptance must be unconditional – *Hyde v Wrench*
- But mere enquiries are not rejections of the offer – *Stevenson v McLean*
- Modern methods of communicating such as fax, e-mail and Internet cause problems in determining when a contract is formed
- Some of these problems have now been resolved by the E-commerce Directive and the Consumer Protection (Distance Selling) Regulations

Activity

Legal problem solving

There are four essential ingredients to answering problem questions:

- Firstly, you must be able to identify the important facts in the problem, the ones on which the answer may depend.
- Secondly, you will need to know and understand the law which is likely to apply in the situation.
- Thirdly, you will need to be able to apply the law to the facts.
- Fourthly, you will need to be able to draw conclusions from that process. This is particularly so where the problem asks you to 'advise'. If you are advising then your client is depending on you to say what to do in the circumstances.

Consider the following situation:

Problem

On 11th May Andy wrote to his friend Brian, offering to sell Brian his Cup Final ticket for £150. Brian posted a letter on 12th May which said:

'Dear Andy,
About the Cup Final tickets. £150 seems a bit on the steep side. I don't mind paying a bit over the odds but I'd be happier paying £100. Or could I pay you £100 now and the other £50 when I'm paid again at the end of the month?
Yours
Brian'

Later in the day, Brian wrote again to Andy:

'Dear Andy,
I've thought again about that ticket. I really want to go and it's cutting it a bit fine to get one from anywhere else. I'll pay you the £150.
Yours
Brian'

He posted the letter the same night.

Andy received Brian's first letter on the morning of 13th May and sold the ticket to another friend, Chris, at work that day.

When Andy returned home that evening, Brian's second letter had been delivered in the later post.

Brian missed the Cup Final and now seeks your advice.

Answering the question

The facts

Unlike in real life, it is common, when a tutor or an examiner makes up a problem, for nearly all of the facts to be relevant in some way. Even so, they may still need to be put into some logical order to connect them to the law you need to use.

Here the key facts seem to be:

1 Andy made an offer to Brian on 11th May of a Cup Final ticket for £150.
2 On 12th May Brian replied that he would prefer to pay £100 to £150, and alternatively asked if he might pay £150 in two instalments.
3 Later on 12th May, Brian sent a straightforward letter of acceptance.
4 Andy sold the ticket to Chris on 13th May, after receiving Brian's first letter.
5 Andy received the second letter later the same day.
6 All of these communications were carried out by post.

The law

We know, because the problem is all about whether Andy is obliged to sell the tickets to Brian or not, that it concerns formation, and particularly offer and acceptance, indeed the word 'offer' is used in the situation.

From this and other facts we can deduce what particular rules are important to solving the problem.

The appropriate law would appear to be:

- A contract can only be formed if there is an agreement, which is a valid offer followed by a valid acceptance.
- An offer must be communicated – *Taylor v Laird*.
- An offer can be withdrawn any time before acceptance – *Routledge v Grant*.

- But this must be communicated to the offeree – **Byrne v Van Tienhoven**.
- A contract is formed once the offer is accepted.
- The acceptance must be communicated to the offeree – **Felthouse v Bindley**.
- Where the post is the normal, anticipated method of accepting then the contract is formed when the letter is posted, not when it is received – **Adams v Lindsell**.
- A counter-offer is a rejection of the offer that is longer open to acceptance – **Hyde v Wrench**.
- But a mere enquiry has no such effect – **Stevenson v McLean**.

Applying law to fact

It is tempting to look at Brian's first letter and see it as a counter-offer. Of course, if we do that there is nothing left to answer about. This should be a pointer in itself, but really in any problem where a particular act can be seen as one thing or the other we need to look at both or all possibilities.

On the other hand, if we do not see it as a counter-offer it means Brian's second letter could be an acceptance ('I'll pay the £150'). We need to examine the first letter, then, to decide whether we think the first part is a definite rejection of the offer, and if not whether the second part is only an enquiry.

If we accept that it is, then our next real concern is that Andy has sold the ticket. Can he do this? Well, if there was a counter-offer he can, with no thought to Brian. If not, then he needs to tell Brian before he sells it.

The final part of the problem is whether the postal rule applies or not. Andy has not sold the ticket until after he receives Brian's first letter. If the letter has no contractual significance then Brian has in effect withdrawn the offer without informing Brian. Brian, on the other hand, has accepted in his second letter. If the postal rule applies, (which appears possible here because all the communications are by letter) then the acceptance takes place when the letter is posted, not when Andy receives it after he has sold the ticket. The contract is formed at the time the letter is posted and Andy would be in breach of contract by selling the ticket to Chris

Conclusions

It just remains now to make a judgement, based on our analysis above, as to whether to advise Brian to sue Andy or not.

Just as in real life, there might not be a definite or straightforward answer. The point is to reach a logical conclusion by using the law correctly.

Chapter 3

PRINCIPLES OF FORMATION: CONSIDERATION

3.1 The nature and purpose of consideration

As we have already seen, the law of contract deals with bargains. The rules of contract seek to differentiate between agreements where there is something to be gained by both parties, as is the case in a contract, and agreements which are purely gratuitous, as are gifts.

Originally, contracts were only recognised if contained in a deed. This was logical in the case of land transfers but otherwise inconvenient. The giving of 'consideration' by both sides became the traditional method of ensuring that other types of agreement were contractual. It was the *quid pro quo*, the proof that a bargain in fact existed, and if no consideration could be found then the agreement could not be enforced. The exception is an agreement made by deed.

3.2 Defining consideration

Originally, it proved impossible to give a simple, single definition of consideration, and the pragmatic view was often taken that it is was no more than the reason why the promise should be binding in law. Often, in any case, it was taken as being no more than a rule of evidence.

Many 19th-century cases looked for definitions based on benefit gained and detriment suffered. So, for instance, it was variously defined as:
- 'loss or inconvenience suffered by one party at the request of the other' – *Bunn v Guy* (1803)
- 'some detriment to the plaintiff or some benefit to the defendant' – *Thomas v Thomas* (1842)

A simple, early way of defining consideration came in *Currie v Misa* (1875) where it was described in terms of benefit and detriment: 'some right, interest, profit or benefit accruing to one party, or some forbearance, detriment, loss or responsibility given, suffered or undertaken by the other'. So, if I contract with you over my contract law textbook for £15, I am gaining the benefit of, the £15 but have the detriment of giving up the book. For you, it is the other way round.

A more sophisticated definition was later provided in *Dunlop v Selfridge* (1915), a case involving issues of both absence of consideration and lack of privity of contract by the party seeking to enforce contractual provisions. Here HL approved Sir Frederick Pollock's definition contained in his *Principles of Contract* that 'an act of forbearance or the promise thereof is the price for which the promise of the other is bought, and the promise thus given for value is enforceable'.

In fact, although the judges are saying that they will not in contract law enforce a promise which has not been paid for in some way, in modern cases they have been shown to be willing to see almost any promise made in a commercial context as contractual. Therefore consideration can be surprisingly little, and it can seem difficult to fit the theory to real situations.

3.3 Executory and executed consideration

Contract law would have no meaning unless it enforced promises as well as actual acts. **Executory** consideration is simply the exchange of promises to carry out acts or pass property at a later stage. If one party breaks their promise and fails to do what they are supposed to do under it, then they are in breach of contract and may be sued.

In unilateral contracts, however, the party making the unilateral offer is under no obligation until the other party performs (executes) their side of the bargain. This is called **executed** consideration, and a common example is a reward. We have already seen this principle in operation in Mrs Carlill's case.

3.4 The rules of consideration

a) Consideration need not be adequate but it must be sufficient

This sounds like complete nonsense because adequacy and sufficiency appear to be the same thing.

Adequacy

In fact, lawyers are using 'adequacy' in its everyday form, i.e. whether the parties are promising things of fairly equal value. Adequacy will be decided by the parties themselves. Freedom of contract would be badly affected if we could not decide ourselves whether we are satisfied with the bargain we have made. In certain circumstances, in any case, it may actually work to our ultimate advantage to make a bargain that on the face of it appears to be a bad one.

The courts, then, are not interested in whether there has been a good or a bad bargain made, only that a bargain exists, and they will seek to enforce the bargain that is actually agreed upon by the parties.

Thomas v Thomas (1842)

A man before his death expressed the wish that his wife be allowed to remain in the house, although this was not in his will. The executors carried out this wish and charged the widow a nominal ground rent of £1 per year. When they later tried to dispossess her, they failed. The moral obligation to carry out the man's wishes was not consideration but the payment of ground rent, however small and apparently inadequate, was.

Sufficiency

On the other hand, 'sufficiency' is used here as a legal term, and it means that what is promised must:

- be real
- be tangible
- and have some actual value.

White v Bluett (1853)

A son owed his father money on a promissory note. When the father died and his executors were trying to recover the money, the son tried to claim that he was not bound to pay. He claimed an agreement with his father that the debt would be forgotten in return for the son's promise not to complain about the distribution of the father's assets in his will. The son failed. The promise was too intangible to be consideration for the father's promise to forgo the debt.

What is real, tangible and of value is not always easily distinguishable.

Ward v Byham (1956)

A father of an illegitimate child promised the mother money towards its upkeep if she would keep the child 'well looked after and happy'. The mother would be doing nothing more than she was already bound by law to do in looking after the child. The court was prepared to enforce the agreement, however, since there is no obligation in law to keep a child happy, and the promise to do so was seen as good consideration.

In fact, even things of no apparent worth have been classed as amounting to valuable consideration.

Chappell v Nestlé Co. (1960)

Nestlé had offered a record, normally retailing at 6/8d (not quite 34p), for 1/6d (7.5p) plus three chocolate bar wrappers, to promote their chocolate. On receipt, the wrappers were thrown away. They were still held to be good consideration when the holders of the copyright of the record sued to prevent the promotion because they would receive substantially fewer royalties from it.

The accusation that if a court wishes to enforce a promise in a commercial context it will always find something to act as consideration seems to be proved when set against the reasoning in certain cases (see later, for instance: *Williams v Roffey Bros. & Nicholls Contractors Ltd* (1990)).

b) Past consideration is no consideration

This is another strange-sounding rule. It simply means that any consideration given cannot come before the agreement but must follow it.

It is a sensible rule in that it can prevent the unscrupulous from forcing people into contracts on the basis of providing goods or services which they have not ordered. Quite simply, in any case it is a promise that has not been agreed to by both parties in their contract.

The basic rule

It will usually occur where one party has done a voluntary act and is trying to enforce the other party's later promise to pay.

Re McArdle (1951)

A son and his wife lived in his mother's house that on her death would be inherited by her son and three other children. The son's wife paid for substantial repairs and improvements to the property. The mother then made her four children sign an agreement to reimburse the daughter-in-law out of her estate. When she died and the children refused to keep this promise, the daughter-in-law sued unsuccessfully. Her consideration for their promise was past. It came before they signed the agreement to repay her.

The exception to the rule

The rule will not always work justly, as the above case shows. In certain circumstances, the rule will not apply. Where one of the parties has requested a service, the law sensibly concludes that (s)he is prepared to pay for it. Even though that service is then carried out without any mention as to payment, or any apparent contractual agreement, a promise to pay coming after the service is performed will be enforced by the courts. This is known as 'the rule in *Lampleigh v Braithwaite*', from the case of that name.

Lampleigh v Braithwaite (1615)

Braithwaite was accused of killing a man and asked Lampleigh to get him a king's pardon. This Lampleigh achieved, at considerable expense to himself, and Braithwaite, in gratitude, promised to pay him £100, which he in fact never did. Lampleigh's claim that there was a contract succeeded. Because the service was requested, even though no price was mentioned at the time, it was clear that both parties would have contemplated a payment. The later promise to pay was clear evidence of this.

In diagram form, it works in the following way:

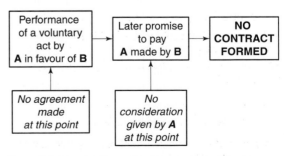

Figure 3.1 *Diagram illustrating the operation of the past consideration rule*

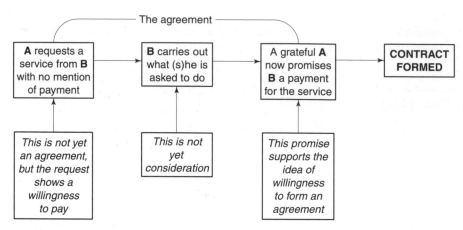

Figure 3.2 *Diagram illustrating the exception in* Lampleigh v Braithwaite *in operation*

Activity

Quick quiz

Consider the following events and decide whether an enforceable contract has been formed or whether consideration is only past.

1 While I was away on holiday in Goa it was very hot at home too. My neighbour Alison noticed that some of my flowers were dying and so she watered them every day, saving them. I was very pleased when I returned and I told her that I would give her £20 for all her trouble. In fact, I have not given Alison the money and she wonders if she is actually entitled to it.

2 Last month I had to go to an exam board meeting in Birmingham. My car would not start so I asked one of my students Neera, who has a car, if she would take me there. She quite happily agreed and gave me a lift there and even waited for the meeting to finish so that she could also give me a lift back. When we had returned I gave Neera the appropriate amount of money for the petrol that she had used, but I also promised her that I would buy her a new copy of a law text book costing £58.50p that she had been saving hard for. However, last week when Neera asked when she could have the money for the book I told her that I no longer intend to buy the book for her.

There are more modern examples of the operation of the exception in *Lampleigh v Braithwaite* operating in a commercial context.

Re Casey's Patent (1892)

Joint owners of a patent wrote to the claimant, agreeing to give him a one-third share of the patents in return for his services as manager of their patents. When the claimant wished to enforce this agreement they then claimed that the agreement was actually in respect of his past services and unenforceable for past consideration. He had in fact supplied no consideration following the agreement. Bowen LJ held that there was inevitably an implied promise that in managing the patents the claimant would be paid for his work. The later agreement to pay was therefore enforceable. It was an example of the exception in *Lampleigh v Braithwaite*.

c) The consideration must move from the promisee (the person to whom the promise is made)

Again, the rule sounds somewhat complex but in fact it simply means that a person cannot sue or indeed be sued under a contract unless (s)he has provided consideration. (This rule is interchangeable with the rule requiring privity of contract.)

Tweddle v Atkinson (1861)

Fathers of a young couple who intended to marry agreed in writing each to settle a sum of money on the couple. The young woman's father died before giving over the money and the young man then sued the executors to the estate when they refused to hand over the money. Even though he was named in the agreement, he failed because he had given no consideration for the agreement himself.

In diagram form, the situation can be expressed as follows:

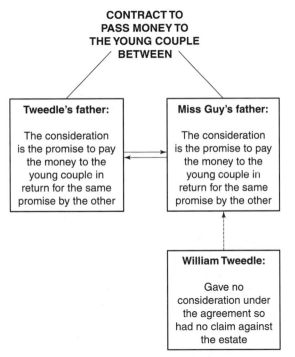

Figure 3.3 *Diagram using the agreement in* Tweddle v Atkinson *to illustrate the rule that consideration must move from the promisee*

d) Performing an existing duty cannot be the consideration for a new promise

The basic rule

Merely doing something that you are already bound to do can never be sufficient to amount to consideration. This applies firstly where the duty is a public one created by law.

Collins v Godefroy (1831)

A police officer was under a court order to attend and give evidence at a trial. It was important to the defendant that the officer attended so he promised to pay him a sum of money to ensure that he did so. The promise to pay was not contractual and unenforceable. There was no consideration for it.

It also applies where the duty has arisen under an existing contract.

Stilk v Myrick (1809)

Two members of a ship's crew deserted. The captain promised the remaining crew that they could share these two men's wages if they got the ship safely home. The promise was held not to be binding on the ship's owner. Sailors were bound by their contract to cope with the normal contingencies of the voyage, which could include these desertions, so there was no consideration for the captain's promise.

The exceptions to the rule

It will be consideration where what is given is more than could be expected from the duty. The extra element is the consideration for the new promise. Again, this will apply where a public duty is exceeded.

Glassbrook Bros v Glamorgan County Council (1925)

During a strike a pit owner asked for extra protection from the police and promised a payment in return. When the strike was over the pit owner refused to pay, claiming that the police were in any case bound to protect his pit. His argument failed. The police had provided more men than they would normally have done, so there was consideration for the promise.

The exception to the basic rule has also been seen even in apparently social arrangements, where it is arguable whether it can in reality be considered that there is also an intention to create legal relations.

Shadwell v Shadwell (1860)

At a time when an action for breach of promise to marry was still available in law, a young man became engaged to marry. His uncle wrote to him congratulating him, and promising to pay him £150 per year until he reached an income of £600 per year as a Chancery barrister. The young man did in fact marry and claimed the money from his uncle when it remained unpaid. The court held that even though the claimant was legally bound to marry, doing so was good consideration for the uncle's promise and the promise was enforceable.

Again, it also applies where the existing duty is a contractual one and a party has given more than was identified as necessary in the contract.

Hartley v Ponsonby (1857)

Involved similar facts to *Stilk v Myrick* but here only 19 members of a crew of 36 remained. A similar promise to pay more money to the remaining crew was enforceable because the reduction in numbers made the voyage much more dangerous. In agreeing to continue in these circumstances they had provided good consideration for the promise to pay them extra money.

The exception has been upheld even in situations where the consideration is not straightforwardly identifiable.

Scotson v Pegg (1861)

Claimants contracted with one party to deliver coal to them or to their order. The contracting party then sold the coal to the defendants and instructed the claimants to deliver the coal to a third party, the defendants. The defendants then agreed with the claimants that in consideration of the claimants delivering the coal to them the defendants would unload the coal at a fixed rate per day. The defendants failed to keep this arrangement and the claimants sued. The defendant argued that there was no consideration for the agreement with the claimants. The court rejected their argument and held that the performance of a duty owed to a third party could in fact provide consideration for a promise made by a third party.

It has also been accepted, albeit by the Privy Council, that a promise to perform an existing obligation made to a third party can be valid consideration for a fresh agreement.

Pao On v Lau Yiu Long (1980)

Both parties owned companies. The major asset in Pao's company was a building that Lau wished to purchase. An agreement was made whereby Lau's company would buy Pao's company in return for a large number of shares in Lau's company. To avoid the damage that sudden trading in this number of shares might cause, Lau inserted a clause, in the contract that Pao should retain 60% of the shares for at least one year. (We could call this Agreement 1.) Pao wanted a guarantee that the shares would not fall in value and a subsidiary agreement was made at the same time by which Lau would buy back 60% of the shares at $2.50 each. Pao later realised that this might benefit Lau more if the shares rose in value and therefore refused to carry out the contract unless the subsidiary arrangement was scrapped and replaced with a straightforward indemnity by Lau against a fall in the value of the shares. Lau could have sued at this point for breach of contract but, fearing a loss of public confidence in his company as a result, agreed to the new terms. (We could call this Agreement 2.) When the value of the shares did then fall, Lau refused to honour the agreement and Pao then sought to enforce the indemnity. Lao offered two defences: firstly that the second agreement, the agreement to indemnify Pao, was past consideration, and secondly that Pao had given no consideration for the second agreement since it only involved doing what he was bound to do under the first agreement (pass the company in return for the shares). In response to Lau's first defence the Privy Council applied the rule in *Lampleigh v Braithwaite*. Lau's demand that Pao should not sell 60% of the shares for one year was a request for a service that carried with it an implied promise to pay. This implied promise was later supported by the actual promise to indemnify Pao. The second of Lau's defences also failed. There was consideration. Pao, by continuing with the contract, was protecting the credibility and financial standing of Lau's company and the price payable in return for this was the indemnity.

The same reasoning can be used to find consideration by third parties to a contract where an agency relationship can be identified and where the agreement protects the commercial credibility of the contract.

New Zealand Shipping Co. Ltd v A.M. Satterthwaite & Co. Ltd (The Eurymedon) (1975)

This is a complex case demonstrating how far the courts are prepared to strain the simple meaning of 'consideration' in order to enforce an agreement that they believe must be enforced. Carriers contracted with the consignors of goods to ship drilling equipment. The carriers hired stevedores to unload the equipment, and these stevedores by their negligence caused substantial damage to it. A clause in the carriers' contract with the consignors contained a clause limiting their liability in the event of breach. The clause also identified that the protection offered by the limitation would extend to any servant or agent of the carriers. There were two questions for the court. Firstly, the court had to decide whether there was a contractual relationship between the stevedores and the consignors. If so, the court was then

required to determine whether the stevedores had provided any consideration for the promise by the consignors to be bound by the limitation clause. This was clearly questionable because the stevedores were doing nothing more than they were contractually bound to the carriers to do: unload the ship. The Privy Council accepted that there was a contractual relationship based on agency and that the promise made to the carriers by the stevedores could provide consideration in return for the promise made by the consignors to be bound by the limitation clause.

A very recent exception to the basic rule occurs where, the party making the promise to pay extra receives an extra benefit from the other party's agreement to complete what (s)he was already bound to do under an existing arrangement.

Williams v Roffey Bros & Nicholls Contractors Ltd (1990)

Roffey Bros builders sub-contracted the carpentry on a number of flats they were building to Williams for £20,000. Williams had underquoted for the work and ran into financial difficulties. Because there was a delay clause in Roffeys' building, meaning they would have to pay money to the client if the flats were not built on time, they promised to pay Williams another £10,300 if he would complete the carpentry on time. When Williams completed the work and Roffeys failed to pay extra, his claim to the money succeeded. Even though Williams was only doing what he was already contractually bound to do, Roffeys were gaining the extra benefit of not having to pay the money for delay to the client. Williams was providing consideration for their promise to pay him more for the work merely by completing his existing obligations on time.

One point to remember is that there was no attempt on Williams' part to extract the extra money by threats or coercion. The rules of economic duress would in any case have prevented him from succeeding.

What is clear from the case is that the courts do not want promises made in a business context to be broken. To prevent this they will find consideration even though we may find it hard to find anything real or tangible about it.

Activity

Multiple choice questions

In the following situations, select the appropriate statement from the choices which follow:

1 Mary, a student, asks Donald, her teacher, if he will give her good tuition for which she will pay him £100.
   a) There is a contract. Mary will have to pay the £100 to Donald.
   b) Mary will be able to sue Donald if his tuition is not good.
   c) Donald cannot demand the £100 from Mary. He is only doing his duty.
   d) Donald can sue for the £100 if Mary does not pay it.

2 Sid, the manager of a firm, promises Danny, a packer, £100 on top of his wages if he will stay late at work one evening to get out a rush order.
   a) There is no contract. Danny is only doing his job.
   b) Danny is entitled to the £100. He is doing extra to his normal job.
   c) Danny can only be paid the £100 if he does £100 worth of extra work.
   d) Sid can sue Danny if he refuses to stay late.

e) A promise to accept part-payment of an existing debt in place of the whole debt cannot be enforced because there is no consideration for such a promise

The basic rule

This was first stated in *Pinnel's Case* (1602) which held that payment of a smaller sum than the debt itself on the due date can never relieve the liability of the debtor to pay the whole debt, so the creditor can always sue for the balance of the debt which is unpaid.

The rule can operate fairly where the creditor is giving in to pressure by the debtor to accept less.

D.C. Builders v Rees (1965)

Builders were owed £482 for the balance of work they had completed. After several months waiting for payment, and at a point where they were in danger of going out of business, they reluctantly accepted an offer by Rees to pay £300 in full satisfaction of the debt. When the builders then sued for the balance, they were successful. They were not prevented by the agreement to accept less, which in any case was extracted from them under pressure.

It can also sometimes seem to operate unfairly where the debtor genuinely relies on the promise of the creditor.

Foakes v Beer (1884)

Dr Foakes owed Mrs Beer £2,090 after a court judged against him. The two reached an agreement for Foakes to pay in instalments, with Mrs Beer agreeing that no further action would be taken if the debt was paid off by the agreed date. Later, Mrs Beer demanded interest, which is always payable on a judgment debt, and sued when Foakes refused to pay. She was successful as a result of *Pinnel's* rule.

Exceptions to the rule

There are two basic exceptions where the agreement to pay less than the full debt can be enforced.

1. Accord and satisfaction

In other words, there is an agreement to accept something other than the money from the existing debt. This might take a number of forms:

• An agreement to accept an earlier payment of a smaller sum than the whole debt. (This was in fact what actually happened in *Pinnel's* case.) As an example, say I owe you £100 that I am due to pay on 1st March. You then agree to accept a payment of £80 made on 1st February. You will be unable to sue for the remaining £20. In effect, the earlier payment reflects consideration for the changed agreement.

- An agreement to accept something other than money instead of the debt. Say I owe you £1,000 and you accept instead my stereo hi-fi, worth about £800. You have the opportunity to place whatever value you wish on the goods. If you accept them in place of the money, the full debt is satisfied.
- An agreement to accept a part-payment together with something else, not to the value of the balance of the debt. Say I owe you £100 and you agree to accept £50 together with a law book worth £21.99. In cash value you have received only £71.99 but, again, the debt has been paid.

2. *The doctrine of promissory estoppel*

The doctrine acts as a defence to a claim by a creditor for the remainder of the debt where part-payment has been accepted.

The effect of the doctrine is to prevent (estop) the claimant from going back on the promise because it would be unfair and inequitable to do so.

Lord Denning in *obiter* statements developed the doctrine from the older doctrine of waiver.

Central London Property Trust Ltd v High Trees House Ltd (1947)

From 1937 the defendants leased from the claimants a block of flats in Wimbledon which they sub-let to tenants. When war started, it was impossible to find tenants and so the defendants were unable to pay the rent. The claimants agreed to accept half rent, which the defendants continued to pay. By 1945 the flats were all let and the claimants wanted the rent returned to its former level and sued for the higher rent for the last two quarters. They succeeded but Lord Denning stated, *obiter,* that

had they tried to sue for the extra rent for the whole period of the war, they would have failed. Estoppel would prevent them from going back on the promise on which the defendants had relied so long as the circumstances persisted. As Lord Denning stated:

'A promise was made which was intended to create legal relations and which to the knowledge of the person making the promise was going to be acted upon by the person to whom it was made, and which in fact was so acted upon. In such cases the courts have said that the promise must be honoured . . . the logical consequence, no doubt, is that a promise to accept a smaller sum in discharge of a larger debt if acted upon, is binding notwithstanding the absence of consideration.'

Unfortunately, Lord Denning's final statement here led some judges to the conclusion that the need for consideration to be proved in contracts had somehow been removed. Lord Denning was then called on to develop a more reliable explanation of the application of estoppel in a later case.'

Combe v Combe (1951)

A wife separated from her husband and sued him for a promise that he had quite gratuitously made to her that he would pay her £2 per week (i.e. it was not under a legal maintenance order). The judge at first instance noted the lack of consideration but held that following *High Trees* this was irrelevant and found in the wife's favour. In the CA, Lord Denning apologised for any confusion he had caused in *High Trees* and explained the doctrine further:

'Where one party has by his words or conduct made to the other party a promise or assurance which was intended to affect the legal conditions between them and be acted on accordingly, then once the other party has taken him at his word and acted on it the one who gave the promise cannot afterwards be allowed to revert to the previous legal relations as if no such promise had been made.'

Lord Birkett in the case made one further very significant comment in describing estoppel as 'a shield and not a sword'; in other words, it could operate only as a defence to a claim, not a means of bringing one.

The essential elements of the doctrine, then, as described in the case require the following to be shown in order to be used successfully:

- There must be an existing contractual relationship between the claimant and the defendant.
- The claimant must have agreed to **waive** (give up) some of his/her rights under that contract (the amount of the debt that has been unpaid).
- The claimant has waived these rights knowing that the defendant would rely on the promise in determining his/her future conduct.
- The defendant has in fact acted in reliance on the promise to forgo some of the debt.

The possible subsequent development of the doctrine is uncertain, particularly now that Lord Denning has died. In *Brikom Investments Ltd v Carr* (1979), for instance, Lord Justice Roskill stressed that 'it would be wrong to extend the doctrine of promissory estoppel, whatever its precise limits at the present day, to the extent of abolishing in this back-handed way the doctrine of consideration'.

Certainly application of the principles of estoppel to the area of part-payment of debt as an enforceable replacement for the whole debt is likely to be rejected. See *Re Selectmove* (1995).

Attempts to apply the principle in *Williams v Roffey* to situations involving promises to accept part-payment of debts in full satisfaction of the whole debt have been specifically rejected.

Re Selectmove (1995)

Here, a company which owed tax to the Inland Revenue offered to pay its debt by instalments. The Collector of Taxes stated that he would contact the company if the arrangement was unsatisfactory and the company began to pay off its debt by instalments. The IRC then insisted that all arrears of tax be paid immediately or it would begin winding-up procedures against the company. The company tried to argue, on the basis of *Williams v Roffey*, that its promise to carry out an existing obligation was good consideration for the agreement to pay by instalments. CA distinguished *Williams v Roffey* as that case involved the provision of goods and services rather than payment of an existing debt. The court, as a result felt itself bound rather by the basic precedent in *Foakes v Beer* and held that IRC was not bound by any agreement to accept payment by instalments. There appears still to be a glaring inconsistency here with the reasoning in *Williams v Roffey*.

Activity

Multiple choice questions
In the following situation, select the appropriate statement from the choices which follow:

1 Dave, a builder, owes his supplier £50,000 for materials. Dave has been unable to sell the house he has recently built at a profit, due to a slump in the property market, and has only £45,000. The supplier agrees to accept the £45,000 to prevent Dave from going out of business. Six months later the supplier has learned that Dave has just gained a building contract worth £5 million.
   a) Dave will have to pay the remaining £5,000 to the supplier immediately.
   b) Dave can use the supplier's promise as a defence to a claim for the money.
   c) The supplier can recover the materials used by Dave.
   d) Dave can sue the supplier.

Activity

Self-assessment questions

1 Why did the law first develop the doctrine of consideration?
2 What, in simple terms, is consideration?
3 How do the 19th century definitions based on detriment and benefit differ from the application of the doctrine in recent times?
4 Why is it unimportant whether the consideration is adequate or not?
5 What is the basic difference between something that is sufficient and something that is adequate?
6 How easy is it to accept cases such as *Chappell v Nestlé* in the light of the accepted legal meaning of 'sufficiency'?
7 Why is it impossible to form a contract with consideration that is past?
8 Exactly how does the exception in *Lampleigh v Braithwaite* operate?
9 What is the connection between the rule that consideration must move from the promisee and the rule requiring privity of contract?
10 How does the case of *Shanklin Pier v Detel Products* contradict or modify the basic rule?
11 In what ways could the rule that consideration must move from the promisee be said to be unfair?
12 What is the distinguishing feature, if any, between *Stilk v Myrick* and *Hartley v Ponsonby*?
13 Why is it difficult to see the distinction between the principles in *Stilk v Myrick* and *Williams v Roffey Bros & Nicholls*?
14 Why exactly did Pau On succeed in the case of *Pao On v Lau Yiu Long*?
15 Is there any relevance to promissory estoppel in the modern day?
16 Do the exceptions to *Pinnel's* rule always cover every possible problem?
17 What is the effect of the judgment in *Re Selectmove*?

KEY FACTS

- Consideration is 'the price for which the promise of the other is bought' – *Dunlop v Selfridge*
- Executory consideration is where the consideration is yet to change hands. Executed consideration is consideration that has already passed
- Consideration need not be adequate – *Thomas v Thomas*
- But it must be sufficient, that is it must be real, tangible and have value – *Chappel v Nestlé*
- Consideration must not be past – *Re McArdle*
- Except where it is a service that has been requested – *Lampleigh v Braithwaite*
- A person seeking to sue on a contract must have given consideration under it – *Tweddle v Atkinson*
- Carrying out an existing contractual obligation cannot be consideration for a new promise – *Stilk v Myrick*
- Unless something extra is added to the contract – *Hartley v Ponsonby*
- Or a third party's interests are involved – *Pao On v Lau Yiu Long*
- Or if an extra benefit is to be gained – *Willams v Roffey Bros & Nicholls*
- Part-payment of a debt can never satisfy the debt as a whole – *Pinnel's* rule
- Although there are exceptions to the rule, including accord and satisfaction (where the debt is paid in a different form), and estoppel (where a party waiving rights is prevented from going back on the promise because of reliance by the other party) – *Central London Properties Trust v High Trees House Ltd*
- The principle in *Williams v Roffey* applies only to existing duties as consideration for fresh agreements and cannot be applied to agreements to accept part-payment of a debt in satisfaction of the full debt – *Re Selectmove*

Activity

Legal essay writing

Consider the following essay title:

Critically discuss the extent to which the courts will allow performance of an existing duty to be accepted as providing consideration for an entirely fresh agreement.

Answering the question

There are usually two key elements to answering essays in law:

- firstly, you are required to reproduce certain factual information on a particular area of law and this is usually identified for you in the question
- secondly, you are required to answer the specific question set, which usually is in the form of some sort of critical element, i.e. you are likely to see the words 'discuss', or 'analyse', or 'comment on', or 'critically consider', or 'evaluate', or even 'compare and contrast' if two areas are involved.

Students for the most part seem quite capable of doing the first, but also generally seem less skilled at the second. The important points in any case are to ensure that you only deal with relevant legal material in your answer and that you do answer the question set, rather than one you have made up yourself, or indeed the one that was on last year's paper.

For instance, in the case of the first, in this essay you are likely to provide detail on the following:

- definitions of consideration itself
- explanations of the rules relating to performance of existing duties
- some specific references to the case law on performance of existing duties, both those identifying that it is not consideration and those that represent exceptions to the simple rule.

This is not then the opportunity to write all that you know about consideration. In fact, it is essential that you are selective in the information that you give. Aspects of adequacy and sufficiency, past consideration, movement from the promisee, and the rules on part-payment of debts are irrelevant to the question set. So you should focus on only a very limited range of information from your total knowledge on consideration.

In the case of the second, the essay asks you in effect to analyse the extent to which there are exceptions to a basic rule of contract, the rule on performance of existing obligations. So in this essay again you have to be really selective with the subject of your discussion as well as with the base of knowledge from which it is drawn.

Relevant law

The appropriate law appears to be:

- A brief explanation of the nature of consideration (consideration being the *quid pro quo* – the proof of the existence of a bargain enforceable in law) and an appropriate definition of consideration such as that in *Dunlop v Selfridge* 'an act of forbearance or the promise thereof is the price for which the promise of the other is bought, and the promise thus given for value is enforceable'
- An explanation of the basic rule on performance of existing duties as consideration – that this is not allowable because it is in effect no consideration – *Stilk v Myrick*
- An explanation that this principle applies not merely in the case of contractual duties but in the case of performance of statutory or other legal duties also – *Collins v Godefroy* and *Ward v Byham*
- Explain the various exceptions to the basic rule that the courts have accepted over time which are:
  - Where something more is given over and above that required under the contract – *Hartley v Ponsonby*
  - Where extra is provided over and above that required by the statutory or other legal duty – *Ward v Byham* and *Glassbrook Brothers v Glamorgan CC*
  - Where the promise is made to a third party (*Scotson v Pegg*) or where third-party rights would inevitably be affected (*Pao On v Lau Yiu Long*)
  - Where not to enforce the arrangement might

threaten the integrity of a commercial agreement – *New Zealand Shipping Co. v A. M. Satterthwaite & Co. (The Eurymedon)*
- Where a party gains an extra benefit from the performance of the existing duty
- Use any other relevant cases as examples, e.g. *Shadwell v Shadwell*.

Discussion and evaluation

The essay title asks for a 'critical discussion' of the circumstances in which the courts will allow exceptions to the basic rule on using performance of existing duties as consideration for fresh agreements to stand.

On this basis it is not sufficient merely to rely on a purely narrative approach listing the basic rule and the exceptions as we have done for the knowledge element. Something more must be done to appraise the rule itself and the exceptions to it.

On the basic rule itself, certain comments can be made:

- The rule is obviously a necessary one since it protects against the situation where a party gains more out of the original agreement than he was entitled to without giving anything extra himself.
- In advance of a doctrine of economic duress it could operate to prevent a party from trying to extract more from the agreement after the event by threatening not to perform.
- In the context of *Stilk v Myrick* it may still be seen as unfair – and clearly one of the points in *Williams v Roffey* was to prevent the breaking of a later promise made in a commercial context on which the other party had relied to his possible detriment.

On the exceptions to the basic rule, relevant comments might include:

- That it is perfectly logical and legitimate where something is added to the original consideration to enforce the later agreement which in effect is a new agreement supported by its own consideration.
- That nevertheless very often the reasoning behind the decision to enforce the fresh agreement can be strained or at least somewhat doubtful, e.g.

- in *Shadwell v Shadwell* and in *Ward v Byham* there is the obvious contradiction that the agreements, being domestic, may be seen as lacking an intention to create a legally enforceable relationship
- in *Williams v Roffey* the defendants had the opportunity to sue anyway – in effect, although the extra benefit is taken, the avoidance of penalties, a party could extend the reasoning to avoid bringing an action themselves where the other party may not complete and make an empty promise merely to save themselves the expense of suing on the breach.
- That very often what the court accepts as consideration is difficult if not impossible to identify in terms of being 'real, and tangible' even if it might tenuously be described as having some 'value', e.g. *Scotson v Pegg, Ward v Byham, Williams v Roffey.*
- That many of the cases actually involve third parties so may be conflicting with the basic rules of privity, e.g. *Scotson v Pegg, Pao On v Lau Yiu Long, The Eurymedon.*
- That certain of the cases are in any case Privy Council decisions so are persuasive only, e.g. *Pao On v Lau Yiu Long.*
- That the courts have in any case chosen to restrict the development of these exceptions to the extent, e.g. that they will not allow the principle in *Williams v Roffey* to be used in the case of part-payment of debts in full satisfaction of the whole debt – *Re Selectmove.*
- It may also be discussed whether or not the law on the area is a demonstration of the courts' willingness to protect free bargaining by parties and how much cases like *Williams v Roffey* demonstrate a willingness to intervene to ensure that commercial agreements can be relied upon and respected.
- Any sensible conclusion would do – but it is probably appropriate to conclude by stating that while the basic rule has some logic, the exceptions seem often to be contradictory to the basic principles behind the requirement of consideration.

Chapter 4

PRINCIPLES OF FORMATION: INTENTION TO CREATE LEGAL RELATIONS

4.1 The two presumptions

We all regularly make arrangements with each other, and we may even be doing things in return for something, and this seems as though there is consideration too.

However, we do not always intend that if we fail to keep to an agreement the other party should be able to sue us. Nor would it be sensible for the courts to be filled with actions on all of the broken promises that are ever made. My children may expect their pocket money regularly but would you want them to be able to sue if I forget to give it to them one week?

The law makes a sensible compromise by assuming that in certain situations we would usually not intend the agreement to be legally binding, while in others we usually would. The first covers social or domestic arrangements where it is presumed there is no intention to be legally bound. The second concerns commercial or business agreements where an intention to be legally bound is presumed. In either case the facts can show that the presumption should not apply. So intention is very much decided on the facts in individual cases.

4.2 Social and domestic agreements

Arrangements between family members are usually left to them to sort out themselves and are not legally binding.

Balfour v Balfour (1919)

A husband worked abroad without his wife who had to stay in England because of illness, and promised an income of £30 per month. When the wife later petitioned for divorce, her claim to this income failed. It had been made at an amicable point in their relationship, not in contemplation of divorce. It was a purely domestic arrangement beyond the scope of the court.

Where husband and wife are estranged, an agreement between them may be taken as intended to be legally binding.

Merritt v Merritt (1970)

Here the husband had deserted his wife for another woman. An agreement that he would pay her an income if she paid the outstanding mortgage was held by the court to be intended to create legally binding obligations.

Sometimes, of course, families make arrangements that appear to be business arrangements because of their character. In such cases the court will need to examine what the real purpose of the arrangement was.

Jones v Padavatton (1969)

A mother provided an allowance for her daughter under an agreement for the daughter to give up her highly paid job in New York, study for the Bar in England and then return to practice in Trinidad where the mother lived. When the daughter was finding it difficult to manage on the allowance the mother then bought a house for her to live in, part of which the daughter could let to supplement her income. They later quarrelled and the mother sought repossession of the house. The daughter's argument, that the second agreement was contractual, failed. The court could find no intent.

If money has passed hands then it will not matter that the arrangement is made socially. It will be held as intended to be legally binding.

Simpkins v Pays (1955)

A lodger and two members of the household entered competitions in the lodger's name but paying equal shares of the entry money and on the understanding that they would share any winnings. So, when the lodger won, he was bound to share the winnings.

If parties put their financial security at risk for an agreement, then it must have been intended that the agreement should be legally binding.

Parker v Clarke (1960)

A young couple were persuaded by an older couple to sell their house in order to move in with them, with the promise also that they would inherit property on the death of the old couple. When the two couples eventually fell out and the young couple were asked to leave, their action for damages succeeded. Giving up their security was an indication that the arrangement was intended to be legally binding

4.3 Commercial and business agreements

An arrangement made within a business context is presumed to be intended to be legally binding unless evidence can show a different intent.

Edwards v Skyways Ltd (1969)

An attempt to avoid making an agreed *ex gratia* payment in a redundancy failed. Although *ex gratia* indicates no pre-existing liability to make the payment, the agreement to pay it, once made, was binding.

The offer of free gifts where this is to promote the business can still be held to be legally binding.

Esso Petroleum Co. Ltd v Commissioners of Customs and Excise (1976)

Esso gave free World Cup coins with every four gallons of petrol purchased. Customs and Excise wanted to claim purchase tax from the transaction. Since Esso were clearly trying to gain more business from the promotion there was held to be intention to be bound by the arrangement.

The principle has also been developed to cover situations where prizes are offered in competitions. The purpose of such events is generally to promote the body offering the prize so there is intention to create a legal relationship which is binding and can be relied on by members of the public who enter the competition.

McGowan v Radio Buxton (2001)

The claimant entered a radio competition for which the prize had been stated to be a Renault Clio car. She was told that she had won the competition but was given a four-inch scale model of a Clio. The defendants argued that there was no legally binding contract. The judge held that there had been intention to create legal relations. The claimant entered the competition as a member of the public and that 'looking at the transcript of the broadcast, there was not even a hint that the car would be a toy'.

However, it is possible for the agreement to contain no intention to be legally binding where that is specifically stated in the agreement itself.

Jones v Vernons' Pools Ltd (1938)

The pools company inserted a clause on all coupons stating that 'the transaction should not give rise to any legal relationship . . . but be binding in honour only'. When a punter claimed that the company had lost his winning coupon and sought payment, his claim failed. The clause prevented any legal claim.

The same type of principle applies with so-called comfort letters. Although such letters are worded so that they appear almost to amount to a guarantee, they do not and will not give rise to legal obligations.

Kleinwort Benson Ltd v Malaysian Mining Corporation (1989)

Kleinwort lent £10 million to Metals Ltd, a subsidiary of MMC. The parent company would not guarantee this loan but issued a comfort letter stating their intention to ensure Metals had sufficient funds for repayment. When Metals went out of business without repaying Kleinwort the latter's action based on the comfort letter failed. If they had wanted a guarantee they should have insisted on one.

Sometimes judges will find that parts of an agreement are intended to be legally binding, and other parts are not.

Julian v Furby (1982)

An experienced plasterer helped his daughter and son-in-law to alter and furnish their house. When the couple split up he sued the son-in-law for the price of the materials he had bought and also for his labour. The court agreed that there should be payment for the materials but not for the man's labour which was felt to be no more than any father would do for his daughter.

Activity

Self-assessment questions

1 How do courts decide if an agreement is intended to be legally binding?
2 Why should an agreement within a family not be legally binding?
3 Why are the cases of *Balfour v Balfour* and *Merritt v Merritt* decided differently?
4 Why should commercial agreements generally lead to a legal relationship?
5 How will businesses try to get round the rules on intention?
6 What is an 'honour pledge clause'?
7 What is the reasoning behind making free gifts, prizes in competitions etc. part of a legally enforceable agreement?

Activity

Quick quiz

Consider whether the courts would identify an intention to be legally bound in the following situations:

1 Alan agrees that he will buy his son a book in return for mowing the lawns.
2 James agrees to take his secretary Dawn out for a meal for getting an urgent job finished quickly and at very short notice.
3 I ask my daughter to give up her part-time job for a week to proofread a draft of a textbook, and I promise to pay her the same as she would have earned.
4 Skinny Co. usually give their employees a £50 Christmas box but this year they have decided against it.
5 I agree to take my wife to the cinema but fail to turn up because I have had to stay longer at work.

KEY FACTS

- There are two rebuttable presumptions – that in social and domestic arrangements there is no intention to be legally bound, and that in commercial and business dealings there is
- An arrangement between husband and wife will not normally be legally binding – *Balfour v Balfour*
- Unless the couple is estranged – *Merritt v Merritt*
- An agreement will be binding where the parties have spent money on it – *Simpkin v Pays*
- And also where they have acted to their detriment – *Parker v Clarke*
- An agreement made in a business context is usually binding – *Edwards v Skyways*
- Even where free gifts are promised to promote sales – *Esso v Commissioners of Customs and Excise*
- The same can apply to prizes offered in competitions – *McGowan v Radio Buxton*
- Some agreements are binding in honour only – *Jones v Vernons Pools*
- Comfort letters create no legal obligations – *Kleinwort Benson v Malaysia Mining Corporation*
- Sometimes the judges take a pragmatic view of an agreement – *Julian v Furby*

Chapter 5:

FORMALITIES AND SPECIALITY CONTRACTS

5.1 The requirement of form

Form is not an aspect of contract law that most A Level syllabuses now concern themselves with. However, it can in some instances be an important issue, and it is therefore worth knowing at least the basic rules. It is not, however, ever likely to be a major part of any A Level contract exam.

It is generally fair to say that with the majority of contracts the form in which they are made is not an issue. We make contracts every day, and probably all day long, without ever contemplating their legal significance and certainly without worrying about the specific form in which we have created them.

We can distinguish between 'simple' contracts and 'speciality' contracts.

In the case of **simple** contracts these can be made orally or in writing, or possibly even be implied by conduct. An example is where an auctioneer completes a contract at an auction by the fall of his hammer (although this might also be accompanied by words such as 'sold to the lady in the red dress')
• with contracts made in this way then there is no requirement for there to be any particular form
• and evidence of compliance with the basic rules of formation will be sufficient to make such contracts enforceable in law.

However, with **speciality** contracts these need to have been created in a specific form in order to gain their validity:
• the 'form' in question will be to do with being written or evidenced in writing
• and this formal requirement indicates that a higher level of proof of the existence of the contract is required

• and so speciality contracts are concerned with more significant property such as land or other transferable interests.

Speciality contracts come in one of three types:
• agreements which must be created in the form of a deed
• agreements which must be made in writing
• agreements which need only to be evidenced in writing, e.g. in a memorandum.

5.2 Agreements which must be created in the form of a deed to be valid

Traditionally, any transaction that involved the conveyance of land or an interest in land had to be in a deed in order to be valid.

A deed was a document which was drafted on parchment, signed by the parties to the agreement, an impression made in sealing wax on the document, which was then delivered up by hand. In this way it was signed, sealed and delivered.

Under s1(1) of the Law of Property (Miscellaneous Provisions) Act 1989 the requirement that the document be 'sealed' has been abolished. Now the document will be valid if it is made clear on the face of it that it is intended to act as a deed, and is validly executed. A new requirement is for the document to be formally witnessed, but this is no more than was already standard practice anyway.

A deed is also the standard means used for transferring of gifts that are thus unsupported by consideration. The classic example here is charitable gifts.

5.3 Contracts that must be in writing in order to be valid

A number of these exist. They are usually identified in a statute that will also outline the requirements.

They include cheques and other negotiable instruments and also credit agreements that must be in the prescribed form and conform to the requirements of the Consumer Credit Act 1974.

Finally, they include sale or disposition of other interests in land. Section 40 of the Law of Property Act 1925 and the doctrine of part performance formerly governed these. Now, however, such contracts come under s2(1) Law of Property (Miscellaneous Provisions) Act 1989 which provides that 'a contract for the sale or other disposition of an interest in land can only be made in writing and only by incorporating all the terms which the parties have expressly agreed in one document or, where contracts are exchanged, in each'

The potential problem created by repeal of the doctrine of part-performance is that it makes it less easy for equity to intervene where there is a dispute over form.

5.4 Agreements needing only evidence in writing to be valid

These are those contracts that are governed by the Statute of Frauds 1677.

Following the repeal of s40 Law of Property Act the only contract requiring evidence in writing is a contract of guarantee. This is a promise made by one party to a second party to meet the debts of a third party in the event of the third party defaulting on the debt.

The basic rule is under s4 that requires the agreement to be evidenced in a written note or memorandum. This memorandum must:
- be signed by the guarantor (or his/her agent)
- clearly be a signed admission of the existence of a contract and
- contain all the material terms of the agreement, including the identities of all the parties involved and the precise subject matter of the contract.

The guarantee is enforceable provided it is evidenced in writing in this way.

Activity

Self-assessment questions
1 In what circumstances will form be an issue in determining the contractual validity of an agreement?
2 What is the common thread that runs between agreements requiring specific form?
3 What is a deed? In what ways has the required form of a deed changed in recent years?
4 What is the common characteristic of contracts that must be created in written form?
5 What exactly is a guarantee?

KEY FACTS

- 'Simple' contracts can be made orally, in writing or by conduct
- Speciality contracts will need to be created by the appropriate form or method
- They mostly have to do with land or interests in land
- Under the Law of Property (Miscellaneous Provisions) Act 1989 transfers of land must be in the form of a deed, having been signed and witnessed
- Cheques and other negotiable instruments will need to be in writing
- Guarantees need to be evidenced in writing

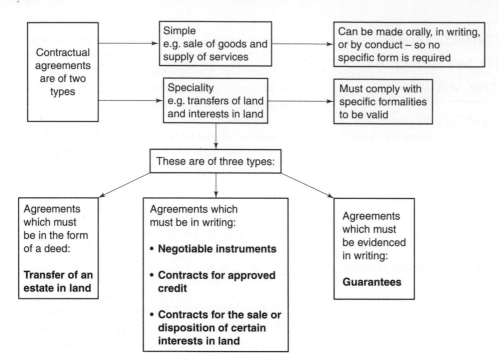

Figure 5.1 Diagram illustrating the ways in which form is significant in contracts

Chapter 6

THIRD-PARTY RIGHTS

6.1 The doctrine of privity of contract

6.1.1 The basic rule

This is possibly the most contentious of all the rules of contract. Simply stated, it is that any person who is not a party to the contract can neither sue nor be sued under it.

This is very similar to the proposition in consideration that a person who has not given consideration under the contract cannot sue or be sued. We have already seen this in operation in *Tweddle v Atkinson*. Here, even though the claimant was named in a written agreement he was unable to claim an enforceable third-party right.

The rule is an old one.

Price v Easton (1833)

Here, Easton had agreed with a third party that if that third party did specified work for him he would pay £19 to Price. While the work was completed by the third party, Easton failed to pay Price who then sued. Price's claim was unsuccessful. He had given no consideration for the arrangement and was not therefore a party to the contract.

The modern statement of the rule is found in Lord Haldane's judgment in:

Dunlop Pneumatic Tyre Co. Ltd v Selfridge & Co. Ltd (1915)

In the contract Dew & Co., wholesalers, agreed to buy tyres from Dunlop. They did so on the express undertaking that they would not sell below certain fixed prices. They also undertook to obtain the same price-fixing agreements from their clients. Dew sold tyres on to Selfridge on these terms but Selfridge broke the agreement and sold tyres at discount prices. Dunlop sought an injunction. They failed for lack of privity. In the House of Lords Lord Haldane said

'only a person who is a party to a contract can sue on it. Our law knows nothing of a jus quaesitum tertio *arising by way of contract. Such a right may be conferred by way of property, as, for example, under a trust, but it cannot be conferred on a stranger to a contract as a right to enforce the contract* in personam.'

6.1.2 Some consequences of the rule

The rule has a number of consequences:
- A person receiving goods as a gift may be unable to sue personally where the goods are defective.
- In such a case it may prove embarrassing to try to enlist the help of the actual purchaser of the goods.
- Even if the purchaser does sue (s)he may be able to recover only for their own loss, not necessarily the loss suffered by the donee of the gift.
- The rule may well prevent enforcement of services that have already been paid for. This was the case in *Price v Easton*.
- The rule may also mean that a benefactor's express wishes are denied, as was the case in *Tweddle v Atkinson*.
- More dramatically still, in commercial contracts, as Lord Dunedin said in *Dunlop v Selfridge* 'the effect . . . is to make it possible

for a person to snap his fingers at a bargain definitely made, a bargain not unfair in itself, and which the person seeking to enforce it has a legitimate interest to enforce'.

6.2 The exceptions to the basic rule

6.2.1 Introduction

Not surprisingly, the rule is unpopular and many attempts have been made to avoid the harsh effects of the rule on enforcing third-party rights in a contract. This is done using a variety of means, none of which has affected the basic rule. This remains intact.

6.2.2 Statutory exceptions

Parliament is not bound by the strict rules of contract in enacting new provisions, and so there are a number of statutory inroads into the rule.

S148(7) of the Road Traffic Act 1988 obliges a motorist to take out third-party liability insurance. Another motorist who is involved in an accident with this motorist can then rely upon it. The insurance is enforceable despite the fact that the other motorist lacks any privity in the insurance contract.

By the Married Women's Property Act 1882 a husband can take out insurance in his own name but for the benefit of his wife and children. They can enforce the terms of the insurance although they are not parties to the contract.

However, the courts will not allow an Act to be used for an incorrect purpose.

Beswick v Beswick (1968)

Here a widow was trying to enforce an agreement between her husband and her nephew for the latter to provide her with a weekly annuity on the death of the former. The agreement was a condition in the sale of her husband's business to the nephew. The widow clearly lacked privity to the agreement and had provided no consideration for it. Her attempt to use a provision in s56 of the Law of Property Act that referred to 'other property' failed. The reasoning was that the Act referred only to real property (land or interests in land) and could not be applied to purely personal property.

6.2.3 Trust law

Despite lacking privity, a party identifying third-party rights under a contract may be able to show that a trust of the rights is created in his or her favour.

Gregory & Parker v Williams (1817)

Parker owed money to both Gregory and Williams. Since he could see no way of organising settlement himself, he assigned all of his property to Williams on the understanding that Williams would then pay off the debt to Gregory. Williams failed to pay over the money to Gregory who, not being a party to the agreement, was unable to sue on it in contract law. The court was nevertheless prepared to accept that a trust of the money had been created in Gregory's favour, which was then enforceable against Williams.

However, the court will not accept that a trust is created unless the claimant can show an express intention that he should receive the benefit.

Les Affreteurs Reunis S.A. v Walford (Walford's case) (1919)

Walford was a broker who negotiated an agreement between a charter party and the owner of the vessel, but was obviously not a party to the agreement. The agreement contained a stipulation that Walford should receive a 3% commission from the shipowners. They failed to pay. The court was prepared to accept that a trust was created only because he was named.

The courts will not in any case accept that a trust is created unless the interest claimed conforms to the general character of a trust.

Green v Russell (1959)

Here, an employer had insurance in his own name that also covered certain employees including Green. There was, however, no such requirement in the contract of employment. When both were killed in a fire, the Court of Appeal concluded that there was no trust in favour of Green since the employer could have surrendered the policy at any time.

In this way the cases in which a claimant might claim that a trust is created are probably quite limited.

6.2.4 Restrictive covenants

This is another device created by equity by which a party selling land retains certain rights over the use of the land. The restriction thus created must be a negative one, for example preventing use of the land for business purposes.

The covenant is said to run with the land. So, if properly created, it will bind subsequent purchasers of the land even though there is no privity between them and the original seller. This will apply even if the land retained by the original seller has also been sold on.

Tulk v Moxhay (1848)

Tulk owned land in London that he sold with an express undertaking that it would never be used to build property on. The land was then re-sold on numerous occasions, each time subject to the same undertaking. Moxhay bought it knowing of the limitation but nevertheless intended to build on it. Tulk successfully sought an injunction. The court accepted that it would be against conscience for Moxhay to buy knowing of the restriction.

The device though operates only in respect of land. The courts have resisted attempts to extend the principle to cover other property. So it will not be available merely as a method of controlling pricing of goods.

Taddy v Sterious (1904)

Tobacco manufacturers sold tobacco to wholesalers with an express clause in the contract requiring that retailers should not sell below fixed prices. When this agreement was breached the manufacturer tried to argue that *Tulk v Moxhay* applied. The court rejected this argument out of hand.

6.2.5 The rule in *Dunlop v Lambert*

This common law rule states that a remedy can be granted notwithstanding the absence of privity of contract 'where no other would be available to a person sustaining loss which under a rational legal system ought to be compensated by the person who caused it'.

The rule has recently been both approved and applied.

Darlington B.C. v Wiltshier Northern Ltd (1995)

The council wanted a new recreation centre. In order to avoid certain financial restraints it was under, it hired Morgan Grenfell who in turn hired the builders of the new centre. A collateral agreement provided for Morgan Grenfell to pay the builders, Wiltshier Northern Ltd, and for the council to reimburse Morgan Grenfell and for Morgan Grenfell to assign all rights they might have against Wiltshier to the council. When £2 million worth of defects were discovered in the building the council obviously wished to sue. Morgan Grenfell would be unable to recover in tort, having no proprietary interest in the building. The council would normally be prevented from suing because of its lack of privity in the building contract. However, Lord Diplock applied the principle in *Dunlop v Lambert* and allowed the action. The justification was that Morgan Grenfell was the fiduciary of the council and had assigned its rights in the building contract over to the council.

But there is also a proviso that the rule will not be applied where the parties to the original contract, the consignor and the carrier, had contemplated that there would be a separate contract between carrier and consignee to regulate liability between them. This proviso has been considered recently.

Alfred McAlpine Construction Ltd v Panatown Ltd (1998)

McAlpine were employed by Panatown to design and build a multi-storey car park. When this contract was formed McAlpine also entered into a duty of care deed with Unex Investment Properties Ltd (UIPL) who were the actual owners of the site. When Panatown sued McAlpine, claiming that the building was so defective that it would need to be rebuilt, McAlpine countered that Panatown had never been the owner of the site and it was UIPL that had suffered the loss, not them – so that

Panatown could claim only nominal damages and UIPL nothing at all since they were not parties to the contract. The Court of Appeal held that the rule in *Dunlop v Lambert* was relevant (that a contracting party could recover damages even though it was a third party that suffered the actual loss). The issue then was whether the proviso applied to prevent recovery by Panatown. The Court of Appeal accepted that the deed with UIPL indicated that contractual rights had been given to the third party but that, on the facts, since all accounts were bound to be settled between Panatown and McAlpine then Panatown must have the right to sue.

6.2.6 Privity of estate in leases

Where an owner of land creates a lease in favour of another person, the terms of the lease are in effect contractual obligations. These terms are more usually known as the 'covenants' of the lease and are enforceable by both parties because there is privity between them.

The principle of 'privity of estate' means that the landowner will be able to enforce the covenants also against anybody to whom the holder of the lease assigns their lease. By ss141 and 142 Law of Property Act 1925 a tenant will also be able to enforce covenants of the lease against a new owner of the freehold, as will that new landlord be able to enforce them against the tenant.

6.2.7 Procedural rules

In very rare instances, rules of procedure have been used to get round the effects of the doctrine of privity. Such a course has succeeded only because to do so has corresponded to the actual promise made, and because all of the parties are present in the court.

Snelling v John G Snelling Ltd (1973)

Three brothers were all directors of their own company, John G Snelling Ltd, which was financed by loans from the three brothers. When the company borrowed money from a finance company the three brothers entered an agreement with one another that, until such time as the finance company loan was repaid, if any of them resigned their directorship in the company they would forfeit the amount of their own loan to the company. The company was not a party to this agreement. One brother later did leave the company and sued the company for his loan. The remaining two brothers applied to join the company as defendants and counter-claimed on the basis of the agreement reached between the three brothers. The court upheld their argument. Even though the company was not a party to the agreement, the brothers and the company were in many ways the same. A stay of execution of the brother's claim was the appropriate order.

6.2.8 The so-called 'holiday cases'

We will discuss the issue of recovery for mental distress and the 'holiday cases' at a later stage under damages. However, significant development was made in these cases in respect of third-party rights.

Jackson v Horizon Holidays (1975)

Mr Jackson had booked a 'family holiday' which fell far short of the contract description. He sued the holiday company not only on his own behalf but for his family also. The company, while accepting liability, disputed that it should pay damages in respect of the family. The House of Lords held that the loss of enjoyment suffered by the family was in effect a loss to the contracting party himself. He had paid for a 'family holiday' but not received it.

Damages were awarded on this basis. This would appear to be straining the law a long way, albeit in order to achieve a just result.

The courts, though, have indicated that this method of getting round the doctrine of precedent is confined to 'holiday contracts'. See later *Woodar Investment Development Ltd v Wimpey Construction (UK) Ltd* (1980) where the House of Lords, while not expressly overruling the *Jackson* case, held that there was no general principle allowing a party to a contract to sue on behalf of third parties injured by a breach of the contract. Lord Wilberforce's view was that *Jackson* fell into a specialist group of contracts involving families where it was intended that the benefit of the contract be shared between the members of the family.

6.2.9 Protecting third parties in exclusion clauses

A party to a contract can include an exclusion clause or a limitation clause in a contract. Traditionally, however, a sub-contractor would be unable to claim the benefit of the exclusion clause, even if named under it.

Scruttons Ltd v Midland Silicones Ltd (1962)

A shipping company was carrying a drum of chemicals for the claimants under a contract containing a clause limiting damages in the event of breach to $500. Stevedores sub-contracted to the shipping company did $1,800 worth of damage, sought to rely on the limitation clause and failed owing to lack of privity. However, Lord Reid did feel that there could be 'success in agency if the bill of lading makes it clear that the stevedore is intended to be protected by the provisions'.

Despite this there have been situations in which such a third party has been able to claim cover under an exclusion clause despite lacking privity.

New Zealand Shipping Co. Ltd v A.M. Satterthwaite & Co. Ltd (The Eurymedon) (1974)

In this Privy Council case, the stevedores were able to succeed and rely on an exclusion clause in a similar action. The reasoning given by Lord Wilberforce was that the stevedores were identified as agents in the contract.

6.2.10 Collateral contracts

This is a mechanism that might succeed when a claimant complains that a contract has been formed through reliance on a collateral promise made by a third party who is not a party to the contract.

Shanklin Pier v Detel Products Ltd (1951)

Owners of a pier were assured by Detel's representatives that their paint was suitable to paint the pier and would last a minimum of seven years. Relying on this assurance, the pier owners instructed their painting contractors to paint the pier with Detel's paint. The paint was in fact unsuitable and peeled. The court held that Detel was liable on the promise despite an apparent lack of privity in the painting contract.

6.2.11 Agency, assignment and negotiable instruments

All of the exceptions we have so far considered are enforceable either because of principles contained in individual cases or because they rely on areas of law other than contract, such as trust law.

There are, however, three major exceptions to the doctrine which are outside of the A Level syllabuses. A detailed analysis is therefore not necessary, but they are worth knowing. They are the rules of agency, the process of assignment, and the rules regarding negotiable instruments.

- Where one party acts as an agent for another (known as the principal) the agent can make and carry out contracts with a third party on the principal's behalf. The significance of this is that the agent can make agreements by which the principal is bound despite the apparent lack of privity. Where all of the appropriate rules are complied with then the principal and the third party are able to sue and be sued by each other under the contract made by the agent.
- Assignment is a specific system devised for the transfer of property rights. This may be appropriate for instance with debts. If the assignment of the debt conforms to the proper rules of assignment then the party to whom the debt is assigned can sue the debtor despite the apparent lack of privity between them.
- Negotiable instruments were originally a device of merchant traders. The rules devised by the merchants were eventually given statutory force in the Bills of Exchange Act 1882. Possibly the most common form of negotiable instrument with which we are familiar in modern times is the cheque. By various processes it is then possible to transfer ownership of the property identified in the instrument. In the case of a cheque a sum of money.

6.3 The Contracts (Rights of Third Parties) Act 1999

We have already seen at the beginning of this section some of the harsh effects that the doctrine of privity can have in preventing third parties from enforcing rights which appear to have been granted them in contracts.

The fact that judges have been prepared to allow so many exceptions to the basic rule is a fair indication of a general dissatisfaction with the operation of the doctrine. In many cases, indeed, judges have themselves called for legislative reform, particularly because of the complexities that are caused by there being so many different exceptions.

This is not a new feeling and as early as 1937 the Law Revision Committee was recommending reforms. In simple terms they suggested that third parties should be able to enforce provisions in a contract which 'by its express terms purport to confer a benefit on a third party'.

More recently, the Law Commission in its Consultation Paper No. 121 argued that there should be a 'third-party rule' in privity. Nevertheless, it rejected various proposed courses of action:
- Extending the number of exceptions – rejected because there were already too many.
- Leaving enforcement of third-party rights to promisees under the contract – rejected as too onerous a burden and no guarantee it would happen.
- Introducing a general rule preventing privity from denying any third-party rights – rejected as too vague, and might 'open the floodgates' to claims.

So the Law Commission favoured a more precise rule whereby third parties would only be able to enforce rights identified in the terms of the contract as intending to confer a legally enforceable benefit on the third party.

Even here, the Law Commission felt that parties to the contract should be able to vary such terms where the contract specifically allowed for such variation.

The Law Commission subsequently prepared a draft Bill in a further report, No. 242. Its major provision is contained in s1(1) by which:

'a person who is not a party to a contract (in this Act referred to as a third party) may in his own right enforce the contract if: (a) the contract contains an express term to that effect; or (b) subject to subsection (2) the contract purports to confer a benefit on the third party'.

The first ground under subsection (a) is self-explanatory. The second ground is subject to subsection (2). It states that ground (b) will be unavailable to a third party where 'on the proper construction of the contract it appears that the parties did not intend the contract to be enforceable by a third party'. In consequence, it seems only those rights actually conferred by the contract can be enforced.

One final recommendation of the Law Commission here was the abolition of the rule that consideration must move from the promisee that would otherwise defeat the reform.

The reforms were presented to Parliament in a draft Bill in January 1999. This has subsequently been enacted as the Contracts (Rights of Third Parties) Act 1999. By s1(3) the Act will apply if a third party is identified in the contract either by name or even as a member of a class. The third party does not have to exist at the time the contract was formed, as long as (s)he is identifiable as part of the class.

The Act contains some amendments from the Law Commission's draft Bill. Certain types of contract are excluded, notably those contracts where other legislation already applies. Another inclusion is a rule preventing a third party from suing an employee who is in breach of his contract of employment. This is to protect workers where they take legitimate industrial action. Another exception is the 'statutory contract' under s14 of the Companies Act 1985, which gives shareholders the right to sue officers of the company on issues arising from the memorandum and articles of association.

The Act has a number of important consequences:
- A wide range of third-party rights will be enforceable under the Act.
- A number of the exceptions to the basic privity doctrine become unnecessary, e.g. the claimant in *Tweddle v Atkinson* would have an enforceable right, as would the family members in *Jackson v Horizon Holidays.*
- Where a third party comes within the scope of an exclusion clause it will be much easier to enforce in their favour.

- Many exceptions will still apply as the Act will have no impact on them, e.g. collateral warranties.
- The Act can still prove ineffective as its provisions can be expressly excluded in a contract.

Activity

Self-assessment questions

1 What are the major justifications for the rule on privity of contract?
2 What is the connection between the doctrine of privity and the requirement of consideration in a contract?
3 In what ways is the doctrine of privity unfair?
4 Why is it not possible to argue that whenever a third-party right is identified in a contract it automatically creates a trust?
5 Is it possible to use the mechanism of a restrictive covenant to protect third-party rights in cases that involve things other than land?
6 To what extent are the judgments in *Scruttons v Midland Silicones* and *The Eurymedon* consistent with one another?
7 Other than where Parliament grants enforceable third-party rights by statute, what are the most effective exceptions to the basic rule on privity?
8 To what extent does the Contracts (Rights of Third Parties) Act 1999 address the problems of all third parties affected by the doctrine of privity?

KEY FACTS

- The basic doctrine of privity is that nobody can sue or be sued under a contract who is not a party to the contract – *Dunlop v Selfridge*
- Put another way, nobody can enforce a contract who has not provided consideration under the contract – *Tweddle v Atkinson*
- Since the rule unfairly prevents third parties identified as gaining rights under a contract from enforcing those rights, a number of exceptions to the strict rule have developed:
- Statutory exceptions, as with third-party insurance under the Road Traffic Acts
- Stating that a trust is created in favour of the third party – *Gregory & Parker v Williams* – but only so long as the interest conforms to the character of a trust – *Green v Russell*
- Restrictive covenants – *Tulk v Moxhay* – but only in relation to land not other interests – *Taddy v Sterious*
- The rule in *Dunlop v Lambert* – *Darlington BC v Wiltshier Northern Ltd*
- Privity of estate in leases
- Procedural rules – *Snelling v John G Snelling Ltd*
- The 'holiday cases' – *Jackson v Horizon Holidays*
- Protection given to third parties in exclusion clauses – *New Zealand Shipping Co. v Satterthwaite*
- Collateral contracts – *Shanklin Pier v Detel Products Ltd*
- Agency, assignment and negotiable instruments
- Now Parliament has passed the Contracts (Rights of Third Parties) Act 1999 to enable third parties to enforce rights that they are given under a contract – so a third party can enforce provisions in a contract if:
  - the contract expressly states that he can
  - the contract purports to confer a benefit on the third party

Activity

Legal essay writing

Consider the following essay title:

'The rule of privity of contract is that only a party to the contract can sue or be sued under the contract. This is intrinsically unfair to third parties who might expect to acquire rights under the contract. However, this criticism has been answered in full by the enactment of the Contracts (Rights of Third Parties) Act 1999.'

Discuss the accuracy of this statement.

Answering the question

There are usually two key elements to answering essays in law:

- firstly, you are required to reproduce certain factual information on a particular area of law and this is usually identified for you in the question
- secondly, you are required to answer the specific question set, which usually is in the form of some sort of critical element, i.e. you are likely to see the words 'discuss', or 'analyse', or 'comment on', or 'critically consider', or 'evaluate', or even 'compare and contrast' if two areas are involved.

Students for the most part seem quite capable of doing the first, but also generally seem less skilled at the second. The important points in any case are to ensure that you deal only with relevant legal material in your answer and that you do answer the question set, rather than one you have made up yourself, or indeed the one that was on last year's paper.

For instance, in the case of the first, in this essay you are likely to provide detail on the following:

- definitions of the basic doctrine of privity of contract itself
- explanations of the various exceptions to the doctrine that have developed through the common law to mitigate the harshness of the doctrine as it affects third-party rights
- specific references to the actual provisions of the 1999 Act and the ways, if any, in which it alters

or mitigates the harshness of the doctrine of privity of contract.

This is then in many ways an opportunity, in knowledge terms, to write most of what you know about third-party rights and the doctrine of privity of contract.

In the case of the second, however, it must be remembered that the essay calls for a critical discussion, however, with a specific question relating to the 1999 Act. You should be careful, therefore, to ensure that, rather than merely giving narrative notes on privity and on the provisions of the Act, that you answer the question set.

Relevant law

- Explain the basic doctrine of privity as in *Dunlop v Selfridge* – a person who is not a party to a contract can neither sue nor be sued under the contract.
- Explain also the link with consideration – a person who has not provided consideration can neither sue nor be sued – *Tweddle v Atkinson*.
- Identify the various exceptions to the doctrine of privity:
  - statutory exceptions such as third-party insurance demanded under s 148(7) Road Traffic Act 1988
  - agreement creates a trust in favour of the third party – *Gregory & Parker v Williams*
  - restrictive covenants allowing a third party to enforce rights over land – *Tulk v Moxhay*
  - the rule in *Dunlop v Lambert*
  - privity of estate in the case of leases
  - certain procedural rules where all parties are actually represented – *Snelling v John G Snelling*
  - the so-called 'holiday cases' – *Jackson v Horizon holidays*
  - protection of third parties through exclusion clauses – *New Zealand Shipping Co. v A.M. Satterthwaite (The Eurymedon)*
  - collateral contracts – where the promise is made by a third party and can be relied upon – *Shanklin Pier v Detel Products*

- agency, assignment, and negotiable instruments.
- Explain also the basic principles of the 1999 Act – enforceable third party rights in two situations:
  - where the contract provides for enforceability by the third party or
  - where the contract purports to confer benefits on a third party.
- Identify also that there is no need for the third party to be named in the contract as long as (s)he fits a class of person described in the agreement.
- Explain also that the third party has the same rights of enforcement as a contracting party would have.

Discussion and evaluation

The essay title asks in effect for a critical discussion of two things: firstly that the doctrine of privity is unfair to third parties; secondly that this unfairness has been fully mitigated by the provisions of the Contracts (Rights of Third Parties) Act 1999. To get into the highest mark levels in an exam, both would have to be addressed.

On this basis the discussion should include:

Points on the unfairness of privity:
- A person receiving defective goods as a gift may be unable to sue personally – leading to embarrassment if the person is then bound to contact the person who made the gift.
- The purchaser in that case would only be able to claim based on the defect, not for any consequential loss.
- The rule may prevent the enforcement of a contract that has already been paid for – *Price v Easton*.
- A benefactor's express wishes may be thwarted by the rule – *Tweddle v Atkinson*.
- As Lord Dunedin said in *Dunlop v Selfridge,* it allows a party to behave unconscionably and shamelessly avoid the consequences of an agreement he has made freely.
- The courts simply would not have accepted so many, and such a variety of, exceptions to a rule that was not unfair in some way.

- Discuss how often before the Act judges themselves classed the rule as unfair and called for legislative reform.
- Consider that the Law Revision Committee called for reform in a paper in 1937.
- Identify the fact that the Act itself followed Law Commission comments in (Consultation Paper No. 121) and an actual Law Commission Report (No. 242).

Points on the extent to which the Act mitigates this unfairness:
- does allow rights to a third party who is named or who expressly or impliedly is intended to benefit from a contract
- but the Act will not apply to all contracts e.g. – contracts where other legislation applies, contracts of employment, the statutory contract in company law
- and the second ground cannot be used if it is clear from the contract that the contract was not intended to be enforceable by a third party
- and most professionally drafted agreements are likely to exclude the Act
- and difficulties may occur for parties who are unaware of the provisions of the Act
- and there is likely to be variable impact on exceptions to the privity rule such as the creation of trusts
- and in any case the existing exceptions to the privity rule are not expressly repealed by the Act so may still operate where necessary.

Conclusion
- Any sensible conclusion would do.
- On unfairness of privity, it is probably appropriate to conclude by stating that while the basic rule has some logic, there must be some intrinsic unfairness or there simply would not have developed such a wide range of exceptions – and so many calls for reform.
- On the extent to which the Act has met the criticisms – obviously concluding criticisms could concern the extent to which it will a) have any impact because of the exceptions to its operation; b) actually replaces the existing exceptions.

Chapter 7

CAPACITY AND INCAPACITY

7.1 The nature of capacity

It would probably make more sense to refer in this section to incapacity rather than capacity since it involves limitations to the general assumption that all parties to a contract have the power to enter into it.

The law ultimately is concerned with promoting freedom of contract. In this way the logic of rules on capacity is aimed at protecting certain types of person who may enter a contract either for their own protection or for the protection of the party who contracts with them. It will do so to avoid an unfair advantage being taken by a party in a superior position. The law does not necessarily prevent such people from entering contracts, but the consequences both for the party who lacks full capacity and the party with whom they deal may be different.

The law sensibly distinguishes between **natural** persons and **artificial** persons, the latter being corporations of whatever type.

In the case of natural persons there are three classes that may be affected by capacity: people who are drunk, mental patients and minors. The last group is probably the most important.

7.2 Minors' contracts

7.2.1 Introduction

The Family Law Reform Act 1969 made some significant changes to the law on minority. Firstly, prior to the Act this group of people was referred to as 'infants' rather than 'minors'. Secondly, the group comprised all those under the age of 21 whereas now it comprises those under 18.

One effect of the Act may have been temporarily to reduce the significance of the rules relating to minors since they now applied to a much smaller group of young people. However, since 1969 time has moved on again. Young people are more mobile and many more are probably now living away from their parents. So minors' contracts may be important once more.

Minors' contracts are divided into three categories representing the consequences for the parties to the contract in each case. They are:

- Contracts which are valid and therefore **enforceable** against the minor.
- Contracts, which the minor may enter but can also back out of if required and which are therefore **voidable**.
- Contracts that are **unenforceable** against the minor and which in practical terms therefore may be difficult for him or her to make.

The nature of these categories means that they can and should serve as much as a guide for the adults who contract with minors as for the protection of the minors themselves.

7.2.2 Valid or enforceable contracts

Those contracts that a party may feel secure in making with a minor themselves divide into two further categories.

a) Contracts for necessaries

The common law traditionally accepted that minors should pay for those goods and services actually supplied to them that are necessaries according to their station in life.

Chapple v Cooper (1844)

A minor whose husband had recently died contracted with undertakers for his funeral. She later refused to pay the cost of the funeral, claiming her incapacity to contract. The court held her liable to pay the bill. The funeral was for her private benefit and was a necessary as she had an obvious obligation to bury her dead husband.

The purpose and effect of such a rule is clear. It is to allow minors to enter into contracts beneficial to them, but at the same time to prevent unscrupulous businesses from taking advantage of their youth and inexperience.

'Necessary' does not have to mean the same as 'necessity'. As Baron Alderson said in *Chapple v Cooper*, 'the proper cultivation of the mind is as expedient as the support of the body'. So it can be more than just food and clothing. As a result, what is a necessary may differ according to the particular minor.

The courts have established a two-part test for determining what is a necessary and therefore what will be enforceable in the individual case:
- The goods or services must be necessary according to the 'station in life' of the particular minor.
- The goods or services must also suit the actual requirements of the minor at the time of the contract.

Nash v Inman (1908)

A Cambridge undergraduate, the son of an architect, was supplied with clothes to the value of £122, including 11 'fancy waistcoats' priced at 2 guineas each (£2.10p) by a Savile Row tailor. While the supply of such clothing could be appropriate to the station in life of the undergraduate, the contract was not enforceable because facts showed that the minor was

already adequately supplied with clothes. Therefore those supplied by the tailor could not be classed as necessaries.

Clearly then what is a necessary varies according to the minor's background. Thus, what is a 'necessary' for the son of the managing director of a large public company may not be a 'necessary' for the son of the car park attendant in the same company.

But, of course, the supplier will have to demonstrate not only that the goods supplied are 'necessaries' in relation to the particular minor, but that the minor also has need of them at the time of the contract.

Under s3 Sale of Goods Act 1979 'Where necessaries are sold and delivered to a minor, or to a person who by reason of mental incapacity or drunkenness is incompetent to contract, he must pay a reasonable price therefor'.

This then leads on to two further points concerning 'necessaries':
- The minor is only liable to pay for goods that are actually supplied. This may mean that executory contracts are unenforceable.
- The minor is even then only obliged to pay 'a reasonable price'. Therefore even though the supplier is able to enforce the contract (s)he may be unable to recover the actual contract price.

One final point concerns contracts containing harsh or onerous terms. Even though a minor has been supplied with 'necessaries' according to the established tests the contract may still be unenforceable if the terms of the contract are prejudicial to the minor's interests.

Fawcett v Smethurst (1914)

The minor hired a car in order to transport luggage. This on the face of it was a 'necessary'. Nevertheless, under a term in the contract the minor was to be held absolutely liable for any damage to the car regardless of how it was caused, on which basis the court felt the contract to be too onerous and therefore unenforceable against the minor.

b) Beneficial contracts of service

The common law again sensibly concludes that the minor may need to support himself or herself financially, and therefore must have the capacity to enter into contracts of employment. School leaving age is 16 and this is two years below the age of majority.

Such a contract would be *prima facie* valid and therefore enforceable. However, from an early time it was accepted that the contract would be binding on the minor only if, on balance, the terms of the contract were substantially to the benefit of the minor.

The court will have to look at the whole contract. The fact that some of the terms act to the minor's detriment will not automatically invalidate the contract of service providing that it still operates mostly for the minor's benefit.

Clements v London and North Western Railway Company (1894)

The minor had taken up employment as a porter with the railway company. He agreed to join the company's insurance scheme, as a result of which he would relinquish any rights he might have under the Employers' Liability Act 1880. In the event of an accident the statutory scheme would be of greater benefit to the minor since it covered a wider range of accidents for which compensation could be claimed, although the levels of compensation were lower. When the minor tried to claim that he was not bound by the employer's scheme, he failed. Viewing the whole contract on balance, it was generally to his benefit.

By comparison, where the contract is made up of terms, which are predominantly detrimental to the minor, then the court will have no choice but to invalidate the contract as a whole.

De Francesco v Barnum (1890)

Here, a 14-year-old girl entered into a seven-year apprenticeship with De Francesco to be taught stage dancing. By the apprenticeship deed the girl agreed that she would be at De Francesco's total disposal during the seven years, and that she would accept no professional engagements except with his express approval. He was under no obligation to maintain her or to employ her. In the event that he did employ her, the scales of pay were set extremely low. She was also obliged not to marry except with his permission. Finally De Francesco was able to terminate their arrangement without notice whenever he wished. When the girl was set to accept other work, De Francesco's action to prevent it failed. The provisions of the apprenticeship deed were held to be unfair and unenforceable against her. They were not substantially for her benefit.

As can be seen from the last case, the principle has not been limited in its application to contracts of service only but has been extended in its application to cover contracts of apprenticeship, education and training, since it is to the general advantage of a minor that (s)he should secure the means of acquiring a livelihood. During this century the courts have taken an even more progressive view of those circumstances which can be classed as a beneficial contract of service.

Doyle v White City Stadium Ltd (1935)

Here the principle was extended to cover a contract between a minor who was a professional boxer and the British Boxing Board of Control. By the agreement the minor would lose his 'purse' (payment for the fight) if he were disqualified. The agreement was held to be binding on the minor since it was not only to encourage clean fighting but also proficiency in boxing, and was therefore for the benefit of the minor.

Chaplin v Leslie Frewin (Publishers) Ltd (1966)

In this case the principle was extended to a contract to write an autobiography.

This was held to be similar to a contract for services and was beneficial to the minor, and so was binding on him.

It follows that, since contracts for necessaries and beneficial contracts of service are enforceable against the minor, if the goods or service are not necessaries or if the contract of service is not beneficial then these contracts are voidable by the minor.

7.2.3 Voidable contracts

This category of contracts made by minors refers to those contracts which though the minor might enter with perfect validity (s)he may nevertheless avoid by repudiating his or her obligations under the contract while still a minor or within a reasonable time after reaching the age of 18.

The common feature of such contracts is that they involve subject matter of some permanency. So they are otherwise known as contracts of continuous or recurring obligations. They involve long-term interests and the law sensibly considers that, while a minor should be able to enter such contracts, (s)he should also be in a position to repudiate all obligations and avoid further liability if so desired, providing the repudiation occurs sufficiently early.

There are four principal classes of contracts falling within this category. They are:
- contracts to lease property
- contracts to purchase shares in a company
- contracts to enter a partnership
- contracts of marriage settlement.

It is clearly the case that such contracts are voidable by the minor because of their potentially onerous nature. Nevertheless, if the minor chooses not to repudiate the contract then (s)he will obviously be bound by all of the obligations falling under the contract, e.g. a minor will be bound by the usual covenants in a lease, and will be bound also by outstanding amounts owed on shares.

Whether the minor has repudiated in sufficient time to avoid the contract is a question of fact in each case.

Edwards v Carter (1893)

Here, a minor sought to repudiate an agreement under a marriage settlement by which he agreed to transfer the money he would inherit from his father's will to the trustees under the settlement. He tried to repudiate more than a year after his father's death and four and a half years after reaching the age of majority. His argument that he was incapable of repudiating until he knew the full extent of his interest under his father's estate failed. His repudiation was too late in time to be reasonable.

Where the minor repudiates the contract before any obligations under it have arisen, then there are no problems, the contract is simply at an end. The minor cannot be sued on any obligation that would have arisen after this point.

However, where obligations have already arisen before this point then the position is not so clear cut. Academic opinion seems to favour the view that the minor is bound by debts arising from the contract prior to the date of repudiation.

Where the minor has transferred money under the contract then it would appear that this is not recoverable unless there is a complete failure of consideration.

Steinberg v Scala (Leeds) Ltd (1923)

A minor was allotted company shares for which she had made the payment due for the allotment and for the first call. Since she was unable to meet the payments for the further calls, she sought to repudiate the contract and also to recover the money which she had already paid over to the company. The court was happy to accept the repudiation. This meant that her name could be removed from the register of shareholders and she would bear no further liability for the company. However, the court was not prepared to grant return of her money. There was no failure of consideration. Even though she had received no dividends or attended any meetings of shareholders, she had received everything she was bound to under the contract. She had been registered as a shareholder.

In contrast the minor may succeed in recovering money paid over if (s)he can prove that (s)he has not received what was promised under the contract.

Corpe v Overton (1833)

Here, the minor reached an agreement to enter a partnership in three months' time, and to pay £1,000 on signing the partnership deed. The minor paid a deposit of £100. When he repudiated the agreement on reaching majority he was able to recover the deposit since he had received no benefits under the agreement. There was a failure of consideration.

7.2.4 Void or unenforceable contracts

At one time much of the law governing minors' contracts was contained in the Infants Relief Act 1874. After much call for change in what was a very complex piece of legislation, its provisions were eventually repealed in the Minors' Contracts Act 1987. This Act took the unusual step of restoring the common law as it was before the prior Act, with some modification. As a result, the law is not without its complexities.

The basic position is that, with the exception of those classes of contracts we have already dis-

cussed, a contract made by a minor will not bind him/her and is therefore unenforceable against him/her. To the sensible party contemplating entering into a contract with a minor, what this means is that the range of contracts open to a minor is necessarily more limited than that available to an adult. There are therefore situations where it is prudent not to contract with a minor.

What it does not mean is that in the case of contracts other than those already considered that they are devoid of legal consequences. For example:

- Even though the minor is not bound by the contract the other party still will be if such a contract is entered.
- If the minor has paid over money under the contract (s)he may be able to recover that money if there is a total failure of consideration.
- If the minor ratifies such a contract on reaching the age of 18 then the ratification will bind the minor. It is not necessary for the contract to be ratified expressly; continuing with the contract may be sufficient for ratification to be implied.

Section 1 of the Infants Relief Act 1874 listed the classes of contract that would be void and unenforceable against the minor. These were:
- contracts for the repayment of money lent or to be lent
- contracts for goods supplied or to be supplied other than necessaries
- accounts stated, i.e. IOUs.

The law has now been somewhat modified by the Minors' Contracts Act 1987. Clearly, in modern circumstances many minors might wish to take advantage of the credit and loan facilities now freely available. Such contracts would have been formerly unenforceable against the minor. Furthermore, by the Infants Relief Act 1874 even a guarantee for a loan given by an adult close to the minor would have been unenforceable since a guarantor is said to 'stand in the shoes of the principal debtor'. So it is understandable that there would be a reluctance to offer loans or contract to supply things other than necessaries to minors. In consequence, their capacity to contract was restricted.

Now under s2 of the Minors' Contracts Act a guarantee can be enforced and minors therefore have perhaps gained greater access to credit facilities.

7.2.5 Minors' contracts and the role of equity

We have seen that the aims of the law governing minors' contracts is not so much to restrict or limit the ability of a minor to enter contracts but rather to protect the minor from those who might exploit him and take advantage of his youth and inexperience.

Logic dictates that the other party to the contract might in certain circumstances require protection from an unscrupulous minor who tries to take full advantage of his contractual incapacity.

Traditionally, while the common law would fail such a party where the contract was unenforceable against the minor, equity could intervene with the remedy of restitution to prevent the minor's 'unjust enrichment'.

R. Leslie Ltd v Sheill (1914)

Here, a minor fraudulently misrepresented his age in order to get a loan from the claimant. At common law the claimant could not recover the amount of the loan since this would have the effect of enforcing an unenforceable contract. However, had the contract involved goods then the minor would have been obliged in equity to return them. Restitution would not apply in the same way to the money lent unless the very coins or notes lent were still identifiable in the hands of the minor.

So the doctrine of restitution would still have limited application in preventing the minor's unjust enrichment.

Now the role of equity has been superseded by s3 of the Minors' Contracts Act 1987. Now, under this provision:

'(1) Where –

(a) a person ('the claimant') has after the commencement of this Act entered into a contract with another ('the defendant'), and

(b) the contract is unenforceable against the defendant (or he repudiates it) because he was a minor when the contract was made,

the court may, if it is just and equitable to do so, require the defendant to transfer to the claimant any property acquired by the defendant under the contract, or any property representing it'.

This provision means that it will no longer be vital to prove fraud against the minor to be able to recover from him provided there is an unjust enrichment and it is equitable for property to be recovered.

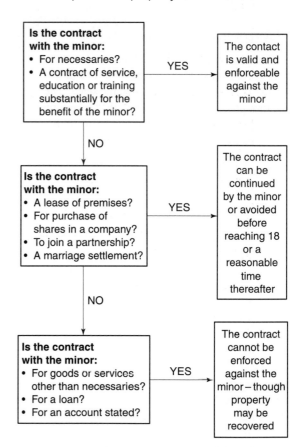

Figure 7.1 Diagram illustrating the different effects of capacity on minors' contracts

Activity

Multiple choice questions

1 From the following choices, select the statement which most accurately describes a contract which is enforceable against a minor:
  a) Brian agrees to lend Sam, aged 17, £5,000 with which Sam is to buy a car.
  b) James, an unemployed 17-year-old, has agreed to buy an ocean-going yacht, price £20,00.
  c) Terry, aged 17, is hoping to become a chef. He has agreed to sign up for a catering course at his local college that will cost him £300 a term.
  d) Sally, who is 17, has signed an agreement to lease a flat from George.

2 From the following choices, select the statement which most accurately describes a contract which is void and unenforceable against a minor:
  a) Tim, who is aged 17, has ordered a suit from Best Man Tailors. His new job in a sales department requires that he wear a suit and a tie.
  b) Helen has agreed to become a partner in a business run by her friends, Sarah and Melanie.
  c) Vanessa is 17 and she got married to Tom when she was only 16. Tom recently died in a car crash and Vanessa has contracted with Boxem, a local funeral directors, for Tom's funeral arrangements.
  d) Simon, aged 16, recently took out a mortgage for a flat. He did so by stating his age as 19 on the application forms.

7.3 Capacity and mentally disordered persons

Mental patients and mental disorder have become the subject of widespread definition in modern times, and the administration of the property of mental patients subject to numerous rules. However, the contractual capacity of such people is still predominantly the subject of common law rules, as with minors.

In considering the capacity of such a party to contract, the first question for the court to determine is whether at the time of contracting that party was suffering from a mental disability to the extent that (s)he was incapable of understanding the nature of their act.

If this is the case then the contract will be voidable by the party with the mental disorder, rather than void, provided also that the other party to the agreement was aware of the disability: *Imperial Loan Co. v Stone* (1892).

A contract made in a period of lucidity, however, is binding upon the mentally incapacitated person even if they lapse back into mental illness.

Where necessaries are supplied to the person suffering a mental illness s3 of the Sale of Goods Act applies once again and (s)he will be obliged to pay a reasonable price for the goods and it will not matter whether the other party is aware of the disability or not.

Under Part VII of the Mental Health Act 1983 the property of a mental patient now falls under the control and jurisdiction of the courts to determine what contracts will bind the individual concerned.

7.4 Capacity and drunkenness

When a party who is also drunk enters into a contract then, provided that he does not know the quality of his actions at the time that the contract is formed, and provided also that his drunkenness is evident to the other party to the contract, then the contract is voidable by the drunken person on his return to a sober state: *Gore v Gibson* (1845).

However, the party making it may later ratify such a contract: *Matthews v Baxter* (1873).

It follows that a contract made with a party who is so drunk as not to know the quality of their act will almost always be voidable since it seems very unlikely that this would then be unknown by the other party.

The same provision concerning necessaries under s3 Sale of Goods Act 1979 that applies to both minors' contracts and to mental patients applies also to those who are incapacitated through drunkenness.

7.5 The capacity of corporations

A corporation is a body which is accepted in law as having its own separate legal personality. In this way a corporation can form contracts and sue or be sued in its own name.

A corporation inevitably is made up of a variety of people, whether employees or officers. But, while it is these individuals who run the business of the corporation and make contracts on behalf of the corporation, they can neither sue nor be sued. An obvious example of a corporation would be a company registered under the Companies Acts. This should be contrasted with something like a local darts club. The club might represent the interests of the members and act on their behalf, but it would be an unincorporated association. Any legal liability would be on the members themselves. They would be held accountable on any contracts, and the club could not as such sue or be sued.

Incorporation inevitably creates only an artificial legal personality. A company is not a person and therefore will have more limited capacity than would an actual person. So the capacity of a corporation will depend on the way in which it has been formed.

A corporation can be formed in one of three ways:
- By **Royal Charter** – These charters were commonly given to the original trading companies such as the East India Company. The capacity was determined by the terms of the charter, though it was usually wide.
- By **statute** – Many of the old nationalised industries and bodies such as the BBC gained their status by Act of Parliament. Their capacity was obviously identified in the statute itself or in regulations made under the statute.
- By **registration as a company** under the Companies Acts – This would be the most common form of incorporation. Each company on formation has to register certain documents for public inspection. One of these is the memorandum of association that includes one important part called the objects clause. This is in effect the constitution of the company and the company may then do anything legal in furtherance of these objects or anything reasonably incidental to them provided it has granted itself the appropriate power. Going beyond the objects is known as acting *ultra vires* and such actions will be illegal.

When a corporation goes beyond its capacity to act in making transactions then it is said to act *ultra vires* (beyond its powers). This could traditionally be unfair on a party contracting with a company that was deemed by company law rules to know of the company's capacity to contract. Now to comply with EU law the Companies Acts have introduced provisions to protect such a party from the company pleading its own *ultra vires* to avoid the consequences of the contract.

Activity

Self-assessment questions

1 Why does the law apply different rules to contracts made by minors?

2 What exactly is a 'necessary', and how does that differ from a 'necessity'?

3 What is the common feature between necessaries and contracts of service or of apprenticeship, education or training?

4 Why does the law allow a minor to 'avoid' the effects of a contract of continuing or recurrent obligations?

5 Why were there different results in *Steinberg v Scala (Leeds) Ltd* and in *Corpe v Overton*?

6 Where a contract has been declared unenforceable against a minor are there any consequences of the contract having been made at all?

7 In what circumstances will equity act against a minor? How different is the provision under s3 of the Minors' Contracts Act 1987?

8 Why are there special rules on capacity when dealing with people who are drunk or who are mental patients?

9 How does the capacity of a company differ from the capacity of an individual?

KEY FACTS

- Nobody can enter a contract who does not have the capacity to do so
- Contracts made with minors are of three types: (i) those enforceable against the minor; (ii) those voidable by the minor; (iii) those unenforceable against the minor.
- Contracts enforceable against the minor include those for necessaries, which are measured against the minor's station in life and current needs – *Nash v Inman*
- By s3 Sale of Goods Act 1979 the minor is only obliged to pay a 'reasonable price' for goods actually delivered
- Enforceable contracts also include contracts of employment, training and apprenticeship, but only if they are substantially to the minor's benefit – *De Francesco v Barnum*
- Voidable contracts are long-term arrangements and include leases, purchase of shares, agreements to enter partnerships etc.
- Any money paid over is only recoverable if there is a total failure of consideration – *Steinberg v Scala (Leeds)*
- Unenforceable contracts include loans and goods other than necessaries
- S2 Minors' Contracts Act 1987 allows that guarantees of such contracts can be enforced
- S3 allows the other party to recover goods handed over to the minor in an unenforceable contract if it is just and equitable
- Rules on incapacity also apply in the case of drunkards and mental patients and contracts made during periods of such incapacity will be unenforceable
- Corporations are also limited in the type of contracts that they can make – their limitation will depend on the type of corporation

Chapter 8

THE CONTENTS OF A CONTRACT: TERMS

8.1 Pre-contractual statements and representations

8.1.1 Introduction

We have so far looked at the methods of creating a contract between two parties and some other factors that may have a bearing on the making of a contract or the ability of the parties to enter into such an arrangement.

The terms of a contract are otherwise known as the contents of the contract and they represent what the parties have agreed to do or to give under the contract, in other words, their obligations to each other. Both sides will have obligations as we have already seen both from the *consensus ad idem* in offer and acceptance and from the doctrine of consideration.

Under a contract, both sides will have to carry out their side of the agreement for the contract to be completed. It is commonly a failure to honour a contractual obligation, and therefore a breach of a term of the contract, that leads to a dispute.

The terms of a contract can be what the parties have expressly agreed upon, but they can also be what the law has said should be included in the contract and therefore is implied into the contract.

8.1.2 The process of defining and distinguishing the express terms

Terms that have been expressly agreed upon by the parties will inevitably arise from the negotiations that have taken place prior to the contract being formed and the statements that each party makes to the other at that time. Such pre-contractual statements are generally known as 'representations'.

A pre-contractual statement may be made orally or in writing or indeed may be implied by conduct, as when a contract is formed on the fall of an auctioneer's hammer. The impact that a pre-contractual statement will have on the contract will depend very much on the character of the statement and the context in which it is made.

In this way certain statements made by the parties will have no significance at all in law, while some will actually form the obligations of the contract as terms, and will therefore be enforceable or their breach will lead to remedies. The significance of certain other pre-contractual statements may depend on whether they have been falsely stated or not in which case they may be actionable.

Thus, in negotiations for the sale of my car I might make the following comments:

- it is a 1978 MGB GT
- it is British Racing Green with gold stripes (in fact, the stripe on one side is missing)
- the price is only £7,000
- it has had only two owners, including myself
- the previous owner only used it to go shopping (in fact, it was a commercial traveller)
- it has done only 65,000 miles (in fact, the true mileage is 165,000)

- it is mechanically perfect
- it has leather upholstery
- it has been serviced 'quite often'
- the petrol consumption is 'reasonable'
- it is an ace little car.

Even a non-lawyer would see the point that the weight attached to these statements varies, as will also then the contractual significance. The fact that a car is mechanically perfect may be of critical importance to the buyer, but what exactly is an 'ace little car'?

Activity

Quick quiz
Try to work out which of the above statements made about the car may be significant enough to be classed as a term and which you think are not sufficiently important to be terms.
There are 11:

- make of car
- colour
- price
- number of owners
- previous use
- mechanical state
- upholstery
- mileage
- service record
- petrol consumption
- 'ace little car'.

Basically, any statement made at the time of the contract or in the period leading up to the contract is a representation. The effect of the statement is to represent that the information contained in the statement is true. One further aspect of the statement at this point is to represent the stated intention of the party making it.

The law rightly has to distinguish between different statements according to the relative significance they will have in law. Where a contract is reduced to writing then the terms are easily iden-

tified in the contract itself. Otherwise the following distinctions can be drawn:

- A statement made by a contracting party which may be intended to induce the other party to enter the contract, but was not intended to form part of the contract is a representation. It may have legal consequences if certain criteria are met. It is not a term since it is not incorporated into the contract.
- A statement made by a contracting party by which (s)he intends to be bound will be incorporated and form part of the contract and is therefore a term. It will have legal consequences, though these may differ according to what type of term it is.

In all cases the court will determine what the intention of the parties was by use of an objective test – what would a reasonable person consider to be the significance of the statement?

There are also some statements made at the time the contract was formed or in the negotiations leading up to it that will attach no liability and have no legal significance. They will be treated as such because the courts can find no reliance placed upon them, or indeed because no sensible person would believe that they would induce a party to enter a contract.

They are of three different types:

Trade puffs

Puffs are the boasts or unsubstantiated claims made by, amongst others, advertisers of products or services to highlight the product they are selling. 'Carlsberg – probably the best lager in the world' is an obvious example of such a boast. It is an exaggerated claim made to boost the saleability of the product. The law will allow the producers some licence to make such statements since it is felt that nobody would be taken in by them: *simplex commendatio non obligat*.

Where a different legal view is taken is when the statement, rather than being identifiable as a mere boast, has included a specific promise or what amounts to an assertion of fact.

Carlill v The Carbolic Smoke Ball Co. Ltd (1893)

Here the Smoke Ball Company argued that the claim in the advertisement that the product would do as it suggested was a mere advertising gimmick, designed to sell more of the product. Its argument failed because of the promise it made to give £100 to anybody contracting one of the prescribed illnesses after using the Smoke Ball correctly. The fact that it had stated in its advertisement that a sum of money was deposited in a bank to cover such claims was even greater proof of its intention to be bound by their promise.

Opinions

Some statements made by a party to a contract attach little legal significance because they lack any weight. An example of this is a mere opinion. An opinion does not carry any liability for the party making it because it is not based on fact.

Bisset v Wilkinson (1927)

Here, a vendor was selling two blocks of land in New Zealand. The purchaser was intending to use the land for sheep farming, though it had not previously been used for that purpose, although sheep had formerly been kept on a small part of the land. The vendor told the purchaser that in his judgement the land could carry 2,000 sheep. In fact, it could support nowhere near that number. The purchaser argued that the statement was an actionable misrepresentation. The Privy Council held that, owing to the inexperience on which it was based, it was nothing more than an honest opinion, and not actionable therefore.

Obviously, if the statement of opinion is known to be untrue by the party expressing it, then it can be actionable as a misrepresentation.

Similarly, a party will be able to sue on the basis of a false opinion which has been stated by a party with specialist expertise in that field, and therefore who is in a better bargaining position than the party to whom it is addressed.

Esso Petroleum Co. Ltd v Marden (1976)

Esso acquired a site on which to build a petrol station. On the basis of professional estimates it represented to Marden, a prospective purchaser, that the filling station would have a throughput of 200,000 gallons per year. In fact, the local authority refused planning permission for the proposed layout so that pumps would be at the back of the site, and access only from side roads at the rear rather than from the main road at the front of the site. Marden queried the throughput figure but Esso assured him it would be possible. Despite Marden's best efforts, sales only ever reached 78,000 gallons, he lost money and was unable to pay back a loan from Esso. Esso sued for repossession and Marden counter-claimed. One of Esso's arguments was that the statement as to the likely throughput of petrol was a mere opinion. This argument failed because of its extensive expertise in the area.

Mere representations

Where a party to a contract has made a representation as to fact, which is intended to induce the other party to enter the contract, but which is not intended to form part of the contract, and it is in fact true, there can be no further contractual significance. The representation has achieved what it was supposed to do but it is accurate so it has also been complied with.

The different significance attached to various types of pre-contractual statements can be expressed in the following table:

Type of statement	Contractual significance	Reasoning
Terms	These will attach liability (and also a range of remedies when they are breached)	Because they are actually incorporated into the contract, and so they become the obligations under the contract
Mere representations	These attach NO liability	Because, while they may induce a party to enter into the contract, they are not incorporated into the contract and are not intended to create binding obligations
Misrepresentations	These attach liability (and also a range of remedies depending on how deliberately the falsehood was made) *Esso v Marden* (1976)	Because even though they are not part of the contract, being false they may have wrongly induced the other party to enter the contract thus vitiating his or her free will
Mere opinions	These attach NO liability in themselves *Bisset v Wilkinson* (1927)	Because the other party's opinion is no more valid than our own, and we cannot be said to rely on it
Expert opinions	These attach liability (possibly as terms if they are important enough to have been incorporated in the contract. If not they may still amount to innocent misrepresentations) *Esso v Marden* (1976)	Because we do rely, and should be entitled to rely, on the opinion of experts
Trade puffs	These attach NO liability e.g. 'Carlsberg – probably the best lager in the world'	Because the law credits us with more intelligence than to take advertiser's boasts too seriously
Puffs with a specific promise attached	These attach liability *Carlill v Carbolic Smoke Ball Co.* (1892)	Because the promise is quite specific and so we can rely on it rather than the puff, since it creates a separate contractual relationship

Figure 8.1 Table illustrating the relationship between different types of representation and the legal consequences attaching to them

Activity

Self-assessment questions

1 In what ways does a term differ from a mere representation?
2 Why is it that some statements made before the contract attach no liability at all?

Activity

Quick quiz

Which of the following situations do you think is likely to contain a term?

1 Jasvinder is a greengrocer. He puts a poster in his window, saying 'The tastiest apples around'.
2 Andrew is selling his caravan. He describes it as a 'family caravan'. It has one double bed and two couches on which it would be possible for other people to sleep.
3 Annie has been given a present of a computer that she cannot use, so she is selling it to Raj. Raj asks if it has a large memory and Annie says that she thinks it has.
4 Sid is selling his motorbike to Colin. He tells Colin that the bike is 'mechanically perfect'. In fact, the bike breaks down as Colin is leaving Sid's house.

KEY FACTS

- The express terms of a contract represent what the parties have agreed upon – these are often identified in the pre-contractual statements
- Pre-contractual statements are known as 'representations
- The law distinguishes between:
  - statements which are sufficiently significant to be incorporated into the contract as terms
  - statements which, while not incorporated into the contract, nevertheless were intended to induce the other party to enter the contract – these are mere representations, but if they are false statements they will be misrepresentations
  - statements intended to have no contractual significance at all – these can include trade puffs and mere opinions
- A trade puff has no effect on the contract because it is a mere boast which is not taken seriously – unless some other promise is attached: *Carlill v The Carbolic Smoke Ball Co.*
- An opinion carries no weight unless it is made by an expert *Bisset v Wilkinson.*

8.2 The process of incorporating express terms

8.2.1 Factors relevant to incorporating terms

Clearly, the dividing lines between some of the above categories of statements are not always obvious. Where a contract is in writing, then generally the terms are as stated in the written contract. Where negotiations leading up to the contract are oral, the courts have developed guidelines to determine whether a particular statement is a term of the contract or not.

In order to be a term of the contract the statement must be incorporated and form part of the contract. Whether or not a statement is incorporated as a term can depend on a number of different factors:

a) The importance attached to the representation

The more importance is attached to the statement by either party then the more likely it is that it is a term. The logic of this is clear. Where a party relied on a statement such that without being incorporated into the contract as a term, then it is unlikely that the party would have entered the contract without the inclusion of the provision identified in the statement as a term.

Birch v Paramount Estates (Liverpool) Ltd (1956)

Here, a couple bought a new house from developers on the basis of a promise that the house would be 'as good as the show house'. In fact, the house was not as good as the show house and the Court of Appeal concluded that the statement was so central to the agreement that it had been incorporated into the contract as a term.

In this way the effect of the statement being so important may make it a warranty of the contract rather than a misrepresentation that it might otherwise have been.

Couchman v Hill (1947)

In a written agreement for the sale of a heifer (a young female cow, usually one that has not yet had a calf) the conditions of sale included a clause that lots were sold 'with all faults, imperfections and errors of description'. The sale catalogue actually described the heifer as 'unserved' (meaning not yet having been used for breeding). Prior to the making of the contract, the buyer asked both the auctioneer and the seller to confirm that the heifer was unserved, and they both assured him that it was. As a result, he bought the heifer. However, not long afterwards he discovered that the heifer was having a calf, and it in fact died as a result of having a calf at too young an age. The Court of Appeal concluded that, despite the written terms in the contract, the representation was so crucial to the buyer in making the contract that it was incorporated as a term.

Where a party has requested specific details about the agreement then this can also be taken to indicate that importance is attached to them and that they are incorporated into the contract as terms.

Bannerman v White (1861)

During negotiations for the purchase of hops the defendant purchaser stated that 'if they have been treated with sulphur I am not interested in even knowing the price of them'. Assurances were given that they had not, which was also repeated when the same question was asked of samples that were produced. In fact, some of the crop had been treated with sulphur. The defendant repudiated the contract. The claimant argued that the discussions were preliminary to the contract, but the court accepted that the stipulations regarding sulphur amounted to a condition of the contract which was therefore breached.

b) Special knowledge or skill affecting the equality of bargaining strength

Thus where the statement is made without any particular expertise or specialist knowledge to back it up it is less likely to be construed as a term.

Oscar Chess Ltd Williams (1957)

The defendants sold a car to motor dealers for £290, describing it as a 1948 Morris 10. They honestly believed that was the correct age of the car since that was the age given in the registration documents. When the car was later discovered to be a 1939 model, the motor dealers sued for breach of warranty. Their action failed. The defendants had no expertise or specialist skill, were reliant on the registration documents and their statement was no more than an innocent misrepresentation.

However, a statement may well amount to a term where the person making it possesses specialist knowledge or expertise and the person to whom it is made is relying on that expertise in deciding to contract.

Dick Bentley Productions Ltd v Harold Smith (Motors) Ltd (1965)

The claimant asked the defendants, who were car dealers, to find him a 'well vetted' Bentley car, in other words, one in good condition. The defendants found a car they falsely stated had only done 20,000 miles since being fitted with a new engine and gearbox. In fact, it had done 100,000 miles. The claimant later found the car to be unsuitable, as well as discovering that the statement about the mileage was untrue, and sued for a breach of warranty. The Court of Appeal upheld the claim since the claimant relied on the specialist expertise of the car dealers in stating the mileage.

c) The time between making the statement and formation of the contract

Sometimes the court may assess that the time lapse between the statement made in the negotiations and the creation of the contract itself is too great to support a claim that the statement is incorporated in the contract as a term.

Routledge v McKay (1954)

A motor cycle had actually first been registered in 1939 but on a new registration book being issued it was wrongly stated as 1941. In 1949 the current owner, who was unaware of this inaccuracy, was selling the motor cycle and in response to an enquiry as to the age by a prospective buyer gave the age in the registration documents. The prospective buyer then bought the motor cycle a week later in a written contract that made no mention of the age. When he discovered the true age and tried to sue for a breach of a term he failed. The lapse of time was held to be too wide to create a binding relationship based on the statement.

d) Reducing the agreement, including the statement, to writing

Where a contract is made in a written document and a statement made orally between the parties is not included in the written document then the court will generally infer that it was not intended to form part of the contract but is a mere representation.

Routledge v McKay (1954)

Here, since the written agreement made no mention of the age of the motor cycle, the court held that it had not been considered important enough to be a term.

Furthermore, where a written agreement is signed this will generally make the contents of the agreement binding irrespective of whether they have been read by the party signing. (A clear warning that we should never sign anything without reading it first.)

L'Estrange v Graucob (1934)

The claimant bought a vending machine from the defendants on a written contract which in small print contained the clause 'any express or implied condition, statement or warranty, statutory or otherwise not stated herein is hereby excluded'. The machine turned out to be unsatisfactory and the claimant claimed for breach of an implied term as to fitness for purpose under the Sale of Goods Act 1893. (Exclusions of liability for the implied terms were possible under the 1893 Act.) She also argued that she had not read the clause and had no knowledge of what it contained. Judgment was initially given to the claimant but on appeal she failed. As Scruttton LJ put it, 'When a document containing contractual terms is signed, then, in the absence of fraud, or, I will add, misrepresentation, the party signing it is bound, and it is wholly immaterial whether he has read the document or not'.

(Of course, judgments like the above would now be subject to the Unfair Contract Terms Act and Unfair Terms in Consumer Contracts Regulations.)

e) The extent to which the term is effectively drawn to the notice of the party subject to it

In general, a term will not be accepted as incorporated into the contract unless it is brought sufficiently to the attention of the party subject to it prior to or at the time the contract is made. This is one of the basic ways in which judges have developed protections for consumers in the case of exclusion clauses. Rules on incorporation of terms are interchangeable with the rules on incorporation of exclusion clauses, and cases such as *Olley v Marlborough Court Hotel* (1949), *Chapelton v Barry UDC* (1940) and *Thornton v Shoe Lane Parking Ltd* (1971) could all also be used to illustrate the basic point. So the party subject to an alleged term must have real knowledge of it before entering the contract or it may not be incorporated.

O'Brien v MGN Ltd (2001)

The claimant bought a copy of the *Daily Mirror* containing a scratch card. On the card was printed 'For full rules and how to claim, see *Daily Mirror*'. The claimant bought another

Daily Mirror containing a scratch card on a later day. The card and paper contained the words 'normal Mirror rules apply'. This second card showed a £50,000 prize, but because of a mistake 1,472 other people were also told that they had won. The competition rules provided for a draw to take place in the event that there were more winners than prize money available. The paper organised a draw with one prize of £50,000 and another £50,000 to be divided between all the others (£34 each). The contract included the phrase 'normal Mirror rules apply' and it was held that this was sufficient to incorporate the terms. The newspaper had done just enough to bring the terms to the attention of the claimant since the rules were referred to on the back of each card and were available at the offices of the paper and in back issues of the paper.

f) The significance of standard forms

It is commonplace in a modern commercial context for parties to contract on their own standard terms and conditions. Very often, this can lead to problems when the terms are mutually conflicting. Where the contract has been formed orally, such terms can be relied on only if they have in fact been incorporated into the contract at the time of its formation.

Lidl UK GmbH v Hertford Foods Ltd (2001)

Here, in a contract for supply of corned beef the seller was able to deliver only part of the order and was unable to get further supplies due to circumstances beyond his control. The buyer then had to obtain supplies elsewhere at extra cost which the buyer then sued for. Both parties then tried to rely on their own standard terms and conditions. The seller's terms included a '*force majeure*' clause which would make them not liable. They had done business with each other before so had seen each other's terms, but the terms were inconsistent and not been incorporated into earlier contracts. As the contract was made on the telephone and neither party had mentioned their standard terms, even though they had later sent them to the other, the Court of Appeal decided that neither set of terms was incorporated. The seller was in breach of contract and liable

It is important to remember that since the passing of the Misrepresentation Act 1967 many of the above claimants would not necessarily have to try to prove that the statement made to them amounted to a term of the contract. The Act allows a claimant an action even in respect of an innocent misrepresentation such as that relating to age of a vehicle found in the registration documents of a vehicle. Prior to this Act there were very limited circumstances in which a claim for misrepresentation could be made. So it was vital for a claimant to prove that a statement was a term otherwise (s)he may have had no remedy at all.

8.2.2 The 'parol evidence' rule

Traditionally, where a party to a written agreement was trying to show that the written document did not fully reflect the actual agreement (s)he would come up against the 'parol evidence' rule. By this rule, oral or other evidence that the party was trying to introduce would not be admissible if it was to be used to add to, vary or contradict the terms contained in the written contract.

The rule can easily be justified. Firstly, if the contract had been reduced to writing then it was only logical to suppose that things omitted from the written document actually formed no part of the agreement. Secondly, the danger is that adding terms in after the written agreement leads to uncertainty.

However, many contracts are partly written and partly oral, and over time a number of exceptions

to the strict rule have emerged rendering the rule unworkable:

a) Custom or trade usage

Terms can invariably be implied into a contract by trade custom (see later on implied terms).

b) Rectification

Where it can be shown that a written contract inaccurately represents the actual agreement reached by the two parties then equity will allow rectification of the written document. Parol evidence can be introduced to show what the real agreement was. The inaccuracies are removed and replaced if necessary with the substance of the real agreement.

Webster v Cecil (1861)

Webster was trying to enforce his purchase of land where the written document identified the price as £1,250. Cecil was able to show that he had already refused an offer of £2,000, so that the accurate price was £2,250. The price was amended accordingly.

c) Invalidation by misrepresentation, mistake etc.

Where a claimant is seeking to avoid the consequences of a contract having discovered that the contract has been made as the result of a mistake or a misrepresentation or other invalidating factor (s)he is clearly entitled to introduce evidence to that effect (see Chapter 11 on vitiating factors).

d) Where the written agreement only represents part of a larger agreement

Clearly in some circumstances, as we have already seen, the court is prepared to accept that oral representations because of their significance are intended to be as much a part of the agreement as those included in the written document.

J. Evans & Son (Portsmouth) Ltd v Andrea Merzario Ltd (1976)

The claimant regularly used the defendants as carriers to ship machinery from Italy and they did so on the defendants' standard forms. Originally the machines, which were liable to rust if left on deck, were always carried below decks. When the defendants started using containers, which would generally be kept on deck, the claimants expressed concern about rusting and were given an oral assurance that their machinery would still be stored below decks. One machine being carried for the claimants was put in a container and by error stored on deck. The container was not properly fastened and subsequently fell overboard. The Court of Appeal allowed the claimant to introduce evidence of the oral assurance, the standard forms did not represent the actual agreement, and the defendants were liable.

e) Where the contract depends on fulfilment of a specified event

Obviously, where the parties have a written agreement but have also agreed that the contract will only come into effect on fulfilment of some other condition, then evidence can be introduced to that effect. There is no attempt to vary the terms of the contract. The evidence of the oral agreement is introduced only to show that operation of the contract has been suspended till fulfilment of the condition.

Pym v Campbell (1856)

Here, there was a written agreement to buy a share of the patent of an invention. The claimant sued for a breach of this agreement. In fact, there was an oral agreement between the parties that the contract would not come into effect until the patent had been examined and verified by a third party. The defendant was allowed to introduce parol evidence of this.

f) Collateral contracts

We have already seen how the collateral contract is an exception to the basic rules on privity of contract, allowing a party to sue the maker of a promise on which they have relied even though that party is not a party to the actual contract.

A collateral agreement can also be relevant as an exception to the parol evidence rule in certain circumstances. For instance, where a promise is made which is dependent on the making of another contract, the promise is collateral, the making of the other contract is the consideration. Though the promise may rank as only a representation in the major contract, it can be raised as evidence of the second or collateral contract.

City and Westminster Properties (1934) Ltd v Mudd (1958)

The defendant rented a shop for six years, together with a small room in which he slept, which was known by the claimant landlords. When the lease was up for renewal the landlords inserted a clause restricting use of the premises to the 'showrooms, workrooms and offices only', the effect of which would be to prevent the defendant from sleeping on the premises. He then gained an oral assurance that he could still sleep in the room, on which basis he signed the new lease. The landlords then bought an action for forfeiture of the lease for the defendant's breach of the new clause. It was held that he had broken the terms of the lease, but the landlords were unable to enforce its terms against him because of the collateral contract.

Activity

Self-assessment questions

1 In what ways can expertise or specialist knowledge be important in determining what the terms of a contract are?
2 What are the benefits of putting a contract in writing?
3 What is the effect of signing an agreement that you have not read?

KEY FACTS

- To form part of the contract, express terms must be incorporated into the contract
- If the contract is written then this presents no problem since the terms are in written form
- Where the contract is oral, a number of factors can be taken into account in determining whether or not representations have been less incorporated:
  - The importance attached to them by the parties – *Birch v Paramount Estates*
  - The relative bargaining strength of the parties – *Oscar Chess v Williams*
  - The extent to which one party relied on the expertise of the other – *Dick Bentley Productions v Harold Smith Motors*
  - Whether the term was sufficiently drawn to the other party's attention before the contract was formed – *O'Brien v Mirror Group Newspapers*
  - Whether the representation was put in writing – *Routledge v McKay*
- A party is generally bound by anything that (s)he has signed, whether or not (s)he has read it – *L'Estrange v Graucob*
- Originally, the 'parol evidence' rule would prevent a party from introducing evidence of oral agreements not actually in the written agreement – but there are now many exceptions to this rule

8.3 Implied terms

8.3.1 General

Generally, the parties to a contract will be deemed to have included all of the various obligations by which they intend to be bound as express terms of the contract.

There are, however, occasions when terms will be implied into a contract, even though they do not appear in a written agreement or in the oral negotiations that have taken place leading up to the contract.

Terms will be implied into a contract for one of two reasons:
- because a court in a later dispute is trying to give effect to a presumed intention of the parties, even though these intentions have not been expressed (these are terms implied by fact)
- because the law demands that certain obligations are to be included in a contract irrespective of whether the parties have agreed on them or would naturally include them (these are terms implied by law – usually this will be as the result of some statutory provision aimed at redressing an imbalance in bargaining strength or seeking to protect a particular group – but it can be by operation of the common law).

8.3.2 Terms implied by fact

Where terms are implied by fact this is usually as a result of decisions in individual court cases. The courts have implied terms by fact in a variety of different circumstances:

a) Terms implied by custom or habit

There is an old maxim that 'custom hardens into right. For instance customary rights gained by long use, otherwise known as prescription, are common features in relation to the use of land. Bridle paths and public rights of way are an example of this.

Hutton v Warren (1836)

Local custom meant that on termination of an agricultural lease the tenant was entitled to an allowance for seed and labour on the land. The court held that the lease made by the two parties must be viewed in the light of this custom. As Baron Parke in the Court of Exchequer said: 'It has long been settled that in commercial transactions extrinsic evidence of custom and usage is admissible to annex incidents to written contracts, in matters with respect to which they are silent.'

b) Terms implied by trade or professional custom

The parties to a contract might be bound by an implied trade custom when it is accepted as their deemed intention even though there are no express terms on the matter.

In marine insurance, for instance, it has long been a custom that there is an implied undertaking on the part of the broker that he will pay the premium to the insurer even where the party insured defaults on the payment.

The custom, however, should operate to give effect to the contract by supporting the general purpose, not to contradict the express terms, and therefore defeat the general purpose.

Les Affreteurs Reunis SA v Walford (Walford's case) (1919)

In this case that we have already seen in privity of contract Walford was suing for a commission of 3% that he felt he was owed for negotiating a charter party between Lubricating and Fuel Oils Co. Ltd and the owners of the SS 'Flore'. One argument of the defendants was that there was a custom that commission was payable only when the ship had actually been hired. In this instance the French government had requisitioned the ship before the charter party had actually occurred.

If the custom was accepted then it would conflict with the clause in the contract requiring payment as soon as the hire agreement was signed, so it was held not to have been implied into the contract.

c) Terms implied to give sense and meaning to the agreement

Sometimes a contract would be rendered meaningless or inoperable without the inclusion of a particular term, which will be implied to give effect and sense to the agreement.

Schawel v Reade (1913)

The claimant wanted to buy a stallion for stud purposes. At the defendant's stables he was examining a horse advertised for sale when the defendant remarked 'You need not look for anything: the horse is perfectly sound. If there was anything the matter with the horse I would tell you'. On this recommendation the claimant halted his inspection and later bought the horse. In fact it turned out that the horse was unfit for stud purposes. Lord Moulton held that, even though the defendant's assurances did not amount to an express warranty as to the horse's fitness for stud, nevertheless they were an implied warranty to that effect.

d) Terms implied to give business efficacy to a commercial contract

Exactly the same point applies in respect of business contracts. Parties would not enter a contract freely that had no benefit for them or indeed that might harm them or cause them some loss. So the courts will imply terms into a contract that lacks them in express form in order to sustain the agreement as a businesslike arrangement.

The Moorcock (1889)

The defendants owned a wharf with a jetty on the Thames. They made an agreement with the claimant for him to dock his ship and unload cargoes at the wharf. Both parties were aware at the time of contracting that this could involve the vessel being at the jetty at low tide. The ship became grounded at the jetty and broke up on a ridge of rock. The defendants argued that they had given no undertaking as to the safety of the ship. The court held that there was an implied undertaking that the ship would not be damaged. Bowen LJ explained that 'In business what the transactions such as this, what the law desires to effect by the implication is to give such business efficacy . . . as must have been intended at all events by both parties who are businessmen'.

This basic principle has been supported in subsequent cases.

e) Terms implied because of the prior conduct of the contracting parties

Quite simply, where the parties to a contract have a prior history of dealing on particular terms, if those terms are not included in a later contract they may be implied into it if the parties are dealing in otherwise essentially similar terms.

Hillas v Arcos (1932)

In a 1931 contract between the two parties for the supply of standard-sized lengths of timber there was included an option clause allowing the claimants to buy a further 100,000 during 1932. The agreement was otherwise quite vague as to the type of timber, the terms of shipment and other features. Despite this the contract was completed and the timber supplied. In 1932 the claimants then wanted the further 100,000 lengths of timber but the defendants refused to deliver them. Their argument was that since the 1931 agreement was

vague in many major aspects and was therefore no more than a basis for further negotiations. The House of Lords held that, while the option clause lacked specific detail, nevertheless it was in the same terms as the contract of sale that had been completed. It was therefore implicit in the original contract that the option be carried out in the same terms if the claimant wished to exercise it.

The process of implying terms by fact

The classic test for identifying whether or not a term will be implied into a contract by fact is that laid down in the judgement of MacKinnon LJ in *Shirlaw v Southern Foundries Ltd* (1939).

'Prima facie that which in any contract is left to be implied and need not be expressed is something so obvious that it goes without saying; so that if, while the parties were making their bargain, an officious bystander were to suggest some express provision for it in their agreement, they would testily suppress him with a common "Oh of course!."'

This is commonly known as the 'officious bystander' test. It is still in use, and on the face of it is an adequate way of showing that what the court is doing is giving effect to the presumed intention of the parties. However, it imposes a very strict standard and possibly an unrealistic one. While one party will usually be all too willing to accept that the implied term at issue was what (s)he actually intended to be part of the contract, the other party almost inevitably will be arguing the exact reverse, or there would be no dispute.

In consequence, there will be circumstances in which the 'officious bystander' rule cannot apply.

One example is where one party to the contract is totally unaware of the term that it is being suggested should be implied into the agreement. In this case it could never have been his intention that it be included, so the test fails.

Spring v National Amalgamated Stevedores and Dockers Society (1956)

There was an agreement between various trade unions, including the defendant union known as the 'Bridlington Agreement', from the meeting of the TUC at which it was reached. The agreement concerned transfer between unions. The claimant joined the defendant union in breach of this rule on transfer but totally unaware of the existence of the agreement. This breach was reported to the TUC Disputes Committee. It then demanded of the defendants that they expel him. When they tried to do so the claimant sued for breach of contract. The defendant union asked that a term should be implied into their agreement with Spring that they it should follow the Bridlington Agreement. MacKinnon's 'officious bystander' test was referred to and rejected. If told about the Bridlington Agreement by an officious bystander, Spring would have no idea what it was.

If it is uncertain that both parties would have agreed to the term even if it had been included in the agreement then it is difficult to demonstrate that it was their presumed intention and include it by implication, in which case the test fails yet again.

Shell (UK) Ltd v Lostock Garage Ltd (1977)

By an agreement between the two parties Shell was to supply petrol and oil to Lostock who in return agreed to buy these products only from Shell. In a later 'price war' Shell supplied petrol to other garages at lower prices, forcing Lostock to sell at a loss. Lostock wanted inclusion of an implied term in the contract to the effect that Shell would not 'abnormally discriminate' against them. The Court of Appeal refused since Shell would never have agreed to it.

Lord Denning took a more relaxed view to the process of implying terms by fact into a contract. He suggested that the process of implication need not be anything more than to include terms that are reasonable as between the parties in the circumstances of the case. The House of Lords rejected his approach.

Liverpool City Council v Irwin (1976)

Here, the council let flats in a 15-floor tower block. There was no proper tenancy agreement though there was a list of tenants' obligations signed by tenants. There were no express undertakings in the agreement on the part of the landlord. The council failed to maintain the common areas such as the stairs, lifts, corridors and rubbish chutes. These became badly vandalised over time, with no lighting and the lifts and rubbish chutes not working. The claimants were tenants in the tower block who withheld the rent in protest. The council sued for repossession. The claimants counterclaimed and argued a breach of an implied term that the council should maintain the common areas. In the Court of Appeal Lord Denning felt that such a term could be implied because it was reasonable in the circumstances. The House of Lords though rejected this approach. Lord Wilberforce said that to do this is to 'extend a long, and undesirable, way beyond sound authority'. Lord Cross stated that 'it is not enough for the court to say that the suggested term is a reasonable one the presence of which would make the contract a better or fairer one' and identifies that the 'officious bystander' test is the appropriate method for a term to be implied into a contract. In the event the House of Lords were not prepared to accept that the council had an absolute obligation to maintain the common areas, though they did accept that there was an implied term to take reasonable care to maintain the common areas, which they did not feel had been breached here by the council.

8.3.3 Terms implied by law – by the courts

Terms implied into the contract are justified on the basis that they represent the presumed but unexpressed intentions of the parties. Had the parties thought of the particular term, they would have naturally included it.

Where a term is being implied into a contract by process of law it is being inserted into the contract irrespective of the wishes of the parties. The justification here is that the law, whether the courts or Parliament itself, wishes to regulate such agreements.

The courts might imply a term by law because it is felt that it is the type of term that should naturally be incorporated in a contract of that type. Once the term has been implied the case will then stand as a precedent for future cases involving the same type of agreement.

Liverpool City Council v Irwin (1976)

Here, the House of Lords could not imply a term as a matter of fact that the landlord was responsible for the common areas because it failed the 'officious bystander' test. However, it did accept that there should be a general obligation on a landlord in tenancy agreements to take reasonable care to maintain the common areas.

8.3.4 Terms implied by law – by statute

In the 19th century the law of contract was most commonly governed by the maxim *caveat emptor* (let the buyer beware). The law was very much concerned with the process of contracting and little attention was paid to the fact that in many circumstances one party to the contract was in a significantly inferior bargaining position to the other party. Early statutes such as the Sale of

Goods Act 1893 did attempt to redress this imbalance. In the latter half of the 20th century there has been much more awareness of the needs of consumers, employees and others in contractual relationships. The old maxim has been found wanting and unacceptable and Parliament, through Acts, has often given greater protection to the party with the weaker bargaining strength in certain types of contracts by the process of inserting or implying terms into the contracts irrespective of the express intentions of the parties.

Such a process is common in Acts governing consumer contracts such as the Sale of Goods Act 1979 (as amended) and the Supply of Goods and Services Act 1982. It is also prominent in employment contracts with not only the Employment Rights Act 1996 but various Acts outlawing discrimination such as the Sex Discrimination Act 1975, Race Relations Act 1976 and Disability Discrimination Act 1995, and many other Acts giving a wide variety of protection to employees by the process of implying terms into the contract of employment.

The importance of such terms is that they provide a statutory protection that can be constantly relied upon because they will usually apply regardless of what is said in the contract.

The Sale of Goods Act 1979

The Act contains a number of these terms which provide a very clear example of the process and its benefits.

S12 – the implied condition as to title

In sale of goods contracts a term is automatically implied that the person selling the goods can pass on good title to the goods, in other words that (s)he has the right to sell the goods.

Niblett Ltd v Confectioners' Materials Co. Ltd (1921)

A seller sold 3,000 tins of condensed milk that were on consignment from America. The tins were marked 'Nissly' which Nestlé argued was too close to their brand name and therefore an infringement of their trademark. The goods were impounded as a result. The buyers then removed the labels as they were required to do and sold the goods on for whatever price they could get. They successfully sued the sellers under s12. The sellers had been unable legitimately to sell the goods in their original state.

The implied term obviously can protect a buyer in those circumstances where the seller does not own the goods and the original owner wants their return.

Rowland v Divall (1923)

The claimant bought a car that turned out to be stolen. When the proper owner took the car back the claimant was able to recover the full price of the car from the seller.

S13 – the implied condition as to description

By this goods sold in a sale of goods contract must correspond to any description applied to them, and this might even include the packaging.

Re Moore & Co. and Landauer & Co's Arbitration (1921)

A contract for a consignment of tinncd fruit was described as being in cartons of 30 tins. When, on delivery, half of the cartons were of 24 tins there was a breach of s13 even though the actual quantity of tins ordered was correct.

S14(2) – the implied condition that the goods are of satisfactory quality

Unlike s12 and s13, this implied term, as with s14(3), applies only when the goods are sold in the course of a business.

Traditionally the requirement was that goods should be of 'merchantable' quality. 'Merchantability' was a legal term with a fairly narrow meaning and as a consequence many parties might be left without a remedy.

Bartlett v Sidney Marcus Ltd (1965)

In this case a car was bought with a defective clutch. The sellers offered either to repair the clutch or to reduce the price by £25. The buyer accepted the price reduction but very soon had to replace the clutch, costing an extra £45. Lord Denning nevertheless rejected the buyer's claim that the defect was more costly meant that it was not merchantable.

The Sale and Supply of Goods Act 1994 amended the section, replacing merchantable with satisfactory, a concept that should be easily understood by consumers generally. It also inserted a new s14(2)(b) explaining what is satisfactory. The definition would include:

a) fitness for all purposes for which goods of the kind in question are commonly supplied
b) appearance and finish
c) freedom from minor defects
d) safety and durability.

There is little case law on the new provisions but they should make it much easier for consumers to bring claims in respect of defective goods.

S14(3) – the implied condition that the goods are fit for their purpose

This provision will apply where the buyer 'either expressly or impliedly makes known to the seller any particular purpose for which goods are being bought regardless of whether or not that is a purpose for which goods of that kind are commonly supplied'.

So the provision mainly applies where the buyer is relying on the skill and judgement of the seller in buying the goods and has expressed a particular purpose for which the goods are required.

Baldry v Marshall (1925)

Here, the buyer claimed that a Bugatti car was not fit for the purpose. He had asked the seller to supply him with a fast, flexible and easily managed car that would be comfortable and suitable for ordinary touring purposes. The Bugatti that he was sold was not such a car.

It may also apply, however, in respect of purposes that are implicit in the contract rather than actually stated.

Grant v Australian Knitting Mills Ltd (1936)

Here, the buyer contracted a painful skin disease from chemicals in underpants that he had bought. The court accepted that the buyer would have impliedly made known the purpose for which he was buying the underpants even if he had not actually stated it to the seller.

S15 – the implied condition that goods sold by sample should correspond with the sample

This provision is particularly appropriate when a seller is being sued by a customer for defective goods and is able to argue that the defect was not apparent in the sample on which was based the decision to buy the bulk for resale. The seller uses s15 to claim against the original supplier.

Godley v Perry (1960)

A boy was injured in the eye by a catapult bought from a retailer when the elastic snapped. The retailer had tested the sample but was able to show that the bulk did not match the quality of the sample.

The Supply of Goods and Services Act 1982

Similar implied terms are contained in the Supply of Goods and Services Act 1982. Since the Act covers situations where goods as well as services

are provided certain of the terms mirror those in the Sale of Goods Act. These include an implied condition as to title (s2); description (s3); an implied condition of satisfactory quality and fitness for the purpose (s4); and an implied condition in respect of sale by sample (s5).

There are also three further significant implied terms of particular relevance to the supply of services:

S13 – In a contract for the supply of a service where the supplier is acting in the course of a business there is an implied term that the supplier will carry out the service with reasonable care and skill

Lawson v Supasink Ltd (1984)

Here, the defendant was contracted to design, supply and install a fitted kitchen for £1,200. Plans were drawn up but the defendant failed to follow them properly. The claimants were able to recover their money. Since the work was shoddy there was no entitlement to payment less the price of repairing defects on the part of the defendant.

S14 – where the time for the service to be carried out is not fixed . . . the supplier will carry out the service within a reasonable time

Charnock v Liverpool Corporation (1968)

The defendant took eight weeks to repair a car when a competent repair should have taken only five weeks and so the defendant was in breach of the implied term.

KEY FACTS

- Terms can be implied into a contract in one of three ways:
  - by fact – because of the presumed intention of the parties
  - by law – because the courts feel that such terms should always be present (*Liverpool City Council v Irwin*)
  - by law – because statutory provisions insert terms into contracts
- Terms are implied by fact because of:
  - custom or common usage – *Hutton v Warren*
  - professional custom – *Walford's case*
  - business efficacy – *The Moorcock*
  - past conduct of the parties – *Hillas v Arcos*
- Terms are implied by fact according to the 'officious bystander' test – if an officious bystander had asked the parties about a term that was missing from the contract they would have replied that it was obviously included (*Shirlaw v Southern Foundries Ltd*)
- Terms are implied by statute for, e.g. consumer protection – Sale of Goods Act 1979, Supply of Goods and Services Act 1982
- Sale of Goods Act terms include, e.g. goods should correspond with description – s13; and be of satisfactory quality – s14(2); and fit for their purpose – s14(3)
- Supply of Goods and Services Act implied terms include – service to be carried out with reasonable care and skill – s13; service to be carried out within a reasonable time – s14; where price not stated, party receiving service to pay a reasonable charge

S15 – where the consideration for the service is not determined . . . the party contracting to with the supplier will pay a reasonable charge

Activity

Self-assessment questions

1 How are terms implied into a contract?
2 What is the difference between an express term and an implied term?
3 What is the difference between a term implied by fact and a term implied by law?
4 In what ways is the 'officious bystander' test ineffective?
5 For what reasons has Parliament chosen to imply terms into contracts through Acts of Parliament?

8.4 The relative significance of terms

8.4.1 Introduction

We have already considered how in representation made prior to the formation of the contract some are more important than others. As a result some are incorporated in the contract and others are not.

In the same way not all terms are equally important to the contract. Some are of critical importance and without them the contract could not be completed. On the other hand some terms are of lesser importance. They may, for instance, be purely descriptive and even if they are breached this will not mean that the contract cannot be carried out.

If terms are of different significance then the effects of a breach of those terms will also vary in significance and there are of necessity different remedies available to the parties in the event of a breach. The courts have traditionally dealt with the issue by classifying terms into different categories. Broadly speaking, then, the courts always distinguished between terms and determined their classification in two ways. Firstly, the term can be categorised according to its importance to the completion of the contract. Secondly, it can be categorised according to the remedies available to a party who is a victim of a breach of the term – a failure to honour the obligation.

8.4.2 Conditions

Until fairly recently, judges recognised only two classes of term. The most important of these was the **condition**, which can be considered in two ways.

Firstly, a condition is a term of a contract which is so important to the contract that a failure to perform the condition would render the contract meaningless and destroy its purpose. As a result, a condition is said to 'go to the root of a contract'.

Secondly, as a result of the significance of the term to the contract, the court allows the claimant who has suffered a breach of the term the fullest range of remedies. When a condition is unfulfilled the claimant will not only be able to sue for damages but will be able to repudiate his obligations, or indeed do both. Repudiation as a remedy is the right to consider the contract ended as a result of the other party's breach of contract. This may be particularly appropriate as it may mean that the claimant can contract with an alternative party and treat himself as relieved of his obligations under the contract, without fear of the defendant alleging a breach by the claimant instead.

Poussard v Spiers and Pond (1876)

Here, an actress was contracted to appear in the lead role in an operetta for a season. The actress was unable to attend for the early performances, by which time the producers had given her role up to the understudy. The actress sued for breach of contract but lost. She had in fact breached the contract by turning up after the first night. As the lead, her presence was crucial to the production and so was a condition entitling the producers to repudiate and terminate her contract for her non-attendance at the early performances.

8.4.3 Warranties

Warranties are regarded as minor terms of the contract or those where in general the contract might continue despite their breach. Almost by default, then, a warranty is any other term in a contract – one that does not go to the root of the contract.

It is a residual category of terms dealing with obligations that are ancillary or secondary to the major purpose of the contract.

As a result, the remedy for a breach of warranty is merely an action for damages. There is no right to repudiate for breach of a warranty.

Bettini v Gye (1876)

In a case with similar circumstances to the last, a singer was contracted to appear at a variety of theatres for a season of concerts. His contract included a term that he should attend rehearsals for six days prior to the beginning of the actual performances. In the event, he turned up only three days before but had been replaced. When the singer sued the producers' claim that the obligation to attend rehearsals was a condition failed. The court held that it was only ancillary to the main purpose and entitled the producers only to sue for damages, not to end the contract and replace the singer.

Thus it can be seen that the way in which the terms are classified is critical in determining the outcome of the contract and the remedies available in the case of a breach of the terms.

8.4.4 The construction of terms

The remedies available to a party who has suffered a contractual breach depend on the classification given to the term that is not complied with. Parties to a contract do not always think to outline prior to the contract the nature of the terms they are incorporating in the contract or the precise remedies they are contemplating will be available in the event of a breach. Where the parties are silent on the classification of terms or the classifications are vague it will be for judges to construe what the terms are and their contractual significance.

Judges use a number of guiding principles:
- Where terms are implied into the contract by law then judges will apply the classification given to the terms in the statute, i.e. the implied terms in the Sale of Goods Act that we have already looked at are stated as conditions.
- Where the terms are implied by fact the judges will construe them according to the presumed intention of the parties.
- Where the terms have been expressed by the parties who have identified how the terms are to be classified or what remedies attach to them then the judges will usually try to give effect to the express wishes of the parties.
- Where the terms are express but the parties have not identified what type of term they are or what is the appropriate remedy in a breach then the judges will construe those terms according to what they believe is the true intention of the parties.

Inevitably, it is very advantageous if a term is a condition since a greater range of remedies is available. This has the potential for unscrupulous

parties to a contract to classify all of the terms of the contract as conditions. In view of the complexities of modern contracting, and particularly the use of the standard form contract, there may well be occasions when the judges feel that it is impossible to follow the express classification of the terms. In this way a term stated as being a condition may be construed in fact as a warranty.

Schuler (L) AG v Wickman Machine Tool Sales Ltd (1974)

In an agency contract Wickman was appointed sole distributor of Schuler's presses. It was stated as a condition of the contract that Wickman's representatives would make weekly visits to six large UK motor manufacturers to solicit orders for presses. A further term stated that the contract could be terminated for a breach of any condition that was not remedied within 60 days. The contract was to last more than four years amounting to more than 1,400 visits. When some way into the contract Wickman's representatives failed to make a visit Schuler sought to terminate the contract. In the House of Lords Lord Reid felt that it was inevitable that during the length of the contract there would be occasions when maintaining weekly visits would be impossible. He also felt that the effect of accepting the term as a condition would be to entitle Schuler to terminate the contract even if there was only one failure to visit out of the 1,400. This would be unreasonable so the term could not be a condition.

Judges may of course be aided in their construction of terms by guidance given in statutory definitions and referring to the market in which the particular contract operates may also assist them.

Maredelanto Cia Naviera SA v Bergbau-Handel GmbH (The Mihalis Angelos) (1970)

A charter party repudiated their contract with ship owners when the contract contained an 'expected readiness to load' clause and it was clear that the vessel would not be ready to load on time. There was a clear breach of a term but the court had to decide of which type. The House of Lords, using guidance from statutory terms as well as from the commercial character of the contract, decided that the term was a condition justifying repudiation. The judges held that in commercial contracts predictability and certainty of relations must be the ultimate test.

So while in general a contract drafted by a lawyer should usually conform to the classification of terms given nevertheless the courts may seek to preserve certainty in commercial contracts whatever the apparent intent of the parties.

Harlingdon & Leinster Enterprises Ltd v Christopher Hull Fine Art Ltd (1990)

Here, defendant dealers sold a painting as a Munter (a German expressionist painter). The sellers declared at the time of the contract that they had no expertise on such paintings whereas the buyers did have. When it was discovered that the painting was a forgery the buyers tried to claim a breach of description by the sellers. They Court of Appeal held that the sale was not one by description entitling the buyers to repudiate. There was no reliance by the buyers who had relied on their own superior judgment.

8.4.5 Innominate terms

The problem of determining which category a term fits usually happens when the parties have been silent on the subject or where the contract

is oral. The effect of the classification is to identify what the term was at the time of the formation of the contract, and therefore all later consequences depend on that classification.

A more recent approach of the courts has been to describe terms as 'innominate', or without specific classification, and in determining the outcome of a breach of the term to consider the consequence of the breach rather than how it is classified in deciding on the available remedy.

The purpose of distinguishing between different classes of term is to ultimately determine what remedies are available to the victim of the breach of the term. The modern concept of the innominate term has developed out of a desire that the right to repudiate a contract should only be available in the event of a breach when it is fair to both sides.

The rather simplistic process of classifying all terms as either conditions or warranties was not without its problems and the innominate term was first considered as an alternative method of deciding the appropriate remedy in the event of a breach of a term in:

Hong Kong Fir Shipping Co. Ltd v Kawasaki Kisen Kaisha Ltd (the Hong Kong Fir case) (1962)

The defendants chartered a ship from the claimants under a two-year charter party. A term in the contract required that the ship should be 'in every way fitted for ordinary cargo service'. In fact, the ship broke down as a result of the incompetence of the engine room staff, and in any case was in a generally poor state of repair and not seaworthy, a fact admitted by the claimants. As a result, 18 weeks' use of the ship was lost by the defendants and they claimed to treat the contract as repudiated and at an end. The claimants sued, claiming that the term was only a warranty, entitling the defendants only to sue for damages. The Court of Appeal agreed. There were, however, some interesting points made in the judgments. Lord Diplock felt that not all contracts could be simply divided into terms that are conditions and terms that are warranties, and that many contracts are of a more complex character. He considered that

'all that can be predicted is that some breaches will, and others will not, give rise to an event which will deprive the party not in default of substantially the whole benefit which it was intended that he should obtain from contract; and the legal consequences . . . unless expressly provided for expressly in the contract, depend on the nature of the event to which the breach gives rise and do not follow automatically from a prior classification . . . as a "condition" or a "warranty"'.

The process seems simple enough. The available remedy is only discovered after the consequences of the breach have first been identified. The innominate term in this way could be particularly useful in contracts such as charters where the results of the breach can vary all the way from rendering the contract impossible to relatively trivial effects.

Nevertheless there is an uncertainty to the innominate term. Nobody can be really sure what the outcome of a particular situation will be until the term has been breached and the judge in the case has construed the term and declared what remedy is appropriate. The doctrine has, however, been accepted.

Cehave N.V. v Bremer Handelsgesellschaft mbH (The Hansa Nord) (1976)

A cargo of citrus pulp pellets to be used as cattle feed was rejected by the buyers because part had suffered overheating and did not conform to the term 'Shipment to be made in good condition'. As the sellers would not refund the price already paid the buyers applied to the Rotterdam court which ordered its sale. Another party then bought the cargo and sold it

on to the original buyers at a much lower price than they had paid the original sellers. The cargo was then used for its original purpose, cattle feed. The buyers argued that the goods were not merchantable within the meaning of the Sale of Goods Act, the term was a condition and therefore justified their repudiation. This was at first successful. The Court of Appeal, however, using the *Hong Kong Fir* approach, accepted that, since the goods had been used for their original purpose, there was not a breach of the contract serious enough to justify repudiation. Only an action for damages was appropriate in the circumstances.

The use of the innominate term is particularly appropriate where there is unequal bargaining strength between the parties or where breaches of the contract are technical rather than material and the traditional methods of classification would lead to an injustice.

Reardon Smith Line Ltd v Hansen-Tangen (1976)

In a contract for the charter of a tanker the ship was described as 'Osaka 354', a reference to the shipyard at which the tanker would be built. In fact because the shipyard had too many orders the work was sub-contracted to another yard and the tanker became known as 'Oshima 004'. When the need for tankers lessened the buyers tried to get out of the contract by claiming a breach of a condition that the tanker should correspond with its description. The court held that since the breach was entirely technical and had no bearing on the outcome of the contract it could not justify repudiation.

However, the court may still classify a term as a condition, regardless of what the possible consequences of a breach might be, where it feels that the circumstances demand it.

Bunge Corporation v Tradax Export SA (1981)

In a contract for the sale of Soya bean meal the buyers were required to give at least 15 days' notice of readiness to load the vessel. In the event they gave only 13 days' notice. This would not necessarily prevent the sellers from completing their obligations. As a result, the first instance court held that since the consequences of the breach were minor it would not justify repudiation. The House of Lords, however, held that, since the sellers' obligation to ship was certainly a condition the obligation to give notice to load in proper time should also be a condition without regard to the consequences of the breach. Lord Wilberforce felt that stipulations as to time in mercantile contracts should usually be viewed as conditions.

Activity

Self-assessment questions

1 What are the major differences between a 'condition' and a 'warranty'?
2 In what circumstances will the court ignore the classification given to a term by the parties themselves?
3 In what ways does a term classed as innominate different from terms classified normally as conditions or warranties?
4 What are the advantages and disadvantages of defining terms as innominate?

KEY FACTS

- There are different types of term – which category a term falls into is determined by how important it is to the contract
- In this way terms also vary according to the remedy available if they are breached
- A condition is a term which 'goes to the root of the contract' – breach of a condition would render the contract meaningless, so that the party who is the victim of the breach can repudiate his/her obligations under the contract as well as or instead of suing for damages – *Poussard v Spiers*
- A warranty is any other term – only damages are available for a breach of a warranty – *Bettini v Gye*
- Where the parties are silent on what type the term is judges must construe it from the surrounding circumstances – while judges try to give effect to the express intentions of the parties, remedies for breach of a term will only be awarded if the condition operates like a condition – *Schuler v Wickman Machine Tool Sales*
- Judges sometimes also view terms as innominate, i.e. the appropriate remedy is judged from the seriousness of the breach – *Hong Kong Fir Shipping case*
- This can prevent the wrong remedy being given for breaches which are purely technical in character – *Reardon Smith Line v Hansen-Tangen*

Activity

Legal problem solving

There are four essential ingredients to answering problem questions:

- Firstly, you must be able to identify the important facts in the problem, the ones on which the answer may depend.
- Secondly, you will need to know and understand the law which is likely to apply in the situation.
- Thirdly, you will need to be able to apply the law to the facts.
- Fourthly, you will need to be able to draw conclusions from that process. This is particularly so where the problem asks you to 'advise'. If you are advising then your client is depending on you to say what to do in the circumstances.

Consider the following situation:

Problem

Brian is a tenant of a flat in a block of twenty flats all owned by his local council, Badborough Council. In the block of flats the stairs are in a very run down and dilapidated state. The handrails are broken and are dangerous and the lighting in the corridors and staircases is frequently out of order so that these common areas are often in darkness. The tenants have repeatedly asked the council to repair handrails and to properly maintain the lighting. The council has, however, refused on the basis that it claims there is nothing in the tenancy agreement that makes it responsible for the common areas inside the block of flats. Some tenants, including Brian, have decided to withhold their rents until the council carries out their demands. The council is now seeking to evict Brian for his non-payment of rent.

Another tenant, George, wanting to improve the outside appearance of his flat, bought a ladder from Dodgy DIY to paint his windows. The manager of Dodgy assured him that the ladder would be suitable for the work in question. In fact, it was too short to reach George's windows properly and in stretching George fell off the ladder and broke his leg.

Advise both Brian and George.

Answering the question

It is sensible when there are two distinct contractual relationships, as with this problem, to separate them in your answer and deal with them individually.

Brian v Badborough Council

The facts

Unlike in real life, it is common, when a tutor or an examiner makes up a problem, for nearly all of the facts to be relevant in some way. Even so, they may still need to be put into some logical order to connect them to the law you need to use.

Here the key facts seem to be:

1 Brian is a tenant in a block of flats owned by Badborough Council.
2 There is apparently nothing in the tenancy agreement making the council responsible for the common areas in the flats.
3 Handrails are broken and dangerous, lighting does not work and is dangerous, corridors are full of litter.
4 Despite requests by tenants the council will not repair or maintain the common areas.
5 Some tenants, including Brian, withhold their rent.
6 The council is seeking to evict Brian.

The law

It is very important, when answering problem questions, that you use only the law that is relevant to the precise facts, if for no other reason that you are not getting any marks for using law that is irrelevant, and so you are wasting valuable writing time. We know because this problem is all about whether the council is obliged to maintain the common areas and whether it can evict Brian for not paying his rent that it is all about terms.

From this and other facts we can deduce what particular rules are important to solving the problem.

The appropriate law would appear to be:

- Terms are the obligations of the parties to a contract which if they are not complied with will lead to a breach of the contract.

- Terms can be either expressed by the parties themselves or implied.
- If express they depend on incorporation – and in a written contract this will be through inclusion in the document itself – *L'Estrange v Graucob*.
- Terms can be implied:
  - by fact – based on the presumed intention of the parties – *The Moorcock*
  - by law – by the insertion of statutory terms, e.g. those in the Sale of Goods Act 1979
  - by law – where judges determine that the term should commonly apply as a matter of law.
- If implied by fact they will depend on the 'officious bystander' test – *Shirlaw v Southern Foundries* – and would probably be implied to make sense of the agreement.
- If implied by the common law it will usually be because there is an area lacking statutory control which the judges feel should be regulated apart from in the current case and the term is 'reasonably necessary' to achieve this – *Liverpool City Council v Irwin*.
- Terms can be either:
  - conditions – going to the root of the contract and if they are breached allowing for repudiation of the contract and/or an award of damages – *Poussard v Spiers*; or
  - warranties – mere general terms which if breached allow only for a claim for damages – *Bettini v Gye*.
- Sometimes alternatively terms are classed as innominate – where the remedy depends on the effect of the breach rather than any prior classification of the term – *The Hansa Nord*.

Applying law to fact:
1 There is nothing express in the tenancy agreement so any rights on behalf of the tenants will have to be implied either by fact or by law. (Ignoring any actual rights to be found in landlord and tenant law which is not in the scope of the syllabus.)
2 There is a possible comparison with cases like *The Moorcock* but the facts are also very similar to those in *Liverpool City Council v Irwin*.

3 Whichever is used, it is likely to regulate the agreement and make the council responsible for the common areas.
4 Brian will have repudiated the contract lawfully only if the implied term is a condition.

Conclusions
It just remains now to make a judgment based on the analysis above whether Brian has lawfully repudiated the tenancy agreement or not.

Just as in real life, there might not be a definite or straightforward answer. The point is to reach a logical conclusion by using the law correctly. It is likely, though, that the term is only a warranty and Brian's repudiation would be unlawful

George v Dodgy DIY
The facts
All the same points apply.
   Here the key facts seem to be:

1 George bought a ladder from Dodgy to paint his outside windows.
2 The shop manager assured George that the ladder was suitable for the use that it was needed for.
3 The ladder was actually too short.
4 George fell when stretching and broke his leg as a result.
5 George wishes to recover damages.

The law
All the same points apply.
   The appropriate law would appear to be:

- Terms are the obligations of the parties to a contract which if they are not complied with will lead to a breach of the contract.
- Terms can be either expressed by the parties themselves or implied.
- If express they depend on incorporation – and in an oral contract this may depend on the importance attached to them by a party – *Birch v Paramount Estates*.
- Terms can be implied by the insertion of statutory terms, e.g. those in the Sale of Goods Act 1979 – here, three possible SGA terms might apply:

- S13 – goods must corresponds to any description applied to them – *Beale v Taylor*
- S14(2) – goods must be of satisfactory quality (i.e. they must not be defective) – *Grant v Australian Knitting Mills*
- S14(3) – goods must be fit for the purpose (the buyer can rely on the skill and judgment of the seller where the buyer has stated the purpose for which the goods will be used) – *Preist v Last.*
- All of these SGA terms are conditions – so if breached allow for repudiation and/or damages.

Applying law to fact
1 S13 is unlikely unless the ladder is seen as being self-descriptive in the circumstances.

2 S14(2) is more arguable – while ladders are of different heights this one was not suitable for its intended use – but we can assume that the ladder was generally fit for normal use.

3 S14(3) is more likely – the shop manager knows of George's purpose for the ladder and has assured him of its suitability – so George can probably rely on this.

Conclusions
Again, it remains to make a judgement based on the analysis above whether. It is possible to argue that George will be able to sue successfully under s14(3) SGA – repudiation can be an issue because the ladder is of no use – so George can have his money back as well as damages for his injuries.

Chapter 9

THE CONTENTS OF A CONTRACT: EXCLUSION CLAUSES

9.1 Common-law control of exclusion clauses

9.1.1 Introduction

A clause in a contract that seeks to either limit or exclude liability for breaches of the contract is itself a term of the contract. It is therefore subject to all of the normal rules regarding terms, particularly those concerning incorporation of the term.

Such terms can be particularly harsh on the party subject to them and they often highlight the inequality of bargaining that can exist between different parties notably providers of goods and services and consumers. Historically, the principle of *caveat emptor* gave a great deal of leeway to a seller and little protection to a consumer. Even where statute intervened to create protections for the consumer, as in the Sale of Goods Act 1893, the sellers' superior position was generally preserved. Thus s55 of the 1893 Act allowed sellers to exclude liability for breaches of the implied conditions in the Act.

As a result, judges gradually developed rules to prevent sellers having an unfettered discretion to avoid liability for their contractual breaches. More recently, a general trend towards consumer protection has seen the introduction of more effective statutory controls and the UK has also had to implement controls created in European law. Judicial controls, though, are still effective in limiting the use of exclusion clauses.

9.1.2 Rules on incorporating exclusion clauses into contracts

Judges have shown a willingness to redress the imbalance that exclusion clauses can give rise to. They have done so initially by insisting on strict rules of incorporation of such clauses. The rules are generally interchangeable with rules regarding incorporation of other terms.

Signed agreements

As with terms in general, the initial proposition is that where a party has signed a written agreement then (s)he is *prima facie* bound by that agreement.

L'Estrange v Graucob (1934)

Here, as we know, the purchaser of the vending machine was bound by the exclusion clause in the contract regardless of the fact that she had not read it.

Express knowledge of the clause

The first principle adopted by the courts is that an exclusion clause will only be incorporated into a contract where the party subject to the clause has actual knowledge of the clause at the time the contract was made.

Olley v Marlborough Court Hotel (1949)

Mr and Mrs Olley booked into the hotel, at which point a contract was formed. When they later went out, they left the key at reception as required. In their absence a third party took the key, entered their room and stole Mrs Olley's fur coat. The hotel claimed that they were not liable because of an exclusion clause in the contract that 'the proprietors will not hold themselves liable for articles lost or stolen unless handed to the manageress for safe custody'. The Court of Appeal rejected the Olleys' claim. The clause was not incorporated in the contract since it was on a notice on a wall inside the Olleys' room.

On the other hand, where the parties have dealt on the same terms in the past it may be possible to imply knowledge of the clause from the past dealings. In which case it may be incorporated in the contract.

Spurling (J) Ltd v Bradshaw (1956)

The defendant had contracted to store goods in the claimant's warehouse over many years. On this occasion he had stored a consignment of orange juice that went missing. The defendant refused to pay and the claimant sued and the defendant counterclaimed the claimant's negligence. The claimant pointed to an exclusion for any 'loss or damage occasioned by the negligence, wrongful act or default' of them or their servants contained in a receipt sent to the defendants. They in turn argued that this was only sent out after the contract was formed. The court accepted the validity of the exclusion since the parties had dealt on the same terms in the past.

However, the courts will not allow a party to rely on past dealings to imply knowledge of an exclusion clause in order to incorporate it into the contract unless the previous dealings represent a consistent course of action.

McCutcheon v David MacBrayne Ltd (1964)

The claimant had used the defendants' ferries to ship his car from Islay to the Scottish mainland on many occasions. Sometimes he was asked to sign a risk note including an exclusion clause and on other occasions he was not. On the occasion in question the claimant's relative, McSporran, took the car to the ferry. He received a receipt on which was printed the exclusion clause, but he did not read it, and he was not asked to sign a risk note. The ferry sank through the defendants' negligence and the car was a write-off. The claimant claimed compensation and the defendants tried to rely on the exclusion clause in the risk note and on the receipt. They failed because there was not a consistent course of action that allowed them to assume that the claimant knew of the exclusion clause so it was not incorporated in the contract. As Lord Devlin put it: 'previous dealings are only relevant if they prove knowledge of the terms actual and not constructive and assent to them'.

Sufficiency of notice of the exclusion clause

In general, the courts will not accept that an exclusion clause has been incorporated into a contract unless the party who is subject to the clause has been made sufficiently aware of the existence of the clause in the contract.

The obligation then is firmly on the party inserting the clause into the contract to bring it to the attention of the other party before it can be relied on and the party who wishes to rely on the exclusion clause is relieved of liability for their contractual breach.

Parker v South Eastern Railway Co. (1877)

The claimant left his luggage in the cloakroom of the station and was given a ticket on paying a fee. On the back of the ticket was a clause stating that the railway company would not be liable for any luggage that exceeded £10 in value. Mr Parker's luggage was worth more than that amount and when it was stolen he claimed compensation from the railway company. Its attempt to rely on the exclusion clause failed since it could not show that it had instructed the claimant to read the clause or to otherwise bring his attention to the exclusion clause.

Clearly, one of the issues in *Parker* would have been whether or not the claimant could have been expected to contemplate that the cloakroom ticket in fact formed the basis of a written contract. An exclusion clause will not be incorporated into the contract when, on an objective analysis, it is not contained in a document that would ordinarily be perceived as being a contractual document or having contractual significance.

Chapelton v Barry Urban District Council (1940)

Here, the claimant hired deckchairs on the beach at Barry, and received two tickets from the council's beach attendant on paying the cost of hiring the chairs. On the back of these small tickets were the words 'The council will not be liable for any accident or damage arising from the hire of the chair' though the claimant did not read it, believing it only to be a receipt. The canvas on one chair was defective and it collapsed injuring the claimant. He claimed compensation and the council tried to rely on their exclusion clause. Their defence failed since the existence of the clause was not effectively bought to the attention of the claimant. It was unreasonable to assume that he would automatically understand that the ticket was a contractual document, and the council was liable for the claimant's injuries.

The exclusion clause might not be incorporated either where reference to it is contained in another document given to the claimant prior to the formation of the contract but where insufficient is done to bring the claimant's attention to the existence of the clause.

Dillon v Baltic Shipping Co. Ltd (The Mikhail Lermontov) (1991)

A woman booked to go on a cruise with her daughter. In the booking form there was a clause that the contract of carriage was 'subject to conditions and regulations printed on the tickets'. In fact, the contract of carriage would only then be issued some time later, at the same time as the tickets. The cruise ship sank and the claimant was injured as a result. In her claim for compensation the defendant shipping company sought to rely on the exclusion clause in the contract of carriage. It failed. The court held that there was insufficient notice given in the booking form to draw the claimant's attention to the existence of the exclusion clause.

One further question concerns the extent to which parties inserting exclusion clauses in contracts must go in order to claim that they are brought sufficiently to the attention of the other party and therefore incorporated in the contract. This is graphically illustrated in a judgment of Lord Denning. The case is also relevant to the requirement that the party subject to the clause must be aware of the clause at the time of contracting. Finally, the case also puts into perspective some of the problems of modern forms of contracting such as dealing with vending machines, ticket machines or other situations where there is no contact with the party seeking to insert the clause or his/her agents at the time of contracting.

Thornton v Shoe Lane Parking Ltd (1971)

The claimant was injured in a car park owned by the defendants. At the entrance to the car park there was a notice that, as well as giving the charges, stated that parking was at the owner's risk. On entering, a motorist was required to stop at a barrier and take a ticket from a machine, at which point a barrier would lift allowing entry to the car park. On the ticket was printed the words 'This ticket is issued subject to the conditions of issue as displayed on the premises'. Notices inside the car park then listed the conditions of the contract, including an exclusion clause covering both damage and personal injury. When the claimant claimed the defendants argued that the exclusion clause applied but their argument was rejected. Lord Denning identified that the customer in such situations has no chance of negotiating. He 'pays his money and gets a ticket. He cannot refuse it. He cannot get his money back. He may protest to the machine, even swear at it. But it will remain unmoved. He is committed beyond recall . . . The contract was concluded at that time'. In consequence, Lord Denning says the customer is bound by the terms of the contract 'as long as they are sufficiently bought to his notice beforehand, but not otherwise'. In other words, for the party including the clause in the contract a very high degree of notice is required for it to be effective. As he had previously stated in *Spurling v Bradshaw*, when looking at what needs to be done to draw a clause to the attention of the party subject to it: 'Some clauses which I have seen would need to be printed in red ink with a red hand pointing to it before the notice could be held to be sufficient'.

One final point worth mentioning on this issue is that the courts have not always felt constrained to apply this strict approach only to exclusion clauses. In certain instances the courts have adopted the same position in contracts containing clauses which are particularly burdensome to the other side regardless of the clause not being an exclusion clause.

Interfoto Picture Library Ltd v Stiletto Visual Programmes Ltd (1988)

Here, the defendants hired photographic transparencies for a visual aid in a presentation, from a party with whom they had had no previous dealings. In the claimants' delivery note, which the defendants did not read, was a clause referring to a holding fee and VAT for each day when the transparencies were not returned past a set deadline, 19th March. When the defendants returned the transparencies on 2nd April they were presented with a bill for £3,783.50 in respect of the holding charge for late return. The claimants sued when the defendants refused to pay. Dillon LJ in the Court of Appeal held that 'if one condition in a set of printed conditions is particularly onerous or unusual, the party seeking to enforce it must show that that condition was fairly bought to the attention of the other party'.

9.1.3 Other limitations imposed by the courts

Inconsistent oral representations

A party is generally bound by a contract which (s)he has signed. In some circumstances, however, the party subject to the clause may have enquired about the existence of the clause or queried the consequences of a clause that they have already read. Where oral misrepresentations have then caused that party to enter the contract with confidence the exclusion clause may be ineffective because it is the misrepresentation that has induced the other party to enter the contract.

Curtis v Chemical Cleaning and Dyeing Co. Ltd (1951)

The claimant took a wedding dress to be cleaned and was asked to sign a document that exempted the defendants from liability for any damage 'howsoever arising'. She sensibly questioned the nature of the document that she was being asked to sign. She was then informed that it only referred to the fact that the defendants would not accept liability for beads or sequins attached to the dress. When the dress was returned it had a chemical stain for which Mrs Curtis tried to claim. The defendants failed in their attempt to rely on the exclusion clause because of the oral assurances made to the claimant.

So, as we have already seen, an oral undertaking made before the contract is formed can override an inconsistent express written term.

J Evans & Son (Portsmouth) Ltd v Andrea Merzario Ltd (1976)

In this case the carriage of the goods was changed to the use of containers. The promise made by the defendants' representative to continue to carry the claimants' machinery below deck was binding and would override any later inconsistent term in the contract.

The same point will apply where a collateral promise or undertaking is made on which the claimant can rely. The effect of the collateral promise may be to prevent the party inserting an exclusion clause into a contract from relying on it in a subsequent dispute.

Webster v Higgin (1948)

The defendant had negotiated to purchase a car from the claimants' garage under a hire-purchase agreement. In a hire-purchase contract while the goods are bought under one contract, the hire-purchase agreement itself is a separate contract. Here, the garage owners promised that the car the claimant planned to buy was in good condition. The hire-purchase agreement contained a clause that 'no warranty, condition, description or representation as to the state or quality of the vehicle is given or implied'. In fact, the car was, as the court described it, 'nothing but a mass of second hand and dilapidated ironmongery'. When the buyer refused to pay the claimant sued for return of the car and the balance of instalments due. The action failed. There had been a breach of the collateral promise that the car was in good condition.

The effect of exclusion clauses on third parties to the contract

The doctrine of privity means that the terms of a contract are only binding on the parties to the contract themselves. We have already seen that in general a party trying to enforce third-party rights under a contract will fail for lack of privity. In the same way, despite the existence of an exclusion clause in a contract, it may not offer protection to parties other than the parties to the contract.

Scruttons Ltd v Midland Silicones Ltd (1962)

Carriers had a contract to ship a drum of chemicals for a company, the claimants in the case. The bill of lading contained a clause limiting the liability of the carriers in the event of a breach to $500. The defendants were stevedores who were contracted by the carriers to unload goods. Their contract with the carriers contained terms that they should have the benefit of the limitation clause in the bill of lading. When the stevedores through their negligence did $583 worth of damage to the drum of chemicals they were sued and tried to rely on the limitation clause in the contract between the claimants and the carriers. Their defence failed because they were not parties to the bill of lading so could not claim any rights under it.

The fact that the doctrine of privity prevents a third party to a contract from relying on exclusions contained in it may mean that a claimant still has a party to sue despite the existence of the clause, where the third party is responsible for the damage, and is financially worth bringing an action against.

Cosgrove v Horsefell (1945)

A passenger on a bus was injured through the negligence of the driver. The contract with the bus company contained a valid exclusion clause which thus protected them from liability. This did not, however, protect the bus driver from an action in negligence.

There have of course been occasions where a party has successfully claimed the protection of an exclusion clause even though not a party to the contract in which the clause was contained. The approach, which is not without its critics, is to argue an agency relationship, and thus to claim that a contractual relationship is created also with the third party.

New Zealand Shipping Co. Ltd v A. M. Satterthwaite & Co. Ltd (The Eurymedon) (1975)

Here there was a contract between a consignor and a carrier to ship drilling equipment to New Zealand. The bill of lading contained an exclusion clause stating that 'it is hereby expressly agreed that no servant or Agent of the carrier (including every independent contractor from time to time employed by the carrier) shall in any circumstances whatsoever be under any liability whatsoever to the shipper, consignee or owner of the goods or to any holder of the bill of lading for any loss or damage or delay of whatsoever kind arising or resulting directly or indirectly from any neglect or default on his part' and also stating that 'every right, exemption, limitation, condition and liberty herein contained . . . shall extend to protect every such servant or agent of the carrier'. In the event, stevedores hired by the carriers negligently damaged the drilling equipment and were sued by the consignors. Their attempt to claim protection under the carriers' exclusion clause succeeded. The Privy Council felt that the issue centred on whether the stevedores had given consideration under the contract. The stevedores had accepted a unilateral offer by the consignors that in return for their promise to carry out duties the consignors would in turn exempt them from any liability. The stevedores had accepted this offer by unloading the ship and could therefore rely on the exclusion clause.

─Activity─

Quick quiz

Consider whether exclusion clauses notified in the following ways will be successfully incorporated into contracts, and say why:

a) A notice placed on the counter in a shop.
b) A notice contained in a signed contract.
c) A notice contained in a delivery note where the parties have regularly dealt on the same terms.
d) A notice posted on a hotel bedroom.
e) A notice contained in a receipt.
f) A notice on the back of a cloakroom ticket.
g) A notice posted on the machine at the entrance to a car park.

9.1.4 Construction of the contract as a whole

Even though an exclusion clause satisfies the above tests and therefore appears to have been successfully incorporated into a contract this does not mean that it will necessarily operate successfully in all cases. The clause might still fail on a construction of the contract as a whole for a number of reasons.

The *contra preferentem* rule

The *contra preferentem* rule is a device that is basically hostile to ambiguities in a contract. The basic proposition is this. If a party wishes to secure an exemption from liability for contractual breaches by means of incorporation of an exclusion clause in the contract then the clause must be specific as to the circumstances in which the exemption is claimed otherwise the clause will fail.

Andrews Bros (Bournemouth) Ltd v Singer & Co. (1934)

A contract for the purchase of 'new Singer cars' contained a clause excluding 'all conditions, warranties and liabilities implied by statute, common law or otherwise'. One car delivered under the contract was strictly speaking a used car because a prospective purchaser had used it. The Court of Appeal held that the supply of 'new Singer cars' was an express term of the contract. Since the exclusion clause applied to 'implied terms' the *contra preferentem* rule would prevent it being used in relation to express terms.

The effect of the *contra preferentem* rule as applied to exclusion clauses then is that, where there is any ambiguity in the contract, ambiguity will work against the party seeking to rely on the exclusion clause. Having inserted the clause in the contract that party cannot rely upon it unless it is clear.

Hollier v Rambler Motors (AMC) Ltd (1972)

Hollier left his car with the garage, as he had done on previous occasions. The normal conditions of the contract were contained in a form that Hollier had signed on previous occasions but not on the one in question. This form contained a term that 'The company is not responsible for damage caused by fire to customers' cars on the premises'. The car was damaged in a fire caused by the defendants'

negligence. The Court of Appeal firstly held that the form was not incorporated into the contract merely by the previous course of dealings in this case. It also concluded that for the garage to rely on the clause it must have stated in it without ambiguity that it would not be liable in the event of its own negligence. Otherwise, the customer might rightly conclude when making the contract that the company would be liable except where the fire damage was caused by other than the defendants' negligence.

It is important also to remember that the *contra preferentem* rule is not limited in its application to exclusion clauses. It can be used in construing other clauses in the contract where the term itself is ambiguous.

Vaswani v Italian Motor Cars Ltd (1996)

In this case the principle was applied to a price variation clause in a contract for the supply of Ferrari cars. The price variation would apply only in limited circumstances. When, on a proper construction of the contract, the suppliers had increased the cost to the purchaser for a reason not falling within those limited circumstances, the supplier was unable to enforce the price variation.

Fundamental breach

Traditionally, the courts were reluctant to allow a party to escape liability for a serious breach by the device of the exclusion clause. One way in which they could control this was by strict construction of the clause and of the contract as a whole, as we have just seen.

Another method that the courts devised and at one time employed to combat the effectiveness of exclusion clauses was the doctrine of fundamental breach. By this doctrine a party who had committed a serious breach by breaching a central term of the contract, a 'fundamental breach', would find their clause rendered ineffective by the court. The fundamental breach would be treated as a breach of the whole contract, and therefore the other party would be able to treat the contract as repudiated. The party inserting the exclusion clause would be unable to rely on it since, by the doctrine, (s)he would be treated as being in breach of every term.

Karsales (Harrow) Ltd v Wallis (1956)

In this case the purchaser arranged to buy a second-hand car on a hire-purchase agreement. In this agreement was a clause stating that 'No condition or warranty that the vehicle is roadworthy, or as to its age, condition or fitness for any purpose is given by the owner or implied herein'. Though the purchaser had previously examined the car and found it satisfactory, when it was delivered the cylinder head had been removed, valves in the engine had burnt out, two pistons were damaged, the tyres were damaged and the radio was missing. The purchaser, not surprisingly, rejected the car. When he was sued the claimants tried to rely on the exclusion clause in the hire-purchase agreement. The Court of Appeal rejected the argument. There had been a fundamental breach of the contract. There was such a substantial difference between the contract as formed and the contract as performed that the breach went to the root of the contract and the claimant could not rely on the exclusion clause.

This approach of the court did not gain universal popularity with judges who found it to be destructive to the general philosophy of freedom of contract. There was also uncertainty as to what actually amounted to a fundamental breach. In consumer contracts judges might be more disposed to accepting the doctrine than they were in commercial contracts where bargaining strength was more equal. As a result, the courts gradually moved to a position of deciding that the doctrine was unsustainable in the form expressed above and was merely a method of construction rather than a rule of law negating

what the parties had freely decided between themselves.

Suisse Atlantique Société d'Armement Maritime SA v NV Rotterdamsche Kolen Centrale (the Suisse Atlantique case) (1967)

The owners of a ship sought to sue the party that had chartered the vessel and were to pay them on the basis of the number of journeys made. The owners claimed, and it was accepted by the court, that breaches of the term concerning loading and unloading meant that the party chartering the vessel had made only eight voyages instead of the 14 that they might have been expected to complete. The charter party argued that their liability was limited to a fixed amount of $1,000 per day by virtue of a limitation clause in the contract rather than the actual loss. The ship owners countered this arguing that there was a fundamental breach as a result of which the limitation clause could not apply. The case was decided on the basis that the clause was not a limitation clause but a genuine liquidated damages clause, and in any case it was felt that there was no fundamental breach. Nevertheless, the House of Lords expressed the view that the doctrine of fundamental breach was a restriction on freedom of contract. Lord Wilberforce was a little more guarded since he recognised that where a breach is so serious that it is almost the same as no performance then it is hard to limit liability and still have a contract left.

The enactment of the Unfair Contract Terms Act 1977 did mean that consumers now had protection against exclusion clauses. The courts have subsequently been prepared to take a more relaxed view towards exclusion and limitation clauses in commercial contracts where the parties contract on the basis of a more equal bargaining strength. In this way a clause may be upheld where the parties have freely and genuinely agreed it at the time the contract was formed.

Photo Productions Ltd v Securicor Transport Ltd (1980)

Securicor was under contract on its own standard terms to provide a night patrol service at Photo Productions factory. A clause in Securicor's standard terms stated that 'Under no circumstances shall the Company be responsible for any injurious act or default by any employee of the company unless such act or default could have been foreseen and avoided by the exercise of due diligence on the part of the Company as his employer'. The duty security officer on the night in question started a fire that got out of control and as a result burnt down a large part of the factory. It was not disputed that he was suitable for the work, nor was it considered that Securicor was negligent in employing him. While the trial judge held with Securicor, the Court of Appeal applied the doctrine of fundamental breach and found in Photo Productions' favour. The House of Lords, however, disagreed. They affirmed that parties dealing in free negotiations were entitled to include in their contracts any exclusions or limitations or modifications to their obligations that they chose. Since the clause was clear and unambiguous there was nothing to prevent its use and it therefore protected Securicor from their employee's actions. It was also fairly critical of the continued use of the doctrine of fundamental breach.

The approach has since been followed. It seems that in common law it is now immaterial how serious the breach is. If the clause seeking to exclude or limit liability occurs in a contract made out of equal bargaining strength then the party inserting the clause can rely on it provided it is clearly and unambiguously stated in the contract.

Ailsa Craig Fishing Co. Ltd v Malvern Fishing Co. Ltd (1983)

Securicor were under contract to the Aberdeen Fishing Vessels Owners Association Ltd, who acted on behalf of various fishing boat owners, to provide a security service in the harbour where boats moored. Following negligence by the security guard, one vessel fouled another vessel; both sank and became trapped under the quay. The contract was on Securicor's standard terms and in the ensuing action they sought to rely on a clause in the contract limiting liability 'for any loss or damage of whatever nature arising out of or connected with the provision of or failure in provision of, the services covered by this contract . . . to a sum . . . not exceeding £1,000 in respect of one claim . . . and . . . not exceeding a maximum £10,000 for the consequences of any incident involving fire, theft or any other cause of liability'. The sums are clearly very small when compared to the likely cost of the damage done to two ships. The court, however, rejected the argument that since Securicor had clearly failed to carry out the terms of their contract at all they should be unable to rely on the limitation clause. The House of Lords stated that limitation clauses are not to be regarded with the same hostility as exclusion clauses because they relate to the risks to which the defending party is exposed, the remuneration he may receive and the opportunity of the other party to insure against loss. As a result, it held that the clause was sufficiently clear and unambiguous to protect Securicor in the case. (The contract was itself made before the enactment of the Unfair Contract Terms Act otherwise there may well have been a different result.)

These two cases, often referred to as the 'Securicor cases', seem to suggest that the doctrine of fundamental breach can no longer apply. They also suggest that, subject now to statutory controls, where there is equality of bargaining strength and free negotiation the parties can include terms however onerous provided that the other side accepts them. These terms will then bind the party agreeing to them even if remedies are lost as a result.

On that level, it is probably the case that the statutory provisions in the Unfair Contract Terms Act may be more effective in controlling exclusion clauses than the common law is.

George Mitchell Ltd v Finney Lock Seeds Ltd (1983)

Seed merchants agreed to supply farmers with 30lb of Dutch winter cabbage seed for £192. A limitation clause in the contract limited liability in the event of breach to the cost of the seed only or to replacement seed. The farmers planned to sow 63 acres with the seed and calculated that their return would be £61,000. The seed was the wrong sort and was not merchantable and there was no crop. The farmers sued for £63,000 in compensation for their lost production. Using the terminology of the Unfair Contract Terms Act the House of Lords held that the clause was unreasonable and could not be relied on.

Overland Shoes Ltd v Schenkers Ltd (1998)

Overland Shoes were importing shoes from China, and Schenkers, who were worldwide freight carriers, were contracted to transport the shoes. The contract was based on the standard forms of the British International Freight Association and included a 'no set-off' clause. When Schenkers sought their freight charges Overland Shoes tried to set off against these sums that Schenkers owed for VAT. Shenkers refused, pointing to the 'no set-off' clause. Overland argued that this was in effect an exclusion clause and was unreasonable under the test in the Unfair Contract Terms Act. The court held that the clause actually satisfied the test of reasonableness since it was based on long-standing established custom.

But in any case there are situations where the courts are reluctant to intervene because the parties are of equal bargaining strength and the clause is a common one. An obvious example is in standard form contracts where the offending clause is based on long-standing trade custom.

Activity

Self-assessment questions

1 For what reasons did judges develop rules to control the use of contractual terms limiting or excluding liability?

2 In what ways does a limitation clause differ from an exclusion clause?

3 In what ways can the rule in *L'Estrange v Graucob* be described as unfair?

4 What complications are created when a person uses a vending machine or a ticket machine, and how do the courts deal with these problems?

5 Why are the courts reluctant to accept that tickets or receipts can contain contractual terms that then bind the parties?

6 Why were the courts prepared to accept exclusions or limitations in the case of such extreme breaches as those in the 'Securicor cases'?

7 To what extent did the common law control of exclusion clauses make statutory intervention inevitable?

8 How does the *contra preferentem* rule help to control the use of exclusion clauses?

KEY FACTS

- An exclusion clause is a term of a contract that aims to avoid liability for breaches of the contract, a limitation clause is one which has the effect of reducing damages if there is a breach of contract
- Again a party is bound by terms where (s)he has signed an agreement – *L'Estrange v Graucob*
- Judges gradually developed controls on the use of exclusion clauses because of their potential unfairness to consumers
- An exclusion clause will not be recognised unless it is incorporated into the contract:
  - The party subject to it must be aware of it at the time of contracting – *Olley v Marlborough Court Hotels*
  - Though it is possible for past dealings to be taken into account if relevant – *McCutcheon v MacBrayne*
  - The party wishing to rely on the clause must bring it to the other party's attention effectively – *Thornton v Shoe Lane Parking*
- Misrepresentations about the clause may mean that the party inserting it in the contract cannot rely on it – *Curtis v Chemical Cleaning Co.*
- In general, third parties to the contract cannot rely on the clause – *Scruttons v Midland Silicones* – but see *Satterthwaite v New Zealand Shipping*
- If the clause is ambiguous it cannot be relied upon – *Hollier v Rambler Motors*
- In recent times the courts have been prepared to take a different view where the parties contract on equal terms – *Photo Productions v Securicor Transport*
- Providing the clause is clear and unambiguous – *Ailsa Craig Fishing v Malvern Fishing*

9.2 Statutory and EC control of exclusion clauses

9.2.1 Introduction

Provisions created by statute or in regulations are clearly the most effective in controlling the operation of both exclusion and limitation clauses in contracts. This is not to say that the common law has no relevance. Quite simply, as we have seen, if an exclusion clause has not been successfully incorporated into a contract according to the normal rules then it will be inoperable anyway.

There are two principal provisions provided by Parliament: the Unfair Contract Terms Act 1977 and the Unfair Terms in Consumer Contract

Regulations 1994, and now the 1999 Regulations, which were passed in order to comply with EC Directive 93/13.

The Unfair Contract Terms Act is an effective brake on the operation of exclusion clauses and as such a serious inroad into the principle of freedom of contract when compared, for instance, with the 'Securicor cases'. The Act applies to exclusions for tort damage as well as contractual breaches.

The 1994 Regulations, and now the 1999 Regulations, are based on the Directive which is obviously aimed at harmonising rules on consumer protection throughout the European Union in order to make the single market more effective. The Regulations are in some senses narrower than the Act. This is because existing UK law already provided many of the features of the

Directive. Nevertheless, in some ways the Regulations are broader than the Act because the directive was intended to apply in a much broader range of circumstances than the Act, and often impose stricter duties.

The consequence is that when construing a given exclusion clause it may be appropriate to have regard to the Act, the Regulations and the common law.

9.2.2 The Unfair Contract Terms Act 1977

When passed, the Act was certainly one of the most significant areas of consumer protection. However, it should be remembered that the Act does not cover every exclusion or indeed every unfair term.

What the Act does try to achieve is to protect the consumer by removing some of the inequalities in bargaining strength. It does this by making certain exclusion clauses automatically invalid, by drawing a distinction between consumer dealings and inter-business dealings, and by introducing a test of reasonableness to apply in inter-business dealings and in certain other circumstances. As a result of this some of the problems caused by unequal bargaining strength are mitigated.

Exclusions and limitations rendered void by the Act

Certain types of exclusion clauses are invalidated by the Act and will therefore be unenforceable even where they have been successfully incorporated in the contract.
- By s2(1) UCTA a person cannot exclude liability for death or personal injury caused by his or her negligence.
- By s5(1) in any consumer contract clauses seeking to exclude liability by reference to the terms of a guarantee will fail in respect of defects which have been caused by negligence in the manufacture or distribution of the goods.
- By s6(1) there can be no valid exclusion of

breaches of the implied condition as to title in s12 of the Sale of Goods Act 1979.
- This same provision applies in respect of Schedule 4 to the Consumer Credit Act 1974 which concerns the same type of condition.
- S6(2) invalidates any exclusion clause inserted in a consumer contract to cover breaches of the implied conditions of description (s13), satisfactory quality (s14(2)), fitness for the purpose (s14(3)), and sale by sample (s15)) in the Sale of Goods Act 1979.
- Again, the provision will invalidate breaches of the same conditions in Schedule 4 to the Consumer Credit Act 1974.
- By s7(2) there can be no valid exclusion in any consumer contract for breaches of the implied terms of reasonable care and skill (s13), reasonable time (s14), and reasonable cost (s15) in the Supply of Goods and Services Act 1982.
- Under s7(1) similar principles to those in s6 apply in respect of goods which are transferred under the Supply of Goods and Services Act 1982.

Definitions of consumer contract and inter-business dealing

The Act inevitably is designed to operate principally for the protection of consumers. As a result the term 'consumer' has to be defined in the Act. The definition is found in s12(1) which identifies that a party acts in a contract as a consumer when:

(a) *he neither makes the contract in the course of a business nor holds himself out as doing so; and*
(b) *the other party does make the contract in the course of a business; and*
(c) *. . . the goods passing under or in pursuance of the contract are of a type ordinarily supplied for private use or consumption.*

If the party inserting the exclusion clause in the contract wants to argue that the party subject to the clause is not a consumer then, by s12(3), (s)he must prove it.

Whether or not a contract involves a consumer dealing is clearly a matter of construction for the courts. There are many situations where a party might buy goods that are ordinarily for business use, or a businessman buys goods but not for business use, so that difficulties can arise. Besides which, a consumer can fall outside the definition in s12 and thus lose the protection it entails if (s)he holds himself/herself out as acting in the course of a business in order to acquire a trade discount.

Activity

Quick quiz

Consider which of the following may be consumer dealings:

1 A solicitor buys 200 square yards of carpet to carpet her offices.
2 A carpet salesman sells at cost price to his brother enough carpet to carpet the whole house.
3 A private individual who owns seven large chest freezers buys enough lambs, and pigs cut into joints to fill the freezers.
4 A young man buys an ambulance second-hand to use as a normal vehicle.

'Business', on the other hand, is defined in s14 as including 'a profession and the activities of any government department or local or public authority'.

Exclusions depending for their validity on a test of reasonableness

The Act identifies a number of contractual situations in which an exclusion clause will be valid provided that it satisfies a test of reasonableness. If it fails to satisfy these criteria then it will be invalid.

- By s2(2) a clause seeking to exclude liability for loss, other than death or personal injury, caused by the negligence of the party inserting the clause can only stand if it satisfies the test of reasonableness in the Act.
- By s3 in those contracts where the party deals as a consumer, or deals on the other party's standard business forms the party inserting an

exclusion clause cannot rely on a clause excluding liability for his/her own breach, or for a substantially different performance, or for no performance at all except where to do so would satisfy the test of reasonableness in the Act.
- By s6(3) a party can only exclude liability for breaches of the implied conditions in ss13, 14(2), 14(3) and 15 of the Sale of Goods Act in inter-business dealings where the test of reasonableness is satisfied.
- This same principle operates in the case of private sellers (those not selling in the course of a business) in respect of exclusions for breaches of ss13 and 15 of the Sale of Goods Act.
- By s7(3) exactly the same requirement of reasonableness operates in respect of exclusions for breaches of the implied conditions in ss3, 4 and 5 of the Supply of Goods and Services Act.
- Under s8 a clause seeking to exclude liability for misrepresentations will be subject to the same requirement of reasonableness.
- By s4, in consumer contracts clauses requiring a party to indemnify the other against loss will only be valid where the clause satisfies the reasonableness test. Such a clause might require the consumer to indemnify the party inserting the indemnity clause for injury loss or damage caused to third parties.

Thompson v T. Lohan (Plant Hire) Ltd & J.W. Hurdiss Ltd (1987)

A plant hire company hired out a JCB and driver. The contract required that the driver supplied should be competent, but the party hiring them would be liable for all claims arising from the use of the equipment or the work of the driver. On top of this the contract required them to indemnify the plant hire company for any claims against them. When the claimant was killed as a result of the driver's negligence the defendants claimed that the clause was a void exclusion clause under s2(1) of the Act. The court held that it was in fact an indemnity clause covered by s4 and thus subject to a test of reasonableness in determining its validity.

The test of reasonableness

Guidelines on what can be classed as reasonable are contained in both s11 of and Schedule 2 to the Act. These are not absolutely definitive so that the test is one really for judicial interpretation, although there is not a great amount of a case law on the area.

S11(5) identifies that it is for the party who inserts the clause in the contract and thus seeks to rely it to show that it is reasonable in all the circumstances.

Warren v Trueprint Ltd (1986)

A contract contained a limitation clause where the defendants were responsible only for a replacement film and would only undertake further liability if a supplementary charge were paid. They were obliged to but were unable to show that this clause was reasonable when they lost a couple's Silver Wedding snaps.

There are in effect three tests of reasonableness.
a) Under s11(1), which concerns exclusion clauses in general, the test is whether the insertion of the term in the contract is reasonable in the light of what was known to the parties at the time when they contracted.

Smith v Eric S Bush (1990)

Here, surveyors negligently carried out a building society valuation, and a defect was missed which later resulted in loss to the purchaser. The purchaser was obliged to pay for the valuation report. This and the mortgage application contained clauses excluding liability for the accuracy of the valuation report. The attempt to rely on the exclusion clause failed since the court were unwilling to accept that its inclusion was reasonable.

b) S11(2) concerns those exclusion clauses referred to in ss6(3) and 7(3), those involving breaches of the implied conditions in the Sale of Goods Act and Supply of Goods Act in inter-business dealings. In the case of these the court should consider the criteria that are set out in Schedule 2:

- Whether the bargaining strength of the two parties was comparable – for instance if the buyer could easily be supplied from another source then it would be.
- Whether or not the buyer received any inducement or advantage from the supplier that might make insertion of the exclusion clause reasonable, particularly if such an advantage could not be gained from any other source of supply.
- Whether the goods were manufactured, processed or adapted to the buyer's specifications.
- Whether exclusions or limitations of liability were customary practice.

Watford Electronics Ltd v Sanderson CFL (2001)

The defendants provided and integrated software into Watford's existing computer system. When Watford terminated the agreement because the system did not work satisfactorily, the cost stood at £105,000. Watford claimed damages for breach of contract for £5.5 million, or for misrepresentation and negligence of about £1.1 million. In the defendant's standard terms there was a clause excluding liability for any claims for indirect or consequential losses whether arising from negligence or otherwise, and limiting any liability to the price of the goods as supplied. UCTA was held to apply so the question was whether or not the clause satisfied the test of reasonableness. The Court of Appeal held that it did since the parties were of equal bargaining power and the limitation clause was subject to negotiation when the contract was made.

c) S11(4) specifically concerns limitation clauses. Here the party inserting the clause must show that a capability to meet liability if it arose. Insurance will also be considered.

George Mitchell Ltd v Finney Lock Seeds Ltd (1983)

Here, the House of Lords considered that the clause limiting damages to the price of the seeds was unreasonable since the suppliers had often settled out of court in the past and could have insured against such loss without altering their profits substantially.

Contracts falling outside the scope of the Act

A number of contracts of specific types will not be covered b the provisions of the Act. These are to be found in Schedule 1:
- contracts of insurance
- contracts for the creation, transfer or termination of interests in land
- contracts that involve patents, copyright and other intellectual property
- contracts for the creation or dissolution of companies
- contracts for marine salvage, charter parties, or carriage of goods by sea or air (except in the case of incidents falling within the scope of s2(1).

9.2.3 The Unfair Terms in Consumer Contracts Regulations 1999

The scope of the Regulations

The Regulations are straightaway significantly different in operation to the Act because they cover contractual terms in general not just exclusion clauses. Nevertheless, they will as their name suggests operate only in relation to consumer contracts.

Consumer dealing is defined in different terms than in the Act.
- A seller or supplier is defined as 'any person who sells or supplies goods or services and who in making a contract is acting for purposes related to his business'. So this is wider than in the Act.
- A consumer is defined as 'any natural person who is acting for purposes which are outside his trade, business or profession'. So this is narrower.

According to Regulation 39(1), the Regulations will apply only where the parties have not individually negotiated the term in question. So the Regulations operate particularly in relation to standard form contracts. In order to avoid the operation of the Regulations, therefore, the seller or supplier will need to show that the contract has been negotiated and is not standard form.

As with the Act the Regulations will not operate in the case of certain types of contract. These are identified in Schedule 1 and include contracts relating to employment, succession, family law rights and partnerships and companies. The Regulations will not cover either insurance contracts where the risk and the insured are clearly defined. Other than this, the scope of the Regulations seems to be much broader than the Act, though their exact scope is uncertain.

Terms falling within the scope of the regulations

The Regulations operate in respect of 'unfair terms'. According to Regulation 4(1), an unfair term is 'any term which contrary to good faith causes a significant imbalance in the parties' rights and obligations under the contract to the detriment of the consumer'. As a result, the Regulations introduce a general concept of unfairness into the making of contracts, which is then subject to controls.

'Good faith' is considered in Schedule 2. This identifies a number of factors that must be looked at in order to establish good faith:

- the relative bargaining strength of the parties to the contract
- whether the seller or supplier gave the consumer any inducement in order that (s)he would agree to the term of the contract in question
- whether the goods sold or services supplied under the contract were to the special order of the consumer
- the extent to which the seller or supplier has dealt fairly and equitably with the consumer.

As well as these general guidelines, the Regulations in Schedule 3 list a great number of terms that may generally be regarded as unfair, though the list is not intended to be exhaustive.

a) Terms which limit or exclude liability for the death or personal injury of the consumer arising from an act or omission of the seller or supplier.

b) Terms which inappropriately limit or exclude liability for a partial performance, a non-performance, or an inadequate performance.

c) Terms that include provisions binding the consumer but which are only at the discretion of the seller or supplier.

d) Terms allowing the seller or supplier to retain sums already paid over by the consumer who cancels the contract where there is no reciprocal term in relation to a cancellation by the seller or supplier.

e) Terms requiring a consumer who is in breach of the contract to pay excessive sums in compensation to the seller or supplier.

f) Terms allowing the seller or supplier to dissolve the contract where the same facility is not made available to the consumer by the contract.

g) Terms that enable a seller or supplier to dissolve a contract that has only indeterminate duration without giving reasonable notice of the dissolution, except where there are serious grounds for doing so.

h) Terms which automatically allow a seller or supplier to extend a contract of fixed duration where the consumer does not indicate otherwise, when the deadline set for the consumer to indicate the contrary desire not to extend the contract is set unreasonably early.

i) Terms which irrevocably bind the consumer to terms which (s)he had no real opportunity to become acquainted with prior to the formation of the contract.

j) Terms that allow the seller or supplier to unilaterally alter terms without any valid reason specified in the contract.

k) Terms allowing the seller or supplier to unilaterally alter without any valid reason the character of the goods or services supplied.

l) Terms enabling the price of goods to be determined at the time of delivery or which allow a seller or supplier to alter prices without the consumer having the opportunity to cancel the contract.

m) Terms giving the seller or supplier the right to interpret terms of the contract or otherwise to determine whether the goods or services supplied correspond to the requirements of the contract.

n) Terms which limit obligations or commitments made by the agents of the sellers or suppliers.

o) Terms requiring the consumer to comply with all obligations under the contract but not imposing a similar obligation on the sellers or suppliers.

p) Terms which grant the sellers or suppliers the right to transfer obligations under the contract which might then have the effect of reducing the consumer's rights under any guarantees.

q) Terms which would have the effect of hindering the right of the consumer to take legal action or which would restrict the availability of evidence.

A further requirement under Regulation 6 is that the terms of a contract should be expressed in plain and intelligible language. If any term is then found to be unfair under the Regulations, it will not bind the consumer.

The Regulations still have certain limitations. They do not apply to any term that has been individually negotiated. This quite sensibly preserves the principle of freedom of contract, but it also has the effect in some cases of presuming an equality of bargaining strength that does not in fact exist. In introducing the Regulations, the Government construed the provisions indicated in the Directive quite narrowly. As a result of this, while the Trading Standards department has the power to challenge the standard form contracts of companies and large corporations, the same facility has not been extended to the consumer groups who may have wished to police contracts. In consequence, the Directive may not be given full effect.

Activity

Self-assessment questions

1 To what extent will the Unfair Contract Terms Act prevent the exclusion or limitation of liability for negligence?
2 In what ways are a consumer dealing and an inter-business dealing different?
3 For what reasons does the Unfair Contract Terms Act make certain exclusions automatically invalid if inserted in a contract?
4 Under the Unfair Contract Terms Act, what exactly does 'reasonable' mean?
5 Is there any difference between who is protected by the Unfair Contract Terms Act and the Unfair Terms in Consumer Contracts Regulations?

KEY FACTS

- Common-law controls of exclusion clauses have also been supplemented by statutory controls through the Unfair Contract Terms Act 1977 and through the Unfair Terms in Consumer Contracts Regulations 1994, and now 1999 (the latter to comply with European Directive 93/13)
- The Act draws a distinction between consumer dealings and inter-business dealings
- Clauses in certain types of contract are made void by the Act, e.g. exclusion of liability for death or injury caused by negligence – s2(1); exclusions of liability for breaches of the implied terms in the Sale of Goods Act and Supply of Goods and Services Act – ss 6(1), 6(2) and 7(2)
- Clauses in certain other circumstances depend for their validity on a test of reasonableness, e.g. damage caused by negligence – s2(2); standard term contracts – s3; breaches of Sale of Goods Act and Supply of Goods and Services Act implied terms – ss 6(3) and 7(3)
- Under s11, what is reasonable depends on the knowledge of the parties at the time of contracting and a number of factors can be taken into account e.g. whether the goods were freely available elsewhere, whether the goods were made to the buyer's specification etc.
- The Regulations are much wider and refer to unfair terms generally, not just exclusion clauses, but apply in consumer contracts only
- In general they are aimed at remedying inequality in bargaining strength and remove unequal conditions

Chapter 10

VITIATING FACTORS: VOID AND VOIDABLE CONTRACTS

10.1 Introduction

We have looked so far at the requirements made on parties when entering into contracts and also at the obligations that parties may make for themselves when they have in fact contracted. If the parties have not complied with all of the necessary requirements that we looked at in Chapter 1 then there will not be a contract in existence anyway.

Nevertheless, the mere fact that all of the rules of formation have been complied with does not make a contract perfect. For instance, where a party has contracted on the basis of false information this is a denial of freedom of contract. That party may clearly have been unprepared to enter the contract if only (s)he had known the true facts.

Thus, even though the various requirements of formation might have been fully met, a party may still have legal rights and remedies because of other defects that are later discovered that are to do with other 'imperfections' at the time the contract was formed. Indeed contracts affected in such a way are often referred to as 'imperfect contracts'.

The defects in question are generally known as vitiating factors. A vitiating factor is one that may operate to invalidate an otherwise validly formed contract, that is one that conforms to all the rules of formation already identified.

To vitiate basically means to impair the quality of, to corrupt or to debase. In contractual terms this means that factors present at the time of the formation of the contract, possibly unknown to one or either party, mean that the contract lacks the essential characteristic of voluntariness, is based on misinformation or is of a type frowned on by the law.

As a result, the role of the law is to provide a remedy to the party who may not have wished to enter the contract given full knowledge of the vitiating factor at the time of formation.

There can be two effects if a contract is vitiated: it may be **void** or it may be **voidable**. Whether the contract is void or voidable in a given case depends on the type of vitiating factor that is complained of.

10.2 Void contracts

In the case of certain vitiating factors, the effect of demonstrating the presence of the vitiating factor to the court's satisfaction is to render the contract **void**. It is as though it has never been.

Stating that a contract is void is in many ways the same as stating that the contract does not exist.

This is because identifying a contract as void is identifying it as having no validity and therefore no enforceability in law.

10.3 Voidable contracts

Where a contract is **voidable** there are different possibilities. The vitiating factor is identified and acknowledged but this does not necessarily mean that the contract is at an end.

A party who has entered a contract that is void-able for a vitiating factor can continue with the contract if that is to his/her benefit.

On the other hand that party can avoid their responsibilities under the contract and in effect set the contract aside.

10.4 The classes of vitiating factors

There are essentially four classes of vitiating factors which themselves are subject to sub-divisions:

- Misrepresentation – where a contract has been formed but as the result of false information about its substance the innocent contracting party who is the victim of the misrepresentation can avoid the contract
- Mistake – where the contract has been formed on the basis of mistakes about contracting terms made by either party or both parties – if the mistake is operative then the contract is void
- Duress and undue influence – duress being a common law area where the contract has resulted from actual or threatened violence and

the contract is voidable – this is now supplemented by economic duress which is improper coercion in a commercial context – and undue influence which is an equitable doctrine concerning contracts that have been made following improper coercion and the innocent party can avoid the contract

- Illegality – of which there are many types where the type of contract will not be accepted at all, sometime by the courts and sometimes by statute, as being legitimate and enforceable – usually for reasons of public policy

Activity

Self-assessment questions
1 What does 'vitiating factor' mean?
2 What are the basic consequences of a contract being declared void?
3 What are the basic consequences of a contract being declared voidable?
4 Will a contract made on the basis of a misrepresentation generally be void or voidable?
5 Will a contract made on the basis of duress generally be void or voidable?
6 Will a contract that is declared illegal be void or voidable?

Chapter 11

VITIATING FACTORS: MISREPRESENTATION

11.1 General

We have already considered, in Chapter 3, that statements made before or at the time of contracting are known as representations. These representations can, if they are incorporated into the contract, be terms of the contract and as such may be actionable if they are breached.

Representations that are not incorporated into the contract will have no contractual significance if they are truly stated. They will have acted to induce the other party into the contract but that is where they end. Alternatively, they may be 'puffs' having no contractual significance.

A falsely made representation, however, is a **misrepresentation** and it can have contractual significance even though it does not form part of the contract. In order to be actionable, therefore, the statement must not only be false but have acted to induce the other party to enter the contract.

Misrepresentation may refer to the false statement itself or it may be the action of making the false statement. The statement may be false or merely incorrect, for it is now possible to claim for an innocent misrepresentation.

The consequences of a contract having been formed on the basis of a misrepresentation are for the contract to be voidable at the request of the party who is the victim of the misrepresentation. It is not void because this denies that party the right to continue with the contract if that is in their interest.

Traditionally, misrepresentation was not actionable at common law. Some relief was available in equity, subject to certain qualifications, and later a remedy was available where fraud could be proved. In general, though, a party had little possibility of claiming against a misrepresentation until the passing of the Misrepresentation Act 1967. For this reason, it was often critical in the past for a party to prove that a statement made to them before the contract was a term.

It may still be advantageous to a party to identify that a representation has been incorporated as a term, though this is obviously more difficult where the contract is written, so that misrepresentation should still be viewed in the general context of pre-contractual statements and representations.

A final point about misrepresentation is that it also shares some features with common mistake. As a consequence, it is not impossible to see both pleaded in a case.

11.2 When a misrepresentation occurs

Definition

A misrepresentation occurs, as we have already said, when a representation made at or before the time of the contract is also falsely stated. A misrepresentation can therefore be defined as a statement of material fact, made by one party to a contract to the other party to the contract, during the negotiations leading up to the formation of the contract, which was intended to operate and did operate as an inducement to the other party to enter the contract, but which was not intended to be a binding obligation under the contract, and which was untrue or incorrectly stated.

This is a very precise definition and if not conformed to it will not give rise to a misrepresentation. The components of this definition then should be considered individually.

a) The statement complained of is required to be one of material fact

- It cannot therefore have been a mere opinion, unless of course the opinion was not actually held at the time of the making of the statement.

Bisset v Wilkinson (1927)

A representation as to the number of sheep land could hold was not based on any expert knowledge so could neither be relied upon nor be actionable as a misrepresentation.

- Neither can it be a statement expressing future intention which would be speculation rather than fact. Though it could be if the statement was falsely representing a state of mind which did not exist.

Edgington v Fitzmaurice (1885)

The directors of a company borrowed money representing that they would use the loan for the improvement of the company's buildings. In fact they had intended from the start to use the loan to pay off serious, existing debts. They had misrepresented what their actual intentions were.

- It could not either be a mere 'puff' which attaches no weight and is not intended to be relied upon at all.

Carlill v The Carbolic Smoke Ball Co. Ltd (1893)

The company's argument, that its promise to pay £100 to whoever contracted flu was only a puff, failed. The maxim *simplex commendatio non obligat* could not apply where it had supported the promise by lodging £1,000 in a bank to cover possible claims.

b) The statement that is claimed to be a misrepresentation must have been made by one party to the contract to the other party

As a result, it will not be a misrepresentation where the false statement that it is argued induced the other party to contract was made by a third party, unless that third party is the agent of the other party.

Peyman v Lanjani (1985)

The defendant took the lease of premises under an agreement requiring the landlord's permission. The defendant did not attend the meeting at which the agreement was struck but sent an agent who he thought would create a better impression with the landlord. He later decided to sell the lease on to the claimant and again this would require the landlord's permission. Once more he sent his agent. The claimant discovered the deception after he had paid over £10,000 under the agreement with the defendant. He then successfully applied to rescind the contract. Using the agent was a misrepresentation of the legitimacy of the lease which had never been agreed between the defendant and the landlord.

c) The statement complained of must have been made before or at the time of the contract

If the statement therefore was made after the agreement was reached then it cannot be actionable as a misrepresentation because it had no effect on the formation of the contract.

Roscorla v Thomas (1842)

After a deal had been struck for the sale and purchase of a horse the seller represented that it was 'sound and free from vice'. In fact, the horse was unruly but the purchaser could not claim since the promise was made after the agreement.

d) The statement has to be an inducement to enter the contract

- Therefore it must be materially important to the making of the contract.

JEB Fasteners Ltd v Marks Bloom & Co. Ltd (1983)

The claimant engaged in a take-over of another company in order to obtain the services of two directors of the other company. In investigating the company it relied on accounts which had been negligently prepared. There could be no claim of misrepresentation since the purpose of taking over the company was to secure the services of the directors and the accounts were no inducement. They were not material to the real purpose.

- Though it will not matter that the representation would not generally be an inducement as long as it induced the claimant.

Museprime Properties Ltd v Adhill Properties Ltd (1990)

Three properties were sold by auction. There was a misrepresentation as to the existence of an outstanding rent review which could result in increased rents and therefore increased revenue. The defendants unsuccessfully challenged the claimants' claim for rescission arguing that the statement could realistically induce nobody to enter the contract.

- It cannot be an inducement where the other party is unaware of the misrepresentation.
- It will not be a misrepresentation where the party to whom it is made already knows the statement to be false.
- It will not be a misrepresentation where the party to whom it was made never actually relied upon the statement in entering the contract.

Attwood v Small (1838)

A mine was purchased and certain information given as to its remaining capacity. This was in fact false. The claimant could not argue a misrepresentation, however, since in buying the mine he had actually relied on his own mineral survey which was also inaccurate.

e) The statement was not intended to form part of the contract

If it were intended to be contractually binding then it would be a warranty rather than a misrepresentation.

Couchman v Hill (1947)

Here, the statement that the heifer was 'unserved' could not be a misrepresentation because of the significance attached to it. It was a term incorporated into the contract.

f) The representation was falsely made

Clearly if the representation was true it would have no further contractual significance once the contract was formed.

11.3 The different types of misrepresentation

11.3.1 The character of a misrepresentation

A misrepresentation can obviously arise in a number of different ways. It could be a merely inaccurate statement, made, for instance, in all innocence, the inaccuracy being unknown to the maker of the statement. This could happen where the maker of the statement is relying on information supplied in manufacturers specifications for example, or oral statements made about goods by a previous owner. A misrepresentation can also be a quite deliberate lie, intended to deceive and stated in full knowledge that it is untrue. In between these points a misrepresentation can be carelessly made by assuming knowledge and failing to check on the actual details.

As a result, misrepresentations can be classified according to type. Since the passing of the Misrepresentation Act 1967 the significance is less marked than it was, but it can still be important in determining what remedy is available to a party who is the victim of the misrepresentation. Traditionally, the character of the misrepresentation was vital since only a fraudulently made misrepresentation was actionable, and in the tort of deceit rather than in the law of contract.

Originally, everything that was not a fraud was classed as an innocent misrepresentation and the only remedy was in equity for rescission of the contract. Now it is possible to identify fraudulent, negligent and innocent misrepresentations, and there are remedies available in common law and under statute.

11.3.2 Fraudulent misrepresentation

At common law, traditionally, the only action available for a misrepresentation was where fraud could also be proved. This action itself is fairly recent coming only at the end of the last century. This demonstrates clearly how vital it was to many litigants in the past to show that a statement on which they had relied had been incorporated into the contract as a term, otherwise they might be left without any remedy at all.

Derry v Peek (1889)

A tram company was licensed to operate horse drawn trams by Act of Parliament. Under the Act it would also be able to use mechanical power by gaining the certification of the Board of Trade. It made an application and also issued a prospectus to raise further share capital. In this, honestly believing that permission would be granted, it falsely represented that it was able to use mechanical power. In the event, its application was denied and the company fell into liquidation. Peek, who had invested on the strength of the representation in the prospectus and lost money, sued. His action failed since there was insufficient proof of fraud. Lord Herschell in the House of Lords defined the action as requiring actual proof that the false representation was made 'knowingly or without belief in its truth or recklessly careless whether it be true or false'.

So those are the three possibilities if an action in deceit is to be successful. 'Knowingly' is straightforward: the representor knew the inaccuracy of his/her statement. In other words, there is a deliberate falsehood. If the representor acted without belief in the statement then this is also a statement falsely made. A recklessly made statement must be something more than mere carelessness. In all cases the essence of liability is the dishonesty of the defendant in making a statement which (s)he did not honestly know to be true. The motive for making the statement is largely irrelevant. If the claimant has suffered loss as a result then there is a claim.

The simplest defence available, then, is to show an honest belief in the truth of the statement. It would not have to be a reasonable belief provided it was honestly held, and as a result fraud is extremely difficult to prove.

Remedies for fraudulent misrepresentation

As we have said, a party suffering loss as the result of a fraudulent misrepresentation can sue for damages in the tort of deceit. The method of assessing any damages awarded then will be according to the tort measure, i.e. to put the claimant in the position (s)he would have been in if the tort had not occurred, rather than the contract measure which is to put the claimant in the position (s) he would have been in if the contract had been properly performed.

This may result in more being recovered by way of any claim for consequential loss. As Lord Denning put it in *Doyle v Olby (Ironmongers) Ltd* (1969): 'the defendant is bound to make reparation for all the damage flowing from the fraudulent inducement'.

This point has been confirmed so that the defendant is responsible for all losses including any consequential loss providing a causal link can be shown between the fraudulent inducement and the claimant's loss.

Smith New Court Securities v Scrimgeour Vickers (1996)

The claimants had been induced to buy shares in Ferranti at 82.25p per share, as a result of a fraudulent misrepresentation that they were a good marketing risk. The shares were actually trading at 78p per share at the time of the transaction. Unknown to either party, the shares were worth considerably less since Ferranti itself had been the victim of a major fraud. When the claimants, on later discovering the fraud, chose not to rescind but to sell the shares on at prices ranging from 49p to 30p per share. The House of Lords held that the losses incurred were a direct result of the fraud that induced the claimants to contract. As a result, any losses awarded should be based on the figure paid of 82.25p rather than the 78p.

The clear consequence of the judgment is that heavier claims can be pursued if fraud is alleged, and there is therefore an encouragement to do so if proof is available.

The claimant who is a victim suffering loss as the result of a fraudulent misrepresentation then has two choices on discovering the fraud. (S)he may affirm the contract and go on to sue for damages as indicated above. But the claimant might also disaffirm the contract and refuse further performance.

If this is the claimant's choice then there are two further possible courses of action. Firstly, if there is nothing at this point to be gained by bringing action against the other party, the claimant can discontinue performance of his or her obligations and do nothing. Then if (s)he is sued by the maker of the fraud (s)he can then use the misrepresentation as a defence to that claim. Alternatively, the claimant might seek rescission of the contract in equity on discovering the fraud.

11.3.3 Negligent misrepresentation

Traditionally, any misrepresentation that was not identifiable as a fraud would be classed as an innocent misrepresentation for which the only possible action was for rescission of the contract in equity.

The reason there was no available action for a negligently made misrepresentation was that negligence falls short of the criteria identified by Lord Herschell in *Derry v Peek*.

There have, however, been developments in both common law and statute meaning that an action is now possible for a negligent misrepresentation. The former is again only possible in tort rather than contract and is a much more limited action than that available under the Act.

Common law

An action for a negligent misstatement causing a pecuniary, that is a financial, loss to be suffered by the other party is now possible.

Hedley Byrne & Co. Ltd v Heller & Partners Ltd (1964)

The claimants were asked to provide advertising work worth £100,000 for another company, Easipower, on credit. Sensibly, they sought a reference as to creditworthiness from Easipower's bankers, the defendants. They wrote back confirming that Easipower was a 'respectably constituted company good for its ordinary business engagements'. The bankers also claimed to reply without any responsibility for the reference they had given. When Easipower went into liquidation with the claimants still unpaid they brought an action in the tort of negligence against the bankers. Their action failed because the bank had validly disclaimed any liability for their reference. Nevertheless, the House of Lords, *in obiter*, considered that such an action would be possible in certain 'special relationships' where the person making the negligent statement

owed a duty of care to the other party to ensure that the statement was accurately made. In reaching this conclusion, the House of Lords approved Lord Denning's dissenting judgment in *Candler v Crane Christmas & Co.* (1951), where he felt that negligently prepared company accounts should be actionable.

Subsequent case law has both accepted and refined the *Hedley Byrne* principle. The requirements of the tort are threefold. The party making the negligent statement must be in possession of the particular type of knowledge for which the advice is required. There must be sufficient proximity between the two parties that it is reasonable to rely on the statement. The party to whom the statement is made does rely on the statement and the party making the statement is aware of that reliance.

It is also possible for the principle to apply to representations as to a future rather than a present state of affairs.

Esso Petroleum Co. Ltd v Marden (1976)

Esso developed a filling station on a new site near to a busy road and let it to Marden. During negotiations for the lease its representative indicated that the throughput would amount to 200,000 gallons per year. Marden queried this figure but contracted on the basis of the reassurance of the more experienced representative. In fact, the local authority then required pumps and the entrance to be at the rear of the site, accessible only from side streets. As a result, throughput was never more than 86,502 gallons per year, and the petrol station was uneconomical. Marden lost all his capital in the venture and gave up the tenancy. Esso sued for back rent and Marden counterclaimed with two arguments, both of which were successful. Firstly, he claimed that the estimate of throughput was a warranty on which he was entitled to rely. Secondly, he claimed that the relationship with Esso was a special one, creating a duty of care. Esso's failure to warn him properly of the changed circumstances and the very different throughput resulting was negligence under *Hedley Byrne*.

Statute

The above case started before the Misrepresentation Act was in force, otherwise a simpler action may have been available.

The Misrepresentation Act was passed in 1967. Its benefit is that an action in terms of it is much broader than any of the actions previously available. It is particularly appropriate where the claimant is unable to prove fraud. It followed the recommendation of the Law Reform Committee that damages should be available for losses arising from a negligent misrepresentation. However, the Act in that sense was based on the law as it existed before *Hedley Byrne* and so takes no account of that principle but rather operates as an alternative to fraud.

Section 2(1) identifies the main means of taking action. By this section:

'Where a person has entered into a contract after a misrepresentation has been made to him by another party thereto and as a result thereof he has suffered loss, then if the person making the misrepresentation would be liable to damages in respect thereof had the misrepresentation been made fraudulently, that person shall be so liable notwithstanding that the misrepresentation was not made fraudulently unless he proves that he had reasonable grounds to believe and did believe up to the time the contract was made that the facts represented were true.'

All that this basically means is that a party who is the victim of a misrepresentation has an action available without having to prove either fraud or the existence of a special relationship in order to fulfil *Hedley Byrne* criteria.

There are then some important differences with the past law.
- Firstly, the burden of proof is partly reversed. Where formerly the claimant would have been required to prove fraud, under the Act it will be for the defendant to show that (s)he in fact held a reasonable belief in the truth of the statement once it is shown to be a misrepresentation.
- If the misrepresentation is negligently made then the claimant has the choice of whether to sue under the Act or under the *Hedley Byrne* principle.
- If the Act is chosen then there is no need to show the relationship required for *Hedley Byrne*-type liability.

Howard Marine Dredging Co. Ltd v A. Ogden & Sons (Excavating) Ltd (1978)

Contractors estimating a price for depositing excavated earth at sea sought advice from the company from whom they intended to hire barges as to their capacity. The Marine manager negligently based his answer of 1,600 tonnes on dead weight figures from Lloyds, register rather than checking the actual shipping register which would have shown a figure of 1,055 tonnes. Delays resulted in the work and the contractors refused to pay the hire for the barges. When sued for payment they successfully counter-claimed using s2(1) of the Misrepresentation Act.

Remedies for negligent misrepresentation

Damages are available as a remedy both under the Act and at common law. If the *Hedley Byrne* principle is applied then damages are calculated according to the standard tort measure. This means that damages will only be awarded for a loss that is a foreseeable consequence of the negligent misrepresentation being made.

Under the Act, damages are again calculated according to a tort measure since the Act is stated as being appropriate where fraud cannot be proved. It is more arguable whether damages will be according to the normal tort measure or whether the test applied in the tort of deceit is appropriate. The latter is more beneficial and has been accepted in *Royscot Trust Ltd v Rogerson* (1991).

One consequence of damages under the Act being calculated according to tort measures of course is that they can be reduced if contributory negligence can be shown.

The only remedy traditionally available if the misrepresentation was negligently made would be for rescission in equity and this is still possible.

11.3.4 Innocent misrepresentation

As has already been stated, any misrepresentation not made fraudulently was formerly classed as an innocent misrepresentation regardless of how it was made. There would be no action possible under the common law only an action for rescission of the contract in equity.

The emergence of the *Hedley Byrne* principle and of s2(1) of the Misrepresentation Act means that possibly the only misrepresentations that can be claimed to be made innocently are where a party makes a statement with an honest belief in its truth. The obvious example of this is where the party merely repeats inaccurate information, the truth of which (s)he is unaware.

In this case an action under s2(1) of the Act would not be possible since this can be successfully defended by showing the existence of a reasonable belief in the truth of the statement. Nevertheless, the traditional action for rescission in equity is still a possibility. There is also a possibility of claiming under s2(2) of the Act.

Remedies for innocent misrepresentation

As we have seen, since damages were not formerly available under common law they will not be available either under s2(1).

However, the court has a discretion under s2(2) to award damages as an alternative to rescission where it is convinced that to do so is the appropriate remedy. The court must consider that 'it would be equitable to do so, having regard to the nature of the misrepresentation and the loss that would be caused by it if the contract were upheld, as well as the loss that rescission would cause to the other party'.

Zanzibar v British Aerospace (Lancaster House) Ltd (2000)

Here the Zanzibar Government purchased a corporate jet aeroplane from British Aerospace in 1992. The Zanzibar Government subsequently alleged that it had been induced to enter the contract on the basis of a false representation by British Aerospace as to both the type of jet and its general airworthiness. Zanzibar claimed rescission of the contract and damages as an alternative. The court denied it on the ground that the delay in bringing the action meant that the right to rescission had been lost and so no damages could be paid in lieu of rescission either.

It is important to consider three significant points regarding s2(2):
- There is no actual right to damages as there may be in a common law action. The award of damages is at the discretion of the court as an equitable remedy would be.
- Since damages are to be awarded as an alternative to rescission, then only one remedy can be granted not both.
- The measure of damages to be awarded is uncertain but since it is in lieu of rescission, then it is unlikely that consequential loss could be claimed.

Prior to the passing of the Act then the only available remedy was rescission. This remedy may be appropriate because, in the words of Sir George Jessell, 'no man ought to seek to take advantage of his own false statements'.

Redgrave v Hurd (1881)

In the case rescission was ordered in a contract between two solicitors for the sale and purchase of the one's practice. He had misstated the income from the practice and when the other backed out tried to claim specific performance of the contract. The other solicitor successfully counter-claimed for rescission.

┌ *Activity* ─────

Self-assessment questions

1 Why was it traditionally so important to prove that a falsely made representation was actually incorporated into the contract?
2 How would a party traditionally prove a fraudulent misrepresentation?
3 How easy or difficult is it to prove fraud?
4 What did negligently and innocently made representations have in common?
5 Which is the more advantageous action: that under *Hedley Byrne* principles for tort or that under s2(1) of the Misrepresentation Act?
6 What are the major advantages of the Misrepresentation Act over other actions?
7 Are the remedies better for any particular class of misrepresentation?

┌ *Activity* ─────

Quick quiz
Suggest what type of misrepresentation is involved in the following examples:

1 James is selling his car to Frank. Frank asks what the capacity of the engine is. James, after looking at the registration documents, tells him that it is 1,299 c.c. Unknown to James, the documents are incorrect.
2 Sally, a saleswoman, tells Rajesh that a three-piece suite is flame resistant, in order to gain the sale, without checking the manufacturers' specifications that would have revealed that it was not.
3 Howard, who has no qualifications at all, tells prospective employers at an interview that he has a degree in marketing.

11.4 Equity and misrepresentation

The availability of damages for a misrepresentation varies, as we have seen, according to the nature of the misrepresentation and the nature of the action bought by the injured party. Rescission, on the other hand, may be available whatever the character of the misrepresentation.

Rescission is of course an equitable remedy and its award is subject to the discretion of the court. It must be remembered that an actionable misrepresentation makes a contract voidable rather than void, so the contract remains valid until such time as it is 'set aside' by the court for the injured party.

The right to rescind is not absolute and it may be lost in a number of circumstances.

- *Restitutio in integrum* is vital to rescission. In essence this means that the party claiming is asking to be returned to the pre-contract position, known as the *status quo ante*. This in fact must be possible to achieve. If it is not, then rescission of the contract will not be granted.

Lagunas Nitrate Co. v Lagunas Syndicate (1899)

A nitrate field was bought by the claimants on an innocent misrepresentation of the defendant as to the strength of the market for nitrates. They made profits for a period but were affected adversely by a general depression in prices, at which point they sought rescission. They failed because they had extracted the nitrates for some time and the field could not be restored to its pre-contract order.

- An affirmation of the contract after its formation by the party seeking rescission will defeat the claim.

Long v Lloyd (1958)

A lorry was bought on the basis of a representation as to its 'exceptional condition'. Several faults were discovered on the first journey that the purchaser then allowed the seller to repair. When the lorry again broke down through its faulty condition the buyer's claim to rescission was unsuccessful. He had accepted the goods in a less than satisfactory condition and was unable to return them.

- Delay is said to 'defeat equity'. So a failure to claim rescission promptly may mean it is unavailable as a remedy.

Leaf v International Galleries (1950)

A contract for the sale of a painting of Salisbury Cathedral described it as a Constable. When the description later proved false, the purchaser's claim to rescission failed because a five-year period had then elapsed.

- If a third party has subsequently gained rights in the goods then it would be unfair to interfere with those rights by granting rescission.

White v Garden (1851)

A rogue bought 50 tons of iron from the claimant using a bill of exchange in a false name, and resold it on to a third party who acted in good faith. When the claimant discovered that the Bill of Exchange was useless he seized the iron from the innocent third party. This was illicit since the third party had gained good title to the iron.

- Under s2(2) of the Misrepresentation Act the judge has a discretion which remedy to apply. Rescission will not therefore be available if the judge has decided that damages are a more appropriate remedy.

It is possible to be granted rescission and an indemnity for other expenses incurred as a result of the misrepresentation.

Whittington v Seale-Hayne (1900)

Poultry breeders took a lease of premises on the basis of an oral representation that the premises were in a sanitary condition. This was untrue. The water was contaminated and the buyer became ill and some poultry died. At the time the claimants were not entitled to consequential loss because they could not prove fraud. However, as well as their claim to rescission of the contract, they were awarded an indemnity representing what they had spent in terms of rent and rates and other costs.

In granting rescission the court must always take into account the seriousness of the breach and the likely consequences of rescission for both parties.

┌─ *Activity* ─────────────────

Self-assessment questions
1 Why was equity traditionally so important to a party who had entered a contract as a result of a misrepresentation?
2 How fair are the 'bars' to rescission?
3 What types of misrepresentation would be classed as innocent following the Misrepresentation Act 1967?
4 What are the advantages and disadvantages of s2(2) of the Act?

11.5 When non-disclosure amounts to misrepresentation

There is no basic obligation at common law to volunteer information that has not been asked for.

Fletcher v Krell (1873)

A woman who had applied for a position as a governess had not revealed that she had formerly been married. Despite the fact that single women were generally preferred, her failure to reveal her marriage was not a misrepresentation.

In fact, silence of itself cannot generally be classed as misrepresentation.

Hands v Simpson, Fawcett & Co. (1928)

A commercial traveller acquired employment without advising his new employers that he was disqualified from driving, even though this was an essential part of the work. Even so, he was not obliged to volunteer the information without being asked.

However, there are a number of situations where the act of withholding or not offering information will amount to misrepresentation.
- Contracts which are *uberrimae fides* or where the 'utmost good faith' is required. This principle is commonly applicable to contracts of insurance on the basis that with full information the insurer may not have been prepared to accept the risk.

Locker and Woolf Ltd v Western Australian Insurance Co. Ltd (1936)

The insured party had not revealed to the insurer when entering the contract that another company had refused him insurance. This was clearly material to the contract.

- Fiduciary relationships where again good faith is required. These may include the relationship between trustees and beneficiaries. A failure to reveal certain information material to the contract may result in its being set aside under the doctrine of constructive fraud.

Tate v Williamson (1866)

A young man dreadfully in debt was persuaded by an adviser to sell his land to raise money to settle the debts. This adviser then bought the land, having not revealed full details as to its value and thus obtaining at half value. The contract was set aside.

- Where a part truth amounts to a falsehood.

Dimmock v Hallett (1866)

A person selling land revealed that the land was let to tenants but not that the tenants were terminating the lease and thus that the income from the land was reducing. This amounted to a misrepresentation.

- Where a statement made originally in truth becomes false during the negotiations. This will then be a misrepresentation.

With v O'Flanagan (1936)

A doctor selling his practice stated the true income at the beginning of negotiations but by the time of the sale this had dwindled to a negligible figure. Since he failed to reveal this, it was a misrepresentation.

Activity

Self-assessment questions
1 What exactly is non-disclosure?
2 In what circumstances will non-disclosure amount to an actionable misrepresentation?

KEY FACTS

- A misrepresentation is a false statement of fact made by one party to the contract to the other, at or before the time of contracting, not intended to be part of the contract but intended to induce the other party to enter the contract
- It will have the effect of making the contract voidable
- A misrepresentation can be made:
  - fraudulently
  - negligently
  - innocently
- If fraudulent there is an action in the tort of deceit *Derry v Peek* – in which case it must have been made:
  - knowingly or deliberately
  - or without any belief in its truth
  - or recklessly as to whether it is true or not – an honest belief is a defence
- If negligent then there is a possible action:
  - in tort under *Hedley Byrne* – provided it is made in a special relationship, where the party making it has expert knowledge relied upon by the other party; or
  - under s2(1) Misrepresentation Act 1967 – *Howard Marine Insurance v Ogden*
- If innocent then traditionally the only remedy was for rescission in equity, now there is also an action for damages under s2(2) Misrepresentation Act
- Rescission is only available if
  - *restitutio in integrum* applies – *Clarke v Dickson*
  - the contract is not affirmed – *Long v Lloyd*
  - there is no undue delay – *Leaf v International Galleries*
  - and no third party has gained rights
- Non-disclosure of information will also amount to misrepresentation
  - in contracts *uberrimae fides* (of utmost good faith) such as insurance – *Locker and Woolf v Western Australian Insurance*
  - where a part truth amounts to a falsehood – *Dimmock v Hallett* and
  - where a true statement later becomes false – *With v O'Flanagan*

Activity

Legal essay writing

Consider the following essay title:

Discuss the extent to which the development of a range of remedies for misrepresentation has ensured adequate protection for parties who have relied on inaccurate information when entering into a contract.

Answering the question

There are usually two key elements to answering essays in law:

- firstly, you are required to reproduce certain factual information on a particular area of law and this is usually identified for you in the question
- secondly, you are required to answer the specific question set, which usually is in the form of some sort of critical element, i.e. you are likely to see the words 'discuss', or 'analyse', or 'comment

on', or 'critically consider', or 'evaluate', or even 'compare and contrast' if two areas are involved.

Students, for the most part, seem quite capable of doing the first, but also often seem to be less confident at the second. The important points in any case are to ensure that you deal with only relevant legal material in your answer and that you do answer the question set, rather than one you have made up yourself, or indeed the one that was on last year's paper.

For instance, in the case of the first, in this essay you are likely to provide detail on the following:

- a definition of misrepresentation
- an explanation of the different classes of misrepresentation
- an explanation of the different remedies available for misrepresentation.

The essay title, although it focuses on remedies, is also in many ways quite wide. So it does give you the opportunity to write a lot of what you know misrepresentation. Although it may seem fairly obvious, the point to remember that it is vital for information on remedies to be given in the answer. A mere narrative on types of misrepresentation would not get into reasonable mark levels.

In the case of the second, however, it must be remembered that the essay calls for a critical discussion, in this case an evaluation of the effectiveness of the law on misrepresentation and its available remedies. You must, therefore ensure that, rather than merely giving narrative notes on misrepresentation you answer the question set and make some evaluative comments.

Relevant law

Identify that, as is the case with terms, misrepresentations begin as representations made before or at the time of the contract.

- Define misrepresentation:
  - a false statement of material fact (not opinion – *Bisset v Wilkinson*; nor future intention – *Edgington v Fitzmaurice;* nor trade puffs – *Carlill v Carbolic Smoke Ball Co.*)

- made by a party to the contract (not by a third party – *Peyman v Lanjani*)
- before formation, not after – *Roscorla v Thomas*
- intended to induce the other party to enter the contract
- but not intended to form part of the contract (which otherwise, if incorporated, would amount to a term).

- Identify the various classes of misrepresentation:
  - fraudulent – based on tort of deceit – *Derry v Peek*
  - negligent – before 1964 negligent misrepresentation was treated as innocent misrepresentation and there was no remedy except in equity – now there are two types: negligent misstatement based on tort negligence and the existence of a special relationship – *Hedley Byrne v Heller & Partners*; and now also under s2(1) Misrepresentation Act 1967
  - innocent – traditionally there was only remediable under equity – but now under Misrepresentation Act 1967 s2(2).

Explain that there are a number of different remedies and the type of remedy depends on the type of misrepresentation action used:

- **Fraudulent:**
  - Sue for damages, under tort measure, including all consequential loss – *Smith New Court Securities v Scrimgeour.*
  - If suing for damage, can also affirm contract and continue; or refuse any further performance.
  - Seek rescission in equity.
- **Negligent:**
  - Damages based on foreseeable loss negligent misstatement.
  - Damages on tort measure under the Misrepresentation Act 1967 – *Royscot Trust Ltd v Rogerson.*
  - Traditionally, rescission was always available in equity.
- **Innocent:**
  - Traditionally, no action or remedy available in the common law.

- So only rescission was available in equity.
- Now under s2(2) Misrepresentation Act 1967 judge has discretion to award damages as an alternative.

Discussion and evaluation

The essay title asks in effect for a critical discussion on the remedies available for misrepresentation. The essay is evaluative in the sense that the title refers to the development of the law. So it is important to put the development of misrepresentation in the context also of the prior law. There are different types of misrepresentation also leading to different types of remedy, so it is also important to get into the highest mark levels to make some critical observations on all of the remedies.

On this basis the discussion should include:

On the development of misrepresentation:

- Before 1899 there was no remedy available at all where a contract had been entered into on the basis of false information – unless equity could be used.
- Even then, liability was limited to a deceit action and was very hard to prove under *Derry v Peek* principles.
- So it was vital for the most part to prove that a representation was incorporated as a term or there could be no redress.
- No further development occurred until 1964, which again was limited by requiring proof of a special relationship.
- The Misrepresentation Act 1967 has actually widened out the law dramatically so that all genuine misrepresentations should be actionable.

Criticisms of the actions and the remedies:

- Fraud under *Derry v Peek* is very hard to prove but if the action succeeds damages are measured very generously
  - so includes all consequential loss where a causative link is proved – following *Smith New Court Securities v Scrimgeour Vickers*
  - there is some discretion in continuing with or ending the contract which can be advantageous

- also there is always an action for rescission in equity still possible.
- *Hedley Byrne* liability is also very narrow and difficult to prove the special relationship
  - but again, damages are set on the tort measure – based on foreseeable loss – but can be reduced for contributory negligence, of course.
- Negligence actions under s2(1) Misrepresentation Act 1967 mean that an action is possible for all misrepresentations.
  - An obvious advantage is the reversal of the burden of proof.
  - Once again, damages are on the tort measure *Royscot v Rogerson*.
- Innocent misrepresentation probably exists now only where inaccurate information is innocently repeated, e.g. from specifications with mistakes in etc.
  - Rescission was always available as a remedy.
  - Now judges have discretion by s2(2) Misrepresentation Act 1967 to award damages in lieu – but can have only one or the other and the claimant may not like the judge's choice.
- Equity always provided rescission as a remedy but it had its own limitations – the 'bars to rescission':
  - not available after too long a delay – *Leaf v International Galleries*
  - not available unless *restitutio in integrum* possible – *Lagunas Nitrate v Lagunas Syndicate*
  - affirmation of the contract *Long v Lloyd*
  - third party acquiring rights – *White v Garden*
  - but on the plus side could be linked to an indemnity – *Whittington v Seale-Hayne*.

Conclusion

- Any sensible conclusion would do,
  - but it is logical to say that the Misrepresentation Act is a massive improvement on the prior law
  - and there are enough classes of action to cover most situations – but they all have their own strengths and weaknesses.

Chapter 12

VITIATING FACTORS: MISTAKE

12.1 Introduction

Mistake is sometimes considered to be a difficult area of law. There are certainly a number of reasons for this. It is quite closely related to the area of agreement since agreement is said to depend on a *consensus ad idem*, a voluntary arrangement mutually agreed by both parties. If a party enters a contract on the basis of a mistake then this is said to negate the *consensus ad idem*, since any consensus could not be genuinely held in that case.

Mistake, certainly common mistake, is also closely related to misrepresentation, since a party might claim that they are mistaken owing to the misrepresentation of the other party, however innocent. In consequence, a claimant sometimes pleads both claims.

Where goods have passed to third parties following a contract that is made as a result of a mistake this can also have quite profound effects since one apparently innocent party is going to lack rights to the subject matter of the contract. If a purchaser under a contract has not been given full title and then sells on to a third party then the maxim *nemo dat quod non habet* might apply. This means that nobody can transfer title who does not already have good title himself. The result of this could be goods being reclaimed from a third party who has acquired the goods in innocence of the defective title. This will become apparent when considering a unilateral mistake as to the identity of the other party to the contract.

For these reasons judges have shown unwillingness in the past to accept a mistake as operative and therefore justifying a declaration that the contract is void. The result of the courts' attitude and the common law constraints imposed on mistake has been for the courts to use equitable solutions, but only in those situations where the common law rules cannot apply.

This is then the first distinction to make in mistake, whether it is the common law or equity that provides the remedy. For the common law to have any effect the mistake must have been an 'operative' one. It must have been a mistake fundamental to the making of the contract such that the contract was only formed because of the mistake.

If the mistake is recognised as being 'operative' then the contract will be void *ab initio*. Not only will the parties be returned to their pre-contract position, but also any further rights coming out of the contract will have no effect, because the contract is as though it had never existed.

If the court cannot accept that the mistake is operative, in other words the mistake was not the reason that the contract was formed, then common law rules can not apply but a solution in equity is possible, subject to the discretion of the court and the normal maxims. Recent case law, however, casts some doubt on this.

If equity can be applied then the effect is for the contract to be voidable. The contract could continue but a party to the contract who has been the victim of the mistake can avoid his/her obligations and the contract may be set aside.

There are basically three classes of mistake, although these themselves sub-divide to cover more specific circumstances.

- A 'common mistake' is one where both parties have made the same mistake. The mistake can concern either the existence of the subject matter of the contract, or its quality, with different consequences depending on which it is.

- A 'mutual mistake' again involves both parties being mistaken, but at cross-purposes over the nature of the agreement rather than making the same mistake.
- A 'unilateral mistake' is one where only one of the parties is mistaken. By implication the other party will usually know of the other party's mistake and be set to take advantage of it.

12.2 Common mistake

12.2.1 Res extincta

This involves a mistake about the existence of the subject matter of the contract at the time that the contract was formed. If at that time the subject matter of the contract did not exist then the mistake is an operative one, because clearly neither party to the contract would contract for something that did not exist, and the contract will be void.

Couturier v Hastie (1852)

The contract was for sale and purchase of a cargo of grain in transit and which both parties believed existed at the time of the contract. In fact, the captain of the ship had sold the cargo, as was customary practice, when it had begun to overheat. When this was discovered the court (while not actually mentioning mistake) declared the contract void rejecting the seller's argument that the buyer had accepted the risk and should pay the price. This basic proposition is now contained in s6 Sale of Goods Act 1979 – 'Where there is a contract for specific goods, and the goods without the knowledge of the seller have perished at the time when the contract is made, the contract is void.'

The above case involved specific goods. If, however, the contract is of a more speculative nature then the consequence of the goods not existing at the time of the contract may be different, since the buyer has bought only a chance.

McRae v Commonwealth Disposals Commission (1950)

Here the contract was for the salvage rights to a wreck. The buyer went to considerable expense to locate the wreck at the approximate position given by the Commission, but could not find it. When they sued for breach of contract the Commission tried to rely on the principle in the last case but failed. There was no operative mistake. The claimants had bought the salvage rights on the clear representation by the Commission that the wreck did exist, who were therefore liable for breach of contract.

If the goods have 'commercially perished' at the time the contract is formed unknown to either party then this still could be an operative mistake leading to the contract being void. Commercially perished would mean that the goods no longer had the value attached to them in the contract.

Barrow Lane and Ballard Ltd v Phillip Phillips & Co. Ltd (1929)

Here the seller bought 700 bags of groundnuts in a particular warehouse and, without ever inspecting the goods, sold them on. When the buyer came to inspect the goods 109 bags had been stolen. The seller could not sue the owner of the warehouse who had become insolvent so he sued the buyer for the price but failed. The goods had ceased to exist in commercial terms and the contract was void.

The classical operation of the principle of res extincta will still apply in modern commercial transactions.

Associated Japanese Bank (International) Ltd v Credit du Nord SA (1988)

A sale and leaseback arrangement over four packaging machines was concluded between the bank and a man called Bennett. Credit du Nord guaranteed Bennett's obligations under the contract. The machines did not in fact exist and the bank was prevented from suing Bennett when he was declared bankrupt. It then sued on the guarantee. Steyn J held that the guarantee was subject to a condition precedent that the four machines existed at the time of the contract. Applying the test from *Bell v Lever Brothers*, for the mistake as to the existence of the machines to be an operative one, the subject matter of the contract must be radically different to that expected by both parties. The guarantee was an accessory contract. The non-existence of the machines was of paramount importance to the guarantor in granting the guarantee. The *res extincta* doctrine applied and the contract of guarantee was void.

12.2.2 *Res sua*

This principle applies to a mistake as to ownership of the goods. If a party enters a contract as a buyer when, in fact, unknown to either party, he owns the title to the goods then the contract is void.

Cooper v Phibbs (1867)

Cooper took a three-year lease for a salmon fishery from Phibbs. At the time of the contract both parties believed that Phibbs owned the fishery when in fact it was subsequently discovered that Cooper was life tenant of the property. He was unable to dispose of the property but was effective owner at the time of contracting. Cooper then tried to have the lease set aside. The House of Lords agreed to this but also granted Phibbs a lien in respect of the considerable expense he had gone to in improving the property.

Although the case was decided on equitable rather than common law principles, law Lord Atkin in *Bell v Lever Brothers* refers to it as an example of *res sua*.

The case can be seen as *res sua*. Equity was applied and the contract declared voidable rather than void because firstly Cooper had only an equitable interest in the property, and secondly Phibbs had spent money on it.

12.2.3 Mistake as to the quality of the contract

This is inevitably a more complex area than either *res extincta* or *res sua*. Generally, however, where the mistake that is common to both parties is that the subject matter of the contract is of a quality different to that anticipated then the mistake has three consequences. The mistake will not be considered an operative one, it will have no effect in common law on the contract, and both parties are still bound by their original obligations.

Bell v Lever Brothers Ltd (1932)

Lever Brothers employed Bell as Chairman of a subsidiary company, Niger Co Ltd, with the brief of rejuvenating the subsidiary. When he was successful in his task and the subsidiary was merged with another company Lever Brothers offered a settlement of £30,000 for the termination of his existing service contract. It was later discovered that Bell was in breach of a clause of the service agreement, having entered into private dealings on his own account. Lever Brothers then sued for return of the settlement, claiming fraudulent misrepresentation, in which they failed, and breach of contract. The Court of Appeal then held that the settlement was invalid for common mistake, the mistake being that Lever were bound to pay the settlement when they could in fact have merely fired Bell. In the House of Lords Lord Warrington felt that the 'mistake' could have no effect on the contract unless it was 'of such a fundamental character as to constitute an underlying assumption without which the parties would not have made the contract they in fact made'. The mistake was not one affecting the consideration or that went to the root of the matter, so the contract of settlement could not be void. Lord

Atkin stated that

> *'Mistake as to quality of the thing contracted raises more difficult questions. In such a case, a mistake will not affect assent unless it is the mistake of both parties and is as to the existence of some quality which makes the thing without the quality essentially different from the thing as it was believed to be . . .'.*

The settlement had not been given as a result of the breach or otherwise of the clause, but in recognition of the work already done by Bell. It was not an operative mistake. The mistake was not fundamental in any way to the making of the settlement agreement. Lever Brothers were merely upset because had they known of the breach before the settlement they could have fired Bell and avoided the expense.

The common law principle then is applied absolutely. Nevertheless, the fact that the mistake is not operative means that an action in equity may still result.

Solle v Butcher (1950)

In an agreement for the lease of a flat both parties mistakenly believed that the rent was not subject to controls under the Rent Restrictions Act. The rent was set at £250 per annum, though if subject to the Act it should have been £140. However, had the landlord realised that it was subject to those controls he might have applied to increase the rent because of considerable repairs and improvements he had made to what was otherwise war-damaged property. On discovering that the rent was subject to controls under the Act the tenant then sued for a declaration that the rent should be £140 and to recover the difference already paid. On appeal the landlord claimed that the mistake was void for mistake. The Court of Appeal held that at common law the mistake had no effect on the contract. It was merely a mistake as to quality. This did not prevent the court from setting the agreement aside in equity.

Although it is possible now that common mistake is such that the contract is neither void nor can it be set aside in equity.

Great Peace Shipping Ltd v Tsavliris Salvage (International) Ltd (2001)

The defendants, who were salvors, had an interest in a ship, the *Cape Providence*, and worried that it might sink they approached London brokers. who contacted a third party (OR), who identified the nearest vessel as the *Great Peace*, which belonged to the claimants. The defendants then agreed a charter party contract to hire the *Great Peace* for five days. However, OR was wrong, and *Great Peace* was several hundred miles away. So the charter contract was based on a common mistake. The defendants then tried to cancel the contract but the claimants refused and claimed for five days' hire. They argued that the mistake made the contract void at common law or voidable in equity. Toulson J held that since the mistake was not as to the existence of the subject matter (and so was not operable) the contract was not void at common law. He also considered that it could not be set aside in equity since it was impossible to determine the nature of the 'fundamental ' mistake that would enable the contract to be rescinded; and he would not exercise any discretion to set the contract aside because the fixing of charterparties is done by professionals and is an area where certainty is important and to set aside the contract would amount to making the correctness of the information given by OR a condition of the contract.

In some situations parties will easily mistake the quality of the contract. This is particularly so in the case of art works or antiques or anything where valuations are a matter of opinion rather than fact, and the attitude taken by the court to the effect of the mistake can vary enormously.

Leaf v International Galleries (1950)

The contract was for the sale and purchase of an oil painting of Salisbury Cathedral that was innocently represented as being a Constable. The buyer discovered that it was not a Constable when he tried to sell it five years later. His claim for rescission failed and he appealed. The Court of Appeal rejected his claim, holding that an action for damages would have been the appropriate action, and also that he had delayed too long for rescission. Lord Denning made some interesting references to mistake: 'There was no mistake about the subject matter of the sale. It was a specific picture of "Salisbury Cathedral". The parties were agreed in the same terms on the subject matter, and that is sufficient to make a contract . . .'. So Lord Denning suggested that the identity of the painter was irrelevant. It was a mistake only as to the quality of the contract.

Nevertheless, the opposite view has been taken in relation to the effect of a mistake as to quality where works of art are concerned.

Peco Arts Inc v Hazlitt Gallery Ltd (1983)

The claimant bought a drawing from a reputable gallery that both parties mistakenly believed was an original. The contract included an express term that the work was an original inscribed by the artist. Eleven years later, the claimant discovered that the work was a reproduction, and tried to claim return of the purchase price and interest. The court, distinguishing *Leaf*, allowed his claim. The time lapse was no problem since it was accepted that, even without due diligence, the truth could not have been discovered at an earlier stage.

Activity

Quick quiz
Consider what sort of common mistake is indicated in the following scenarios:

1 Tracy has bought a set of antique cutlery that both she and the shopkeeper believed to be solid silver. In fact, the cutlery is only silver plate.
2 Geoff today contracted to buy my old 1966 Ferrari sports car. Unknown to either of us, the car was destroyed in a fire last week when the garage where it was kept burnt down.
3 I have contracted to take the lease of a boating lake from Tom, who both of us believe has inherited the property. In fact, after we form the contract we discover that I have been given a life interest in the property.

12.3 Mutual mistake

A mutual mistake occurs where the parties to the contract are at cross-purposes over the meaning of the contract. One of the problems here is that it is doubtful whether any meaningful and sustainable agreement has ever been reached.

What the courts will do is to try to make sense of the agreement that does exist in order that it can continue. To do this they will implement an objective test and will try to identify a common intent if one exists.

If, however, the promises made by the two parties so contradict one another as to render any performance of the agreement impossible then the court will deem that an operative mistake exists and the contract will be declared void.

Raffles v Wichelhaus (1864)

The contract was for the sale of cotton on board a ship named *Peerless* that was sailing out of Bombay. In the event, there were two ships both named *Peerless* both sailing from Bombay on the same day. The seller was selling the cargo other than the one that the buyer was intending to buy. There was no way of finding a common intention. The contract could not be completed and was declared void.

So ambiguity surrounding the subject matter of the contract may well make a mistake operative and result in the contract being declared void.

Scriven Bros & Co. v Hindley & Co. (1913)

There are different qualities of hemp. One is called 'tow' and is generally of inferior quality. Auctioneers were selling hemp that was actually 'tow' though this was not made absolutely clear in the catalogue. The purchaser bid extravagantly, under the mistake that he was actually bidding for the superior product. He rejected the goods on discovering the mistake. The auctioneer's action to enforce the contract failed owing to the mutual mistake. There could be no reconciling the situation to mutual satisfaction.

However, where one party is merely mistaken as to the quality of the contract then the mistake is not mutual. The contract can be continued, although it is not to the liking of that party and the contract will not be declared void.

Smith v Hughes (1871)

Smith was offered a consignment of oats that he examined a sample of and bought. On delivery he discovered that the oats were 'new oats' rather than oats from the previous year's crop. He refused delivery and when the seller sued for the price claimed that the contract should be void for mistake. He believed he had been offered 'good old oats' rather than 'good oats'

as the seller claimed. The court felt that it could not declare a contract void merely because one party later discovered it was less advantageous than he believed it to be.

12.4 Unilateral mistake

12.4.1 Introduction

The cases in unilateral mistake show two particular lines: the mistake will either be as to the terms of the contract or will be as to the identity of the other party to the contract. In either case the significant point is that only one of the parties to the contract is actually mistaken, hence unilateral mistake.

The basic principle is simple. Where one party contracts on the basis of a mistake known to the other party then the contract is void because there is no consensus in this instance. The mistake must obviously be a fundamental one. A mistake as to quality will not suffice.

12.4.2 Mistaken terms

If one party to the contract makes a material mistake in expressing his/her intention and the other party knows, or is deemed to know, of the mistake then the mistake may be operative, with the result that the contract may be void.

Hartog v Colin & Shields (1939)

The contract was for 30,000 Argentine hare skins. The price was stated at 10d and 1 farthing per lb. The regular practice was to sell per piece. Since there were about three pieces per lb. this would reduce the cost of each piece to a third. The buyers tried to enforce the contract on the basis of the mistaken term. The sellers countered that the offer was wrongly stated, as would be common knowledge in the trade. The court declared the contract void for the mistake.

The test of whether or not such a mistake is operative and therefore voids the contract appears to have three parts:

- One party to the contract is genuinely mistaken over a material detail that had the truth been known would have meant (s)he would not have contracted on the terms stated. (This was clearly the position of the sellers in the above case.)
- The other party to the contract ought reasonably to have known of the mistake. (Again the court accepted in the above case that the buyers were taking advantage of a situation that they would have been aware of because of usual custom in the trade.)
- The party making the mistake was not at fault in any other way.

Sybron Corporation v Rochem Ltd (1984)

Having opted for early retirement, a manager was awarded a discretionary pension. It was subsequently discovered that the manager, together with other employees, had engaged in a fraud on the company. The company sought to have the pension agreement set aside, and succeeded. The Court of Appeal held that it was the manager's breach of duty that had induced the company to believe that it was obliged to grant him the pension. It had done so under a mistake of fact.

However, the mistake cannot be operative if the other party is unaware of it.

Wood v Scarth (1858)

A landlord agreed to lease premises to a tenant, mistakenly believing that his clerk had made plain to the tenant before the agreement that a premium of £500 was expected as well as rent. The court held that the mistake could not be operative since the tenant contracted on terms not including the premium in good faith and without knowledge of the landlord's mistake.

The contract for rent only was therefore not affected.

12.4.3 Mistaken identity

Again, the area is at first sight complex and it raises different issues to those already considered. However, the occasions when the principle arises are not straightforward. The common scenario will be when a rogue has made off with property belonging to another party after making false representations as to his/her identity. This then is the mistake made by the other party. The goods will then usually have been transferred to an innocent third party from whom the original owner is trying to recover them.

The cases are distressing because the courts will have to decide which of two seemingly innocent parties to disappoint. If the contract is one covered by the Sale of Goods Act 1979 then the rogue, as a seller, has no title to pass in disposing of the goods. If the original owner identifies the title as only voidable sufficiently early, then he may have rights as against a subsequent purchaser. If the third party buying the goods from the rogue does so in good faith and without notice of the defective title then (s)he may have a good title as against the party from whom the rogue acquired the goods.

The case law shows some confusion and contradictions. There are some basic requirements that the original owner must satisfy in order to claim that (s)he retains ownership.

- In order to claim a mistake on the basis of a mistaken identity, the party seeking to claim rights in the goods must first of all show that (s)he intended to contract with a person other than the one with whom they did contract. So there must have been another person.

Kings Norton Metal Co. Ltd v Edridge, Merrett & Co. Ltd (the Kings Norton Metal case) (1897)

Wallis contracted under the name Hallam & Co. for the purchase of expensive items of brass rivet wire. The goods were supplied but never paid for. The Metal Co. sued the party who eventually purchased them from Wallis to recover the goods. The court was not prepared to void the contract for mistake. The Metal Co. was not so much mistaking the identity of Wallis, since Hallam & Co. did not exist, as mistaking the creditworthiness of Wallis with whom it had in fact contracted.

- In order to claim that the mistake is operative and therefore makes the contract void the mistake must be shown to have been material to the formation of the contract.

Cundy v Lindsay (1878)

Blenkarn hired a room at 37 Wood Street where a highly respectable firm, Blenkiron & Co., conducted its business at number 123. He then ordered a large number of handkerchiefs from Lindsay's, with a signature designed to be confused with that of the reputable firm. The goods were supplied and Blenkiron was billed. Blenkarn had sold some goods on to Cundy before the fraud was discovered. Lindsay then tried to recover the goods. On appeal the House of Lords held that the contract was void for mistake. The mistake was operable because Lindsay's were able to show that the identity of the party trading from 37 Wood Street was material to the formation of the contract. Unlike the *Kings Norton Metal case*, there was a party here with whom the claimants wished to contract. The third party acquired the goods from Blenkarn without any title.

- If the one party is to be able to claim that the mistake is to be considered material then the other party to the contract must have known of it.

Boulton v Jones (1857)

The defendant ordered certain goods from Brocklehurst in order to take advantage of a set-off (a legal means of keeping the goods in return for a debt already owed to the defendant). Unknown to the defendant Brocklehurst had assigned his business to the claimant. When the goods were delivered and the defendant refused to pay, he then tried to have the contract set aside for mistake as to the identity of the party with whom he had contracted. The court would not void the contract. The other party knew nothing of the mistake and had merely responded to an order to supply goods. The mistake was not operative.

12.4.4 Mistaken identity and face-to-face dealing

Where a party negotiates a contract in person then the party is deemed to be contracting with the other party who is physically present at the negotiations, whatever the identity that the other party assumes. In this way the mistake is not as to the identity but as to the creditworthiness of the other party. This is not material to the forming of the contract so the mistake is not operative and the contract cannot be void.

Phillips v Brooks Ltd (1919)

North, a rogue, selected jewellery in a shop including a necklace worth £2,550 and a ring worth £450. He wrote a cheque for £3,000, misrepresenting himself as Sir George Bullough, whose address the jeweller found in the directory. North persuaded the jeweller to let him leave with the ring, leaving the rest of the jewels till his cheque cleared. The cheque bounced and when the jeweller later discovered the ring in a pawn shop where North had sold it he tried to sue for its recovery. His argument, that the contract with North was based on mistaking North's identity for that of Sir George Bullough, failed. He could have only intended to contract with the party he met face-to-face. The pawn shop gained good title because it bought in good faith, without notice of any defect in title.

One case actually cast doubt on this principle and caused some confusion.

Ingram v Little (1960)

Sisters jointly owned a car that they advertised for sale. The rogue who came to buy it offered to pay by cheque. The ladies initially refused the cheque but were persuaded when the rogue passed himself off as an important local figure, and found the name offered in the telephone directory. The cheque bounced and when the ladies discovered the car in the hands of an innocent third party to whom the rogue had sold it they sued to recover the car. The Court of Appeal, strangely, accepted that the mistake as to identity was material to the contract, as it was shown that the ladies initially rejected the cheque, and so relied on the identity of the important local figure.

The case is seen as being either decided on the particular facts or indeed wrongly decided, and subsequent cases have reiterated the original principle.

Lewis v Avery (1972)

A rogue buying a car represented himself as a famous actor of the time, Richard Greene, and showed a false studio pass after his cheque was at first rejected. When the cheque was dishonoured and the seller later discovered the whereabouts of the car, he sued the new owner for recovery. His action failed. The claimant had been induced into believing that the party he contracted with was somebody different but had

still contracted with that party. The mistake was not operative and the contract could not be void.

It follows that, for a party to claim that the identity of the other party is material to the making of the contract, he must have taken adequate steps to ensure the true identity of the other party.

Citibank NA v Brown Shipley & Co. Ltd; Midland Bank v Brown Shipley & Co. Ltd (1991)

A rogue passed himself off as a company officer and persuaded a bank to issue a bankers' draft to pay for large amounts of foreign currency he was buying from another bank. The currency was passed once the legitimacy of the bankers' draft was established. When the fraud was discovered the issuing bank tried to recover from the other bank but failed. They had done insufficient to establish the *bona fides* of the rogue for his identity to be material and their mistake to be operative.

The principle of face-to-face dealing may apply where the contract is made by the claimant's agent but if the contract is made through a mere intermediary then general principles of mistaken identity will apply.

Shogun Finance Ltd v Hudson (2001)

A rogue, giving a false name and address, completed hire-purchase forms to buy a car and showed a stolen driving licence in the name of D. Patel to confirm his identity. The car dealer faxed a copy of the licence and draft HP agreement, signed by the rogue in Mr Patel's name, to the claimant finance company. They then checked the credit rating of the real Patel and accepted the deal. The rogue paid 10% party in cash and partly by cheque and drove the car away and then sold it to the defendant. When the finance company realised the mistake they brought proceedings against the defendant.

The rule *nemo dat quod non habet* was applied, i.e. a seller cannot pass on a title if he does not have one. The Court of Appeal considered the 'face-to-face' cases but decided that they did not apply. The offer of finance was made to Mr Patel, not the rogue; there was no contract between the rogue and the finance company. The situation was more like *Cundy v Lindsay* since the finance company never saw the rogue, dealt only with documentation, and the salesman in the showroom was not their agent, but only an intermediary. The rogue gained no title that he could pass on, and the innocent purchaser had to bear the loss.

Activity

Self-assessment questions

1 In what ways is mistake close to
   a) agreement and
   b) misrepresentation?
2 Why is it easy to confuse common mistake with misrepresentation?
3 Why might a party prefer to sue for a mistake rather than for misrepresentation?
4 In what circumstances will a contract be void in common law as a result of a mistake?
5 In what sense is it possible to say that a common mistake as to quality has no effect on the contract?
6 What is the difference between a common mistake and a mutual mistake?
7 What are the possible effects of a mutual mistake on the contract?
8 What is meant by the requirement in unilateral mistake that the mistake must be a material one?
9 Why is identity such a key factor in unilateral mistake?
10 In what ways does the case of *Ingram v Little* seem to be wrongly decided?

Activity

Quick quiz
Suggest what type of mistake is involved in the following scenarios:

a) I contracted with Farmer Giles to buy his horse called Silver. He has two horses called Silver. He believes that he has sold me his brown stallion with the white flash on the nose. I believed that I was buying his grey mare.
b) A man calling himself Tony Blair knocked on my door one evening and bought my car by cheque. I accepted the cheque because I believed he was the Prime Minister but I have now discovered that this was not the case, as his cheque has been returned.
c) In the pub tonight I agreed to sell my collection of Elvis records to a man called Stan. However, when I went home and asked my wife where they were she said that she had thrown them away years ago because they were never played.

12.5 Mistake and equity

12.5.1 Introduction

If a mistake has been shown to be operative then the common law rather than equity may apply. If it is not an operative mistake and therefore not void, then an equitable solution may be sought in one of three ways:
- **rescission** of the contract, with the contract being set aside and new terms substituted
- **a refusal to grant** the other party's claim for specific performance of the contract
- **rectification** of a document containing a mistake which is material.

12.5.2 Rescission

If the party claiming rescission can show that it is against conscience to allow the other party to take advantage of the mistake then the court may allow rescission, though usually at the same time substituting more equitable terms as an alternative.

Solle v Butcher (1950)

At common law the mistake as to the application of rent review rules had no effect. Nevertheless, the court set aside the original terms that were unworkable in the circumstances and was prepared to allow the tenant the choice of terminating the lease or continuing it with the rent set at £250. This would be appropriate since the improvements justified the increase.

Rescission will often be the appropriate remedy in the contracts made as the result of an innocent misrepresentation.

Magee v Pennine Insurance Co. Ltd (1969)

An insurance agent had filled out the proposal form for the proposer. The details as to the people driving the car was inaccurately stated as including Magee, who was stated as having a provisional licence, and his eldest son, a police driver, since only his youngest son was to drive the car. Magee himself did not have a licence and, when the car was in an accident, the insurance company agreed to pay £385 being the true value of the car. When the company later discovered the inaccuracies in the proposal they refused to pay and Magee sued to enforce the agreement. On appeal, Lord Denning affirmed his own principle in *Solle v Butcher*, held that the agreement to pay was made as a result of a common mistake and was voidable in equity.

It has recently been restated, however, that equity intervenes with the remedy of rescission only to allow a party to escape from an unconscionable bargain but it will not intervene to allow a party to avoid having made a bad bargain. See *Clarion Ltd v National Provident Institution* (2000). Besides this, the case of Great Peace Shipping casts doubts on the use of equity in mistake.

12.5.3 Refusal of specific performance

As an equitable remedy, specific performance depends on the discretion of the court. So it can also be refused where one party entered the agreement on the basis of a mistake and:
- it would be unfair or harsh to expect him to perform the contract or
- the mistake was actually caused by the other party's misrepresentation or
- the other party knew of the mistake and tried to take advantage of it.

Webster v Cecil (1861)

Webster offered to buy land from Cecil and Cecil who stated that the land had cost him more than that rejected his offer of £2,000. Webster then tried to enforce a written agreement for sale of the land for £1,250. His claim to specific performance failed since the written agreement clearly ran contrary to any oral one.

The court will not, however, refuse an order merely because it means one party has made a worse bargain than he thought he had.

Tamplin v James (1880)

James bought an inn at auction. He believed that he had also bought adjoining land but had not. He had made no check of the plans and he could not resist an order of specific performance of the contract.

12.5.4 Rectification of a document

The court can rewrite a written document that does not conform to the actual agreement between the two parties, as happened in *Webster v Cecil*.

The two sides in dispute will usually have a different view of what the agreement is so the side seeking rectification must show that a complete and certain agreement was reached, and that the agreement remained unchanged up to the time of contracting.

Craddock Bros Ltd v Hunt (1923)

Craddock agreed to sell his house to Hunt not intending an adjoining yard to be included in the sale. By mistake the yard was included in the conveyance so Craddock immediately sought rectification of the document and succeeded.

Activity

Self-assessment questions

1 When will a party claiming mistake be able to look for a solution in equity?
2 Why could the mistake in *Solle v Butcher* not lead to the contract being void under the common law – and why was equity able to be used?
3 When will the courts refuse to grant an order of specific performance?
4 What happens to the contract when rectification is applied as a remedy?

12.6 Non est factum

This is literally translated as 'this is not my deed'. It is a doctrine that operates only in respect of written agreements. Usually the principle in *L'Estrange v Graucob* applies and a party is bound by written agreements that (s)he has signed.

However, in some circumstances a party is able to claim that they only signed as a result of a genuine mistake as to the nature of the document signed. The doctrine is subject to strict requirements. It will only be appropriate because the party signing is subject to some weakness that has been exploited by the other party, for instance blindness or senility. Also the other party must have represented that the document is something different than that which has been signed.

If this is so and the party signing has taken the precautions available to check on the authenticity of the document before signing then the contract is void. However, before the court will declare the contract void it must be satisfied that the document is of a kind materially different to what it was represented to be, and that the party has not been negligent in signing it.

Saunders v Anglian Building Society (1970)

This case, which began as *Gallie v Lee*, involved an elderly widow who decided to transfer her property to her nephew on the stipulation that she could live there for the rest of her life. She did this so that he could borrow money on the property in order to start a business. The document was drawn up by Lee, a dishonest friend of the nephew, and was in fact a conveyance to him rather than a deed of gift to the nephew. Lee then borrowed against the property and defaulted on the loan. The widow in answer to the claim for repossession initially succeeded with a plea of *non est factum*. On a later appeal the House of Lords rejected her plea. There was insufficient difference between the documents that she did sign and had intended to sign. Both gave up her rights to the property and she had not done enough to check its nature.

The class of mistake	The character of the mistake	The legal consequences of the mistake
Common mistake: ♦ *Res extincta* (*Couturier v Hastie*) ♦ *Res sua* (*Cooper v Phibbs*) ♦ **Mistake as to quality** (*Bell v Lever Bros*)	The same mistake is made by both parties: ♦ The mistake concerns the existence of the subject matter at the time the contract is made ♦ The mistake is about who owns the subject matter at the time of contracting ♦ Mistake is merely as to the quality of the bargain made	♦ The mistake is 'operative' and the contract is void ♦ The mistake is 'operative' and the contract is void ♦ The mistake is not 'operative' – contract continues but may be set aside in equity (*Solle v Butcher*)
Mutual mistake:	Both parties make a mistake but not the same one – they are at cross-purposes	♦ If performance is impossible then the contract is void (*Raffles v Wichelhaus*) ♦ If the court can find a common intent then the contract may continue (*Smith v Hughes*)
Unilateral mistake: ♦ **Mistake as to terms** (*Hartog v Colin & Shields*) ♦ **Mistaken identity not face-to-face** (*Cundy v Lindsay*) ♦ **Mistaken identity face-to-face** (*Lewis v Avery*)	Only one party is mistaken – the other party knows and takes advantage of the first party's mistake: ♦ (i) One party mistaken over a material detail; (ii) other party knew of mistake; (iii) mistaken party not at fault ♦ (i) Mistaken party intended to contract with someone else; (ii) mistake material to contract; (iii) mistake known to other party ♦ Party contracts in person with someone who claims to be someone else	♦ If all three, mistake is 'operative' and contract void – if not then may be voidable in equity ♦ If all three, mistake is 'operative' and contract void – if not then may be voidable in equity ♦ Not an 'operative' mistake – mistaken party deemed to be contracting with person in front of him
Non est factum	♦ Mistake concerns nature of the document being signed ♦ The document is (i) materially different to what it was represented to be; (ii) there is no negligence by the person signing it	If both are present then there is an 'operative mistake' – the contract is void – but if not then there is no effect on contract (*Saunders v Anglian Building Society*)

Fig. 12.1 Table illustrating the different types of mistake and their legal consequences

KEY FACTS

- A mistake can occur in one of three principal ways:
  - both parties are making the same mistake – known as common mistake
  - the parties are at cross-purposes and so are both mistaken but making different mistakes – known as mutual mistake
  - only one of the parties is mistaken and the other party knowingly takes advantage of this – known as unilateral mistake
- If a mistake is operative (i.e. the contract was only made because of the mistake) then the contract is void at common law
- Only if the mistake is not operative it may be possible to rescind the contract or set it aside in equity
- A common mistake can void a contract where the mistake is as to the existence of the subject matter of the contract – *res extincta* – *Couturier v Hastie*
  - but it will not void the contract where the mistake is only as to the quality of the contract made – *Bell v Lever Brothers*
  - authenticity of art works is a difficult area – *Leaf v International Galleries*
- A mutual mistake will void the contract when the parties are so at odds that it is impossible to make any sense of the agreement – *Raffles v Wichelhaus*
  - but if the mistake is only about the quality of the contract then the contract will continue – *Smith v Hughes*
- With unilateral mistake the mistake can be about the terms of the contract or about the identity of the other party to the contract
  - If the mistake is about the terms of the agreement then it is operative and the contract void if the one party through no fault of his own is mistaken over a material detail and the other party knows or ought to know of the mistake – *Hartog v Colin & Shields*
  - If the mistake is the identity of the other party then that mistake must have been material to the formation of the contract – *Cundy v Lindsay*
  - If the parties contract face to face then they are said to be contracting with the party in front of them regardless of what identity they assume – *Lewis v Avery*
- Where the mistake is not operative equity can be used in one of three ways:
  - to rescind the contract or set it aside on terms – *Solle v Butcher*
  - to refuse a request for specific performance of the contract – *Webster v Cecil*
  - to rectify a document which contains the mistake – *Craddock Brothers v Hunt*
- It is possible to claim *non est factum* (this is not my deed) in relation to a document signed provided that:
  - a party has some disability which is being taken advantage of and
  - (s)he thinks (s)he is signing an entirely different type of document – *Saunders v Anglian Building Society*

Chapter 13

VITIATING FACTORS: DURESS AND UNDUE INFLUENCE

13.1 Introduction

The courts have always been keen to preserve freedom of contract. A necessary element of this freedom is that the agreement should be reached voluntarily. This means that no force or coercion should be used in order to secure the agreement. If a party does enter a contract because of coercion by the other party then the law accepts that the contract should be set aside and the party coerced should be relieved of their own obligations.

Such principles have been developed so that there is an action under common law for duress, and an action in equity for undue influence. In the first a remedy will be automatic on proof of the duress and the contract can be set aside. In the second the remedy is at the discretion of the court. In either case the contract will be voidable rather than void.

13.2 Duress

Duress is a common law area which was traditionally associated with intimidation that was real or at least sufficiently real and threatening to vitiate the consent of the other party, and mean that (s)he acted not by free will.

Cumming v Ince (1847)

An inmate in a private mental asylum was coerced into signing away title to all of her property or she was threatened that the committal order would never be lifted. The contract was set aside. It was not made of her free will.

The law developed so that the threat vitiating the contract was associated with violence or even death.

Barton v Armstrong (1975)

A former chairman of a company threatened the current managing director with death unless the managing director paid over a large sum of money for the former chairman's shares. It was shown in the case that the managing director was actually quite happy to buy the shares and would have done so even without any threat being made. Nevertheless threats had been made and were therefore sufficient to amount to duress, vitiating the agreement they had reached as a result.

Threats to carry out a lawful action, however, cannot amount to duress.

Williams v Bayley (1866)

A young man had forged his father's signature on promissory notes (IOUs) which he then gave to the bank, causing it to lose money. The bank then approached the young man's father and demanded that he should mortgage his farm to it to cover the son's debt or it would prosecute the son. The threat was for lawful action and so could not amount to duress. However, the court was disturbed by the manner of the threats and accepted that they did amount to undue influence.

Traditionally, for duress to apply to allow the contract to be set aside the threat should be a threat of violence against the other party not against their property.

Skeate v Beale (1840)

A promise given in return for recovery of goods that had been unlawfully detained was not duress.

13.3 Economic duress

This last point had been the subject of some criticism. A doctrine has subsequently developed in the commercial field whereby a contract may be set aside not because of threats of violence but because extreme coercion has rendered the contract otherwise commercially unviable. It was first discussed in cases without actually being applied.

D.C. Builders v Rees (1965)

In this case, as we have already seen, the Reeses forced the small firm of builders to accept a cheque of £300 in full satisfaction of the actual bill of £462 or take nothing. They had no choice in the circumstances but to accept. Lord Denning considered the issue of inequality of bargaining strength and felt that coercion in such circumstances justified avoidance of the agreement.

The point was then taken further and a more formal doctrine was developed.

Occidental Worldwide Investment Corporation v Skibs A/S Avanti (The Siboen and the Sibotre) (1976)

During a world recession in the shipping industry, charterers demanded a renegotiation of their contract with the ship owners. They claimed that they would otherwise go out of business and that with no assets they were not worth suing. The ship owners had no choice but to agree. Because of the recession they would have little chance of other charters of their vessels. Kerr J suggested that the question to ask was 'was there such a degree of coercion that the other party was deprived of his free consent and

agreement'. He also identified a two-part test to establish if economic duress had occurred: (i) did the party alleging the coercion protest immediately, and, if so, (ii) did that party accept the agreement or try to argue openly about it?

Lord Scarman then also accepted the basic doctrine in *Pao On v Lau Yiu Long* (1980) 'there is nothing contrary to principle in recognising economic duress as a factor which may render a contract voidable provided always that the basis of such recognition is that it must always amount to a coercion of will which vitiates consent'. Lord Scarman also outlined the test for coercion 'whether the person alleged to have been coerced did or did not protest . . . did or did not have an alternative course open to him . . . was independently advised . . . took steps to avoid it'.

The doctrine and the tests deriving from it have been subsequently and satisfactorily applied.

Atlas Express Ltd v Kafco (Importers and Distributors) Ltd (1989)

Atlas, a national carrier, contracted with Kafco to deliver Kafco's basketwork to Woolworth stores. It was estimated that each load would be between 400 and 600 cartons and a price of £1.10p per carton was agreed. In fact the loads were only about 200 cartons each and Atlas refused to carry any more without a minimum £440 per load. Kafco had no immediate alternative and were forced to agree to protect their contract with Woolworth. However, they later failed to pay the agreed rate and Atlas sued. Tucker J held for Kafco and said

> 'I find that the defendant's apparent consent to the agreement was induced by pressure which was illegitimate . . . In my judgment can properly be described as economic duress, which is a concept recognised by English law, and which in the circumstances of the present case vitiates the defendant's apparent consent'.

The doctrine has been extended to apply wherever there is an intentional submission to improper pressure. Although what the difference is between legitimate pressure and improper pressure is not always certain.

Universe Tankships Incorporated of Monrovia v International Transport Workers Federation (The Universal Sentinel) (1983)

One of a number of cases involving action by the ITWF in respect of a campaign to improve conditions on ships 'flying flags of convenience'. Here, the ship was blacked by the union and forced to pay towards the ITWF welfare fund to secure the ship's release. This was economic duress, the pressure being illegitimate. Though the court were undecided on the difference between what was legitimate pressure and what was not.

The doctrine is still developing and is subject to uncertainty. Even though the economic duress can be shown this is no guarantee of a remedy.

North Ocean Shipping Co. Ltd v Hyundai Construction Co. Ltd (The Atlantic Baron) (1978)

A shipyard agreed to build a tanker for a shipping company, payment to be in five instalments. As part of the contract the shipyard opened a letter of credit for repayment of payments already made if they should fail to build the ship. After payment of the first instalment the shipyard demanded an increase in the price. The shipping company reluctantly agreed, as they needed the ship to complete other contracts. The letter of credit was increased as a result. Months after completion of the ship the shipping company sued for return of the excess. While the court accepted that there was economic duress, it was felt that the increase in the letter of credit was sufficient consideration for the fresh promise, and also the delay meant that the contract was affirmed.

Activity

Self-assessment questions

1 What is the main limitation on a claim to duress?
2 What is the effect of:
   a) a successful claim of duress and
   b) the alternative when duress is not available as an action?
3 Why has the doctrine of economic duress developed?
4 In what circumstances will a claim of economic duress fail and in what circumstances will it succeed?
5 Will there always be a remedy available where the court accepts that economic duress has in fact occurred?
6 What was the traditional difference between a claim of duress and a claim of undue influence?

13.4 Undue influence

Traditionally developed under equity and so any remedy is at the court's discretion. Undue influence developed to cover those areas where improper pressure prevents a party from exercising their free will in entering a contract. Since equity is inevitably more flexible than common law the doctrine could be applied whenever a party has exploited the other party to gain an unfair advantage.

Clearly, there is nothing wrong with trying to induce another to enter a contract, so it is the degree of influence and the context in which it occurs that the court is concerned with in determining what is and is not acceptable.

Traditionally, a distinction was made between those situations where undue influence was presumed from the relationship of the two parties and where undue influence had to be proved. The courts have recently redefined these classes.

Bank of Credit and Commerce International SA v Aboody (1990)

Here, a wife was able to avoid liability to the bank in respect of a surety transaction which she was induced to enter by her husband. She succeeded because the bank was said to have either constructive or actual notice of her husband's actions in either exercising undue influence over her or misrepresenting the amount of money he owed the bank.

The court drew distinctions between the two classes of undue influence:

Class 1 – actual undue influence – representing the original situation where there was no special relationship between the parties and so the party alleging the undue influence is required to prove it.

Class 2 – presumed undue influence – representing the traditional class where there was a special relationship and so undue influence is automatically presumed unless the contrary is proved.

The classifications were subsequently approved in the leading case.

Barclays Bank plc v O'Brien (1993)

The bank granted an overdraft of £135,000 for O'Brien's failing business on the security of the jointly owned marital home. The bank's representative failed to follow instructions to ensure that both O'Brien and his wife receive independent before signing. In the event, the company went further into trouble and the bank then sought to enforce the surety to recover the debt. Mrs O'Brien succeeded in showing that she had been induced to sign as a result of her husband's undue influence and had an inaccurate picture of what she had signed. The House of Lords considered that:

- there was a presumption of undue influence against the husband
- such a presumption could also apply with cohabitees

- a surety of this type could not be enforced where it had been gained by the presumed undue influence of the principal debtor
- unless the creditor took reasonable steps to ensure that the surety was entered into with free will and full knowledge then the creditor would be fixed with constructive notice of the undue influence
- constructive notice could be avoided by warning of the risks involved and advising of the need to take independent legal advice at a meeting not attended by the principal debtor.

Class 1: Actual undue influence

This type of undue influence applies where there is no special relationship between the parties. In this way it is impossible to show that an abuse of confidence or trust has occurred and as a result the party alleging the undue influence must show it.

Undue influence will be accepted in these circumstances where it is possible to show that the coercion amounted to a dominance to the extent that the party subject to it was unable to exercise free will or act independently of the influence in contracting.

Williams v Bayley (1866)

A young man forged endorsements on promissory notes, causing loss to a bank. His father was then approached by the bank to stand the son's debts. This was acceptable behaviour but the threat that the bank would have the son arrested and deported amounted to undue influence.

It was originally defined in *Allcard v Skinner* (1887) as 'some unfair and improper conduct, some coercion from outside, some overreaching, some form of cheating'.

Lord Denning felt it should apply where there is any inequality in bargaining strength.

Lloyds Bank v Bundy (1979)

An elderly farmer, his son, and a company owned by his son were customers of the same bank. The farmer was persuaded by his son and the bank manager to use his farm as security for a loan to the son's company. When the company defaulted on the loan and the bank sought possession of the farm, the farmer successfully pleaded undue influence. There was a clear conflict of interest because the bank represented all parties.

However, Lord Scarman subsequently rejected this in *National Westminster Bank plc v Morgan* (1985).

Lord Browne-Wilkinson in CIBC Mortgages Ltd v Pitt (1993) has more recently explained that 'actual undue influence is a species of fraud . . . a man guilty of fraud is no more entitled to argue that the transaction was beneficial to the person defrauded than a man who has procured a transaction by misrepresentation', rejecting the previously held view that the party claiming actual undue influence was required to show some manifest disadvantage.

Traditionally, such relationships as husband and wife and banker and client were felt to fall within actual undue influence, but the class as a whole seems to be becoming more rare.

Class 2: Presumed undue influence

This class applies whenever the party claiming it can show a relationship of trust and confidence with the party against whom the undue influence is alleged. The claimant only need prove the relationship, and then undue influence is presumed and it is for the other party to disprove that it has in fact occurred. This can only be done by showing that the party alleging the undue influence entered the contract with full knowledge of its character and effect. In order to achieve this the party against whom undue influence is alleged will need to show that the other party had the

benefit of independent, impartial advice before entering the contract.

Traditionally, presumed undue influence applied in relationships such as parent/child.

Lancashire Loans Co. v Black (1933)

A domineering woman induced her daughter to stand guarantor for a loan with a bank. When she defaulted on the loan and the bank sought to enforce the guarantee the daughter successfully claimed undue influence. She was dominated by her mother, did not properly know the nature of what she was signing and had been given no independent advice.

Also a relationship based on spiritual leadership gave rise to the presumption.

Allcard v Skinner (1887)

A woman belonging to a religious sect was persuaded to join a closed order and to give all of her property up to the order. When she later left the order she then tried to recover railway stock that she had owned. While it was accepted that she had been subjected to undue influence her action failed because she waited until five years after leaving the order before claiming, and 'delay defeats equity'.

Other relationships such as trustee/beneficiary, doctor/patient, and other fiduciary relationships have been held to create a presumption of undue influence.

Such relationships are now identified as Class 2A, and arise automatically, merely because of the type of the relationship. It is also now possible to establish a relationship where the one party proves that (s)he has placed trust and confidence in the other where the presumption will apply even though not falling within one of the traditional categories. This is now known as Class 2B.

The most common case is that of husband and wife, which traditionally fell under the category of actual undue influence, requiring proof of the undue influence by the party alleging it, usually a wife. The court in *Bank of Credit and Commerce International SA v Aboody* (1990) rejected the proposition in *Midland Bank v Shepherd* (1988) that the wife/husband relationship gave rise only to actual undue influence, and therefore proof of the undue influence by the husband.

It has been argued both that the party subject to undue influence in these cases is protected because the other party is seen as the agent of the creditor, or alternatively that the wife in such situations has a special protection in equity. The most common means of protecting the weaker party, however, is by application of the 'doctrine of notice'. That is the creditor, usually a bank or building society, will be unable to enforce the defaulted loan against the wife where it has actual or constructive notice of her equitable interest in the property which stands as surety for the loan.

Since *Barclays Bank plc v O'Brien* wives are able to show a relationship of trust and confidence in their husbands and thus qualify for presumed undue influence under Class 2B. The informality of the relationship, it is accepted, means that there is a greater risk of the wife being taken advantage of in order to secure a loan based on the surety of the matrimonial property. This is then sufficient to put the creditor on notice providing that the contract is not on the face of it to the wife's advantage, and there is a risk that the husband has unfairly induced the wife's acceptance. Lord Browne-Wilkinson, in the case, also suggested that the principle should apply also to cohabitees where the relationship is actually known to the creditor.

So the creditor will be unable to enforce the surety against the loan unless he has 'taken reasonable steps to satisfy himself that the surety entered into the obligation freely and in knowledge of the true facts'. Reasonable steps might include: personally interviewing the person stand-ing surety for the loan in the absence of the principal debtor; explaining the full extent of the liability; explaining all of the risks involved; encouraging the person to seek independent legal advice before standing surety on the loan.

The creditor of course has no duty to enquire what goes on when the solicitor gives this independent advice.

Massey v Midland Bank (1995)

Mrs Massey was persuaded to give the bank a charge on the property she shared with Potts, the father of her children, as security for his business overdraft. The bank suggested that Mrs Massey would need independent legal advice. This was arranged with Potts' solicitor, and Potts himself attended. Potts defaulted and the bank sought to enforce the charge. The bank had notice of the relationship, and of the risk that the charge was not to Mrs Massey's advantage. However, the solicitor confirmed to the bank that she had received independent advice, and it was not bound to make any further enquiries.

On this basis the creditor is entitled to assume that the solicitor will act honestly and competently. As Steyn LJ put it in *Banco Exterior Internacional v Mann* (1994) 'I do not understand Lord Browne-Wilkinson to be laying down the only steps to be taken which will avoid a bank being faced with constructive notice . . . rather he is pointing out best practice'.

However, in the recent case of *Royal Bank of Scotland plc v Etridge (No 2)* (2001) the House of Lords has considered the issue of whether a solicitor appointed by the bank to give the wife independent advice is agent of the bank. It reviewed all the leading authorities on undue influence, setting significant guidelines in the process. It has set out some major rules. The case would also seem to suggest that the distinctions between Class 1, Class 2A and Class 2B are now in many ways irrelevant.

Royal Bank of Scotland plc v Etridge (No 2) and other appeals (2001)

Here, the wife claimed undue influence by her husband and argued that the solicitor had not explained the charge to her on her own. She claimed that the bank was therefore fixed with constructive notice of the undue influence. The House of Lords reviewed all of the law on undue influence in the banking cases where a wife has stood surety for her husband's debts. The Lords appear to have decided that there are not two types of undue influence. Presumed undue influence is merely an evidential 'lift' in helping prove undue influence. They also expressed dislike with the words 'manifestly disadvantageous' and preferred instead the 19th-century language 'transactions which are not to be accounted for on terms of charity, love or affection'. They considered that it was out of touch with life to presume that every gift from a child to a parent was undue influence. They also thought that most cases where a spouse guarantees a husband's business debts would be explicable and are reasonably accountable. This view might lead to fewer cases being successful. The Lords issued general guidelines as follows:

1 A bank should be put on enquiry whenever a wife offers to stand surety for her husband's debts or vice versa, or even in the case of unmarried couples where the bank was aware of the relationship.

2 A bank should take reasonable steps to satisfy itself that a wife had been fully informed of the practical implications of the proposed transaction. This need not mean a personal meeting if a suitable alternative was available and the bank could rely on confirmation from a solicitor acting for the wife that he had advised her appropriately. But if the bank knew that the solicitor had not properly advised the wife or ought to have realised that the wife had not received appropriate advice then it was risk of being fixed with notice.

3 A solicitor advising the wife can act for both her and her husband (and/or the bank) unless

he realised that there was a real risk of conflict of interests, in which case he should cease acting for her or be liable.

4 The advice given by a solicitor should include explanation of the following:
  • the nature of the documents and their practical consequences for the wife
  • the seriousness of the risks involved – i.e. the extent of her financial means and whether she has other assets out of which repayment could be made
  • that she has a choice of whether to proceed or not
  • the solicitor should be sure that the wife does wish to proceed, and the discussion should take place at a face-to-face meeting with the wife in the absence of the husband.

5 The bank has a duty to obtain confirmation from the solicitor.
  a) For future cases:
  • the bank should take steps to check directly with the wife the name of the solicitor she wishes to act for her
  • this communication and response must be direct with the wife
  • the bank should send the solicitor the necessary financial information
  • in exceptional cases, where the bank believes or suspects the wife is being misled by her husband, the bank should inform the solicitors of the information giving rise to that suspicion
  • in every case the bank should obtain written confirmation from the solicitor.
  b) For past transactions:
  • it would be sufficient if the bank obtained from a solicitor acting for the wife confirmation to the effect that he had brought home to the wife the risks she was running by standing surety.

6 *In obiter* the court also identified that the *O'Brien* principle is not confined to husband/wife relationships but also to others who are in a sexual relationships or whenever there is a risk of undue influence (e.g. parent and child). If the bank knows of the relationship, that is enough to put the bank on enquiry.

The effects of pleading undue influence

Where a claimant succeeds in a plea that undue influence has taken place then the contract is voidable by the party alleging the undue influence. The contract will be set aside subject to the principle of *restitutio in integrum*.

However, in certain circumstances a party may be denied an effective remedy despite a successful plea if the actual value of the property has changed.

Cheese v Thomas (1994)

Cheese, who was aged 84, contributed £43,000 to the purchase of a property costing £83,000. His nephew provided the remaining £40,000 by way of a mortgage. The property went in the nephew's sole name, but was to be solely occupied by the uncle until his death. The nephew then defaulted on the mortgage. The uncle then sought return of his £43,000 fearful of his security. The court accepted a claim of undue influence and ordered the house sold. However, the slump in property prices meant that the house could only fetch £55,000 and the uncle was then entitled to only a 43/83 share.

Activity

Self-assessment questions
1 Why did the doctrine of undue influence develop in equity?
2 What was the traditional difference between claims made under duress and those made under undue influence?
3 What differences were there traditionally between actual undue influence and presumed undue influence?
4 Why was undue influence traditionally presumed in the case of certain relationships?
5 Were the classes of relationships covered by this principle sensible?
6 What is the difference between the new classes 2A and 2B in undue influence?
7 What is the role of the 'doctrine of notice' in undue influence?
8 When will a bank have constructive notice of the undue influence, and how can it avoid this?
9 What is the basic rule in *Barclays Bank v O'Brien*?
10 What impact do cases such as *Massey* have on the basic rule?
11 When are banks in a special relationship with their clients?
12 How has the case of *Royal Bank of Scotland plc v Etridge (No 2)* in HL developed or help clear up the rules on undue influence?

KEY FACTS

- To preserve freedom of contract the courts have traditionally invalidated a contract which has been formed as the result of any coercion
- Duress is a common law action where a contract has been procured by violence or threats of violence – *Barton v Armstrong*
- Economic duress is a modern area where in a commercial contract a party is coerced into a change of arrangements under the threat of a commercially damaging course of action – *The Siboen and the Sibotre*
- The party raising it must have (i) protested immediately, and (ii) shown a reluctance to enter the arrangement otherwise any remedy may be lost – *The Atlantic Baron*
- Undue influence is traditionally an equitable area where one party has been induced by coercion to enter a contract – it is a question of degree what level of persuasion is acceptable and what amounts to undue influence
- There are now identified two types of undue influence – Class 1 or actual undue influence, and Class 2 or presumed undue influence – *BCCI v Aboody*
- Actual is where there is no special relationship and the party alleging the undue influence must prove it – *CIBC Mortgages v Pitt*
- Presumed undue influence occurs in certain relationships such as parents and children – *Lancashire Loans v Black* – and spiritual adviser/follower – *Allcard v Skinner*
- The party against whom the undue influence is alleged must disprove it
- Class 2B now extends this type of undue influence to those situations where a wife is induced to place the family home as security for a loan made to the husband – *Barclays Bank v O'Brien*
- In such situations the creditor is put on notice of the possibility of the undue influence and must take reasonable care to ensure that the wife only agrees to the arrangement after having full knowledge of the risks involved, having been given independent legal advice
- Many cases such as *Massey, Mann, Camfield,* and *Etridge* concern whether or not the creditor has done sufficient to discharge their duty towards the wife to escape actual or constructive notice
- Now the major rules are contained in HL judgment in *Etridge*
  - Bank put on enquiry when she stands as surety for husband's debts
  - Bank should take steps to see that she is fully informed
  - Solicitor can act for both parties unless he realises that it involves a conflict of interests
  - Solicitor should inform wife of nature of documents, seriousness of risk, that she has choice to back out
  - Bank should get confirmation of advice from solicitor
  - *O'Brien* principles extend beyond husbands and wives into other similar relationships

Chapter 14

VITIATING FACTORS: ILLEGALITY

14.1 Introduction

Most vitiating factors represent some sort of defect in the formation, for instance that the agreement does not truly represent the consensus of the two parties because the agreement is based on a mistake or a misrepresentation. Illegality on the other hand is more about the character of the agreement itself. It is of a type that for some reason the law frowns on.

The basic principle involved is straightforward enough: the law will not enforce a contract that is tainted with illegality. However, the area is not a simple one for a number of reasons. Firstly, the types of contract that have been declared illegal are not only numerous but also diverse. Secondly, while judges frequently refer to contracts being illegal or void or unenforceable, they do not always fully distinguish between these terms. Thirdly, there is the added complication that over time both the common law and statute law have both been used to render different types of contract illegal. Fourthly, the area is one that is heavily influenced by public policy.

Despite these difficulties it is possible to identify some loose groupings in which to categorise such contracts.

- Certain contracts are said to be void and therefore unenforceable – in other words, there is nothing to prevent their creation and so long as the parties comply with the terms of their agreement they create no problems, but if one party breaches a term of the agreement the other will have no redress in law;
- Certain other contracts are said to be illegal and therefore unenforceable – with these it is possible that they should not have been made at all, in any case other connected transactions may be tainted with their illegality.

Since contracts can be illegal by statutory provision or by common law it is possible to classify illegality into four groups:

- contracts **void by statute**
- contracts **declared illegal by statute** (with the further division between contracts that are illegal in their formation and those declared illegal because of the manner of their performance)
- contracts that are **void at common law** – an area that is heavily influenced by public policy
- contracts that are **illegal at common law** – again for public policy reasons.

14.2 Contracts void by statute

These are of two types:

Contracts of wager

Wager was defined in *Carlill v The Carbolic Smoke Ball Co.* as where 'two persons mutually agree that one shall win from the other money or other stake upon the determination of some event, neither party having an interest in the contract apart from the stake'.

By virtue of s18 Gaming Act 1845 such contracts are null and void. So it is possible to make a contract of wager but not to enforce it. Money passed as a result of the wager is not recoverable and contracts that are associated with the wager may also be affected.

There are of course a number of contracts involving betting that are now regulated by various Acts and are consequently enforceable. These include the lottery and the pools, on course tote betting, and casino gambling under the Gaming Act 1968.

Restrictive trade practices

Public policy originally prevented enforceability of agreements aimed at restricting free competition. Now such agreements fall under the Restrictive Trade Practices Act 1976, and are regulated by the Director General of Fair Trading. They are also subject to the control of EU competition law in Articles 81 and 82 of the EC Treaty.

14.3 Contracts illegal by statute

Here the contract could be illegal in one of two ways:

- it could be illegal to make such contracts at all – generally this would be for reasons of public policy, Parliament does not wish such contracts to be made
- it could be legal to engage in such a contract but the manner in which the contract is performed is illegal.

Contracts illegal when formed

Where the contract is illegal as formed then the contract is void *ab initio* and unenforceable as a result.

Re Mahmoud and Ispahani (1921)

The Seed, Oils and Fats Order of 1919 prohibited unlicensed trading in linseed oil. One party had a licence and contracted to supply the defendant who did not but who falsely stated that he did. When the defendant backed out of the agreement the claimant sued for the failure to accept delivery. He was unsuccessful because the contract was void and unenforceable for the lack of the licence.

The justification for this is that the contract would be 'a transgression of the positive laws of our country' – Lord Mansfield.

Cope v Rowlands (1836)

An Act made it illegal for stockbrokers to deal without a licence. Cope set up business in London without obtaining a licence. As a result, when he sued Rowlands for payment for work done, he failed. His lack of a licence made the contract illegal and unenforceable. The purpose of the provision was to protect the public from the harm that could be caused by unregulated brokers.

Sometimes, however, the contract will not be illegal because the provision in the Act is for a different purpose than to prevent the contract from being made.

Smith v Mawhood (1845)

A tobacconist failed to get the appropriate licence to sell tobacco products. The purpose of the licensing was to impose a penalty for the revenue so the contract was not unenforceable.

Contracts illegally performed

A contract may be created legitimately but become illegal and therefore unenforceable because the manner in which it is performed is illegal.

Anderson Ltd v Daniel (1924)

A statute provided that, in sales of fertilisers, an invoice listing chemicals contained in the product must be given to the buyer. Fertiliser was supplied without the proper invoice. When the buyer failed to pay for the goods, the seller's action for the price failed. The contract could be made lawfully but the absence of the invoice rendered it illegal and the seller could not enforce it.

But the fact that performance is not by the proscribed manner does not mean that it will be automatically unenforceable on all occasions.

St John Shipping Corporation v Joseph Rank Ltd (1956)

The court refused to hold that a contract for the carriage of goods at sea was illegal and therefore unenforceable merely because the captain loaded his ship beyond the legal loading line. To do so would have allowed the other party to avoid payment with no justification.

The point that the case clearly makes is that the illegality must relate to the contract's central purpose if the contract is to be declared invalid and unenforceable.

14.4 Contracts void at common law

The central issue here is again whether the type of contract offends public policy. Again, as void contracts there is nothing to prevent parties agreeing to their formation but the parties will be unable to enforce the terms of the contract when there is any dispute.

Contracts unenforceable under this heading fall into three distinct categories:

Contracts seeking to oust the jurisdiction of the courts

Generally, the courts will reject any attempt to remove their jurisdiction through clauses in contracts to that effect.

An exception to this is arbitration clauses, known as *Scott v Avery* clauses. Many bodies will contain a clause referring any dispute, at least initially, to a qualified arbitrator expert in the specific field.

Also, Parliament directs a number of contractual disputes to bodies other than the courts. An obvious example of this is employment disputes and employment tribunals.

Contracts prejudicial to the family

The courts traditionally have seen themselves as the defenders of moral values and marriage is seen as a sacred institution requiring the protection of the courts. Traditionally, then, any arrangement which might have the effect of harming marriage would be deemed void by the courts.

Obvious examples of this would be taking a fee not to marry or indeed procuring a marriage for a fee, or otherwise threatening a marriage.

Originally the courts would also view contracts which relinquished parental responsibility as void, as where a parent sold the child. Now this principle may be complicated by the practice of surrogacy.

Contracts in restraint of trade

These are clearly the most important category of contracts void at common law and they are probably also the most contentious.

A restraint of trade clause is a clause of a contract by which one party agrees to limit or restrict his ability to carry on his trade, business or profession.

Judges have always viewed such arrangements as *prima facie* void for two principal reasons:
- firstly, the courts are reluctant to endorse an arrangement whereby one party effectively gives up his right to his livelihood as a requirement of the stronger party to the contract
- secondly, the judges are similarly reluctant to see the public deprived of that party's skill or expertise.

Nevertheless, the courts have always tried to protect the idea of freedom of contract and only intervene in a contractual relationship reluctantly. As a result, while restraint clauses are *prima facie* void, the courts will allow them to stand where they are demonstrated as reasonable.

Reasonable in this context is measured in two ways:
- firstly, the restraint must be reasonable as between the two parties to the contract. 'Reasonable' here means that the restraint is no wider than is needed to protect the legitimate

interests of the party inserting the restraint clause into the contract. Merely preventing legitimate competition through use of the restraint is unacceptable and the clause will fail

- secondly, the restraint must be reasonable in the public interest. A restraint would not be considered reasonable that deprived the public of a benefit that might otherwise be enjoyed or that unduly restricted choice.

Restraint clauses generally operate in one of three distinct contexts:
- employee restraints
- vendor restraints
- agreements of mutual recognition between businesses.

Employee restraints

These are clauses contained in the contract of employment that restrict the activities of the employee on leaving the employment. The employer seeking to rely on such a clause will succeed only where he is actually protecting a legitimate interest of his business. No clause will succeed which merely tries to prevent legitimate competition and which has its logical outcome therefore that the employer is effectively prevented from working. The employer then will be able legitimately to use such a clause to protect only things such as his trade secrets and his client connections, and sometimes to reduce the damage that could be done by a high-level employee.

The courts must decide what is reasonable in the circumstances. They will measure what is reasonable against a number of factors:

a) Whether or not the work is specialised

– in which case the restraint is more likely to be seen as reasonable.

Forster v Suggett (1918)

A clause in a glass blower's contract prevented him from working for any competitor of his employers on leaving. The court held that the skill was so specialist at the time that it amounted to a trade secret and the glass manu-

facturers were entitled to the protection of the clause.

b) The position held by the employee in the employer's business

The higher up and the more important the employee, the more likely it is that inclusion of the restraint is to be reasonable.

Herbert Morris Ltd v Saxelby (1916)

The restraint clause prevented the ex-employee from involvement with the sale or manufacture of pulley blocks, overhead runways, or overhead travelling cranes for a period of seven years after leaving the employment. This covered the whole range of the employer's business and was too wide to succeed despite the key position held by the employee.

c) Soliciting clients

In general, since an employer is able to protect his client contact, a clause that prevents the employee from soliciting those clients will be upheld provided that it is not too wide.

Hanover Insurance Brokers Ltd and Christchurch Insurance Brokers Ltd v Schapiro (1994)

Here, a number of brokerages including Hanover Insurance Brokers (HIB) were sold on to Christchurch. After the sale three directors of HIB left and set up on their own and were accused of soliciting clients. A restraint clause in their contract prevented them from soliciting the clients of Hanover Associates (of which HIB was a subsidiary) and all its other subsidiaries. The three ex-directors argued that the clause was too wide and should be declared void since they had only worked for HIB. The court accepted this, but held also that since the purpose of the restraint was to prevent soliciting of insurance clients, and only HIB engaged in this activity, then the clause could be upheld against the three directors in respect of the clients of HIB.

d) The geographical area covered by the restraint

This must not be wider than necessary to protect the legitimate interest.

Fitch v Dewes (1921)

A restraint in a conveyancing clerk's contract prevented him from working in the same capacity for any firm within a seven-mile radius of Tamworth Town Hall for life. The restraint was reasonable because of the rural nature of the community and the clerk's contact with the solicitor's client base.

e) The duration of the restraint

This must not be longer than necessary to protect the legitimate interest.

Home Counties Dairies Ltd v Skilton (1970)

A milk roundsman had an employment contract containing two restraints. Clause 12 prevented him from entering any employment connected with the dairy business. The second, Clause 15, provided that he should not work as a roundsman or serve any existing customer for a period of one year after leaving the employment. Clause 12 was too wide to be reasonable. Clause 15 was successful since it only protected legitimate interests and for only a short period of time.

f) The restraint must be no wider than is necessary to protect the legitimate interests of the employer

The restraint must be against activities only, which would protect the employer's legitimate interests. Any attempt to widen the clause to activities not relevant to the employee's actual work will be void.

Mont (JA) (UK) Ltd v Mills (1994)

This restraint clause was against a 43-year-old managing director in the paper tissue industry and was contained in a severance agreement. The clause prevented him from joining any company within the paper industry for a period of 12 months after ending his employment. The court decided that it was much too wide. It effectively prevented him from working in the paper industry which was all that he knew. The clause only needed to prevent him from revealing confidential information.

g) Achieving restraint through other means

It will also generally be classed as unreasonable to attempt to achieve the restraint through other means than a direct restraint clause.

Bull v Pitney Bowes (1966)

There was no restraint clause in the contract but there was a clause whereby employees forfeited their pension rights in the event that they took up work with a competitor of the employer. This was held to be void for public policy.

A similar line would be taken when employers agree among themselves on an arrangement that has the effect of a restraint of trade.

Kores Manufacturing Co. v Kolok Manufacturing Co. (1959)

Two electronics companies reached an agreement not to employ the other's staff for five years in the event of their leaving. This had the same effect as a restraint clause and was held to be void.

A similar point applies where the restraint is achieved through rules of associations.

Eastham v Newcastle United FC Ltd (1964)

Here, George Eastham, a well-known footballer, challenged the rules of the Football Association on the legitimacy of the then transfer system. These rules meant that a club could retain a player's registration even after his contract ended and so effectively prevent him from playing again. Also, players could be placed on the transfer list against their will. The court determined that these rules did amount to an unlawful restraint of trade. (Of course, subsequently the whole area of transfers has become subject to control under Article 39 EC Treaty through the *Bosman* ruling.)

Vendor restraints

These will occur where sellers of business agree under the contract of sale not to unfairly compete with the purchaser of the business. Again, such agreements are *prima facie* void. Declaring such restraints void has been justified as preventing an individual from negotiating away his livelihood, and also for preventing the public from losing a valuable benefit where the one party is prevented from trading by the other.

They are, however, more likely to be accepted as reasonable by the courts because the bargaining strength of the parties is more likely to be equal.

Again, to be reasonable and enforceable, they must protect only legitimate interests and not merely aim to prevent legitimate competition.

British Reinforced Concrete Co. v Schelff (1921)

A business that specialised in the production of steel reinforcement for roads was sold. In the contract a restraint clause prevented the vendors of the business from engaging in any similar business. One of the vendors then entered another business as manager of the reinforced concrete section. The clause was held to be too wide to protect legitimate interests and could not be applied.

Again, the same tests apply as for employee restraints and no clause will be enforced that is too wide in its application, though what is too wide is a question of fact dictated by the circumstances of each case.

Nordenfelt v Maxim Nordenfelt Co. (1894)

Nordenfelt had established a worldwide business manufacturing and selling guns and ammunition. When he sold the business, it was subject to a clause in the contract preventing from engaging in the armaments business anywhere in the world for a period of 25 years. This seems an unusually wide clause. However, the court was prepared to enforce it since the world was the appropriate market.

Mutual undertakings

Often, agreements between merchants or manufacturers or in other trades of different types will amount in effect to restraints. Similar rules apply and they will not in any case be declared reasonable and valid unless a clear benefit is gained by both sides.

One example is agreements based on the rules of associations.

English Hop Growers v Dering (1928)

Here, Dering was held to be bound by his agreement to deliver all of his hop crop to the association for onward sale. This arrangement was actually the way in which hop growers eliminated competition. It also ensured that any loss as well as any profit was shared equally amongst the members of the association in any given year. So it was a genuine protection of the members and of obvious mutual benefit.

Another area where the same principles can obviously apply is in the agreements between artists and performers etc and their various agents, particularly where there is an obvious imbalance in the bargaining strength of the parties.

Schroeder Music Publishing Co. Ltd v Macaulay (1974)

An unknown composer entered into an agreement with music publishers. Under this agreement the publishers would receive world copyright on any composition he produced, there would be no general payment for compositions and royalties were payable only on those compositions that were commercially exploited, and the publisher gave no guarantee that any work would be published. The original five-year agreement could automatically be extended by the publishers but they could also terminate the agreement at any time with only one month's notice. The court held that this regulation of trade was plainly unreasonable and unlawful, particularly in the light of the inexperience and unequal bargaining strength of the young composer.

While the same rules generally apply, this can be contrasted with situations where, while a contract may have been originally entered into where one party may have taken advantage of the immaturity and unequal bargaining strength of the other, subsequent compromises have been to the advantage of the other party.

Panayiotou v Sony Music International (UK) Ltd (1994)

This case involved George Michael and his attempts to improve the degree of control he had over his recording contract and gain greater freedom from the restrictions it imposed on him. Originally, he and Andrew Ridgeley had a recording contract as the group 'Wham', and they had tried to get their recording contract declared void for restraint of trade. This in fact was changed in 1984 under an agreed compromise and the group moved to CBS. Michael then established himself as a

solo artist and in 1988 his contract was changed to reflect his new 'superstar' status. CBS was also taken over by Sony at this time. When Michael later wanted to change his image and became dissatisfied with Sony he sought to have this agreement declared void for restraint of trade. As the 1988 contract was based on and was an improvement on the 1984 agreement which the court accepted as a genuine compromise, it refused his claim as being contrary to public policy.

A further area where the courts have applied the principles of restraint of trade and discussed in detail the tests for determining reasonableness is in the case of so-called 'solus agreements'.

Esso Petroleum Co. Ltd v Harper's Garage (Stourport) Ltd (1968)

Under the solus agreement here, Esso lent Harper's Garage money and it could sell only Esso petrol from its two garages. In the case of the first garage, known as the Corner Garage, there was a loan, the agreement was to last for 21 years, and by the same agreement Harper's were bound to pay back the loan over that 21-year period and not any shorter period. In effect, then, they were tied into the agreement to sell only Esso petrol for those 21 years. Under the agreement for the second garage, known as the Mustow Green garage, the duration of the agreement was for only four years and five months and there was no loan attached to the garage. HL discussed in length and restated the various rules for determining the validity of restraint of trade clauses. Applying these rules, it declared the Corner Garage agreement void on the basis of excessive duration of the restraint. Using the same basis of duration, HL declared the Mustow Garage agreement valid as both fair and reasonable.

Activity

Problem

Try the following problem:

Lisa agreed to sell her hairdressing business in Wickton to Alison for £50,000, including the lease, all fixtures and fittings, and the goodwill. Lisa had planned to marry and begin a family, and thus give up hairdressing for a number of years.

In a clause in the written contract that had been insisted upon by Alison, Lisa agreed that she would not 'for a period of ten years following transfer of the business open a salon or other hairdressing establishment within a twenty five mile radius' of the salon in Wickton. By a further clause in the contract Lisa was prohibited from 'approaching, soliciting for business, or contacting with a view to entering any business arrangement, for a period of five years, any client of the business'.

Three years later, Lisa has found that she is unable to have a family, and so she plans to return to hairdressing. She has taken the lease on a hairdresser's in Sockington which is only five miles from Wickton.

Alison is concerned that she may now lose business and seeks your advice on any remedies which may be available to her.

14.5 Contracts illegal at common law

This is potentially a very wide group of contracts and it includes any type of agreement that is prejudicial to the general notion of freedom of contract. The basis for judges declaring such arrangements illegal is that to allow them to stand would be harmful to the public good. So, like most aspects of illegality at common law, the reason for the illegality is public policy.

The categories of such agreements are numerous and varied. The common characteristic seems to be some form of immorality in each case. They include:

a) A contract to commit a wrong

This might be a tort, a fraud, and even a crime.

Dann v Curzon (1911)

Here, the claimant had been hired to start a riot in a theatre. When he sued for the unpaid fee of £20 he was unsuccessful. The judges, as a matter of policy, could not enforce an agreement to carry out a crime.

b) A contract to benefit from the crime of another

Beresford v Royal Insurance Co. Ltd (1937)

Relatives were prevented from benefiting from the life insurance of a suicide.

c) A contract to defraud the Revenue

Napier v The National Business Agency (1951)

Under his contract of employment the claimant received expenses of £6 per week where his actual costs were no more than £1. This was a deliberate agreement between the parties with the purpose of avoiding income tax. When the claimant was dismissed he was unable to sue for back pay since the contract was unenforceable.

There is also an interesting recent development of this point.

Carnduff v Rock and another (2001)

Here, the Court of Appeal held that there could be no enforceable agreement between a police informer and the police for payment for information. It would be against the public interest to allow an informer to sue for payment. Laws LJ identified that to resolve the issue fairly would involve examining the operational methods of the police in detail. This would transfer the 'difficult and delicate business of tracking and catching serious professional criminals from the confidential context of police operations to the glare of a court of justice'.

d) Contracts aimed at corruption in public life

Parkinson v The College of Ambulance (1925)

The claimant, who was wealthy, was asked to donate funds to a company, in return for which the other party promised he would be able to gain him a knighthood. When the claimant made the donation but was not given any honour he sued for return of his money. He failed because this was purely a corrupt practice.

e) Contracts to interfere with justice

Harmony Shipping Co. SA v Davis (1979)

An agreement by a witness not to give evidence in return for a cash payment was void and unenforceable.

f) Contracts to promote sexual immorality

Pearce v Brooks (1866)

A prostitute hit on the idea of conducting her trade from hired carriages. When she did not pay the fee owed, the owner's action for the price failed. The contract was for immoral purposes and was unenforceable.

14.6 The consequences of the contract being void

Where the contract is declared void the significant difference in effect is between contracts void under common law and contracts void because of statute.

Common law

Where the contract is declared void by the courts, as may be the case with a contract in restraint of trade, there are a number of possible consequences:

a) Firstly, depending on the wording of the contract, the whole contract itself is not necessarily void, though the offending clause may be.

b) Money that has been paid over under the contract may be recoverable as a result of the contract being declared void, as in *Hermann v Charlesworth* (1905) where the procurement of a marriage for a fee was declared void.

c) It is possible to sever the clause that is void from the rest of the contract to avoid voiding the whole contract.

Goldsoll v Goldman (1915)

A restraint in the sale of a jewellery business specialising in the sale of imitation jewellery inside the UK, prevented the vendor from engaging in the sale of real or imitation jewellery throughout most of Europe and America. The court severed the word 'real' from the contract, and also the clauses relating to those areas outside of the UK, and the rest of the clause stood.

d) But the court will not sever parts of a contract where to do so would alter the whole character of the agreement.

Attwood v Lamont (1920)

A tailor's cutter was restrained, on leaving his employment, from taking up work as 'tailor, dressmaker, general draper, milliner, hatter, haberdasher, gentleman's, ladies' or children's outfitter at any place within a ten mile radius'. The court saw this not so much as a list but a comprehensive description of the employer's whole business and as such severance was not possible and the contract was void and unenforceable.

e) Also, the court will not employ severance if to do so would defeat public policy which rendered the contract void in the first place.

Napier v The National Business Agency (1951)

Here, because of the tax avoidance mechanism, the contract was void and the claimant was unable to recover any of the money owing.

Statute

The effects if the contract is void because of a statutory provision may obviously vary and will depend on the wording of the Act itself.

However, where the statute itself is silent on the effects of the contract being declared void then the common law effects above will apply.

14.7 The consequences of the contract being illegal

Here, the principal difference is not between the common law and statute but between contracts that are illegal as formed and those that are legally formed and only become illegal by the manner of their performance.

Illegal as formed

Where statute or the common law has declared that a class of contract will be illegal if made then such a contract can never be legally formed or performed and will be illegal from the moment of formation. There are then a number of consequences for such agreements:

a) Since the contract is illegal it is also unenforceable by either party.

Dann v Curzon (1911)

Since the agreement to start the riot was illegal then there was no legal way of enforcing payment.

b) As a result, property or money transferred in advance of the agreement cannot generally be recovered, as was the case with the claimant in *Parkinson v The College of Ambulance* (1925) where the court would not permit recovery of the donation.
c) This may be the position even where the parties are unaware of the illegality of the agreement.

J.W. Allan (Merchandising) Ltd v Cloke (1960)

Fees to hire a roulette wheel for an illegal game under the Betting and Gaming Act 1960 were not recoverable although the parties were unaware that the game was illegal.

d) However, there are certain exceptions to this basic rule where property transferred may be recoverable:

    (i) where not to allow recovery is 'an affront to public conscience'.

Howard v Shirlstar Container Transport Ltd (1990)

The contract was to recover an aircraft impounded in Nigeria, so in effect it meant stealing it for the owner. When it was completed and the aircraft owner refused to pay claiming that the arrangement was void for illegality the court held that the claimant could recover in the circumstances.

    (ii) where the illegality is not vital to the cause

Tinsley v Milligan (1993)

The claimant and defendant bought a house, putting it in the claimant's name so that the defendant could carry on claiming benefits, thus making the agreement illegal. The defendant later claimed a share of the property under a resulting trust arising out of the contribution to the purchase. The claimant argued illegality but the House of Lords accepted that the right arising out of the trust was enforceable.

    (iii) where the party seeking recovery is not *in pari delicto*, i.e. is not as culpable as the other party

Kirri Cotton Co. Ltd v Dewani (1960)

A landlord demanded a premium from a tenant even though this was illegal under legislation. The tenant could recover the cost because he had no choice but to go along with the illegal arrangement.

    (iv) where the agreement has been induced by a fraud

Hughes v Liverpool and Victoria Legal Friendly Society (1916)

The claimant was induced by the fraud of an insurance agent to take out on parties who were not insurable by her. When the fraud was discovered she was entitled to return of the premiums paid.

    (v) where the one party repents before the contract is performed.

Illegal as performed

If both parties are equally culpable for the illegal performance then the rules are basically the same as for contracts illegal in their formation.

However, if one party is unaware of the illegality then (s)he may have remedies available including recovery of any money handed over in advance of the contract.

Marles v Trant (1954)

A seed supplier sold seed to Trant as 'spring wheat' seed which in fact it was not. Trant then sold it on to Marles, but without an invoice required by statute. When Marles discovered that the seed was 'winter wheat' seed he was able to sue despite the illegality of the contract.

Activity

Self-assessment questions

1 In what ways does illegality differ from other vitiating factors?
2 How are restrictive trade practices regulated in modern times?
3 What is the difference between a contract illegally formed and a contract illegally performed?
4 How important do you think control of contracts prejudicial to marriage is in the present day?
5 Why are contracts in restraint of trade *prima facie* void?
6 When will a restraint clause be upheld?
7 How is reasonableness measured in restraint of trade?
8 What are the common characteristics of contracts declared illegal by the common law?
9 In what circumstances can a party recover money or property handed over under an illegal contract?
10 What are the purposes of severing a contract?

KEY FACTS

- Illegality is a difficult area because judges refer to contracts being illegal, void and unenforceable, and also because a contract can be invalidated by statute or by the common law
- Contracts void by statute include contracts of wager, and restrictive trade practices
- A contract can be illegal by statute in its formation – *Re Mahmoud and Ispahani* – in which case it is unenforceable
- Or a legally formed contract can be illegal in its performance – *Anderson Ltd v Daniel*
- Contracts void at common law include:
  - contracts to oust the jurisdiction of the court
  - contracts harmful to family life
  - contracts in restraint of trade
- Contracts in restraint of trade are *prima facie* void but may enforced if they are accepted as reasonable as between the parties, and in the public interest
- Reasonableness depends on:
  - geographical extent – *Fitch v Dewes*
  - duration of the restraint – *Home Counties Dairies v Skilton*
- A party is able to protect only legitimate interests – *British Concrete v Schelff*
- A vendor restraint is more likely to be held reasonable than an employee restraint – *Nordenfelt v Maxim Nordenfelt*
- A party cannot either try to use other means to effect a restraint – *Bull v Pitney Bowes*
- Contracts illegal at common law are all for reasons of public policy and include:
  - a contract to commit a wrong – *Dann v Curzon*
  - a contract to commit a crime – *Beresford v Royal Insurance Co.*
  - a contract to defraud the Revenue – *Napier v The National Business Agency*
  - contracts aimed at corruption – *Parkinson v The College of Ambulance*
  - contracts to interfere with justice – *Harmony Shipping Co. v Davis*
  - contracts promoting immorality – *Pearce v Brooks*
- If a contract is void by statute, the effect depends on what the statute says
- If a contract is void at common law then money paid over may be recovered – *Hermann v Charlesworth* – and sometimes the offending clause can be severed to save the rest of the agreement – *Goldsoll v Goldman*
- A contract illegal as formed is unenforceable and money paid over is generally unrecoverable, though there are exceptions
- A contract legally formed but illegally performed will have remedies available to a party who is unaware of the illegality – *Marles v Trant*

Chapter 15

DISCHARGING THE CONTRACT

15.1 Discharge by performance

15.1.1 Introduction

Discharge of the contract refers to the ending of the obligations under the contract, so that where we have thought of formation being the beginning of the contract discharge is concerned with its end.

In its simplest form discharge will be the point at which all of the primary obligations created by the contract have been met. However, the situation is not always that simple or straightforward and there are times when we refer to the contract being discharged even though the obligations under the contract remain uncompleted.

The obvious example of this latter point is where the contract has been breached. Secondary obligations in this case may be substituted for the primary obligations, and a party not carrying out his/her obligations under the contract may be required to pay damages.

Where all of the obligations under the contract have been carried out this is referred to as performance of the contract. The contract is discharged, but even then the area can be complicated by one party completing some but not all of the obligations.

15.1.2 The strict rule on performance

The rule in *Cutter v Powell*

The starting point for performance of the contract, sometimes known as the 'perfect tender'

rule, is that there should be complete performance of all of the obligations under the contract. If this is the case then the contract is in effect complete and discharged.

On the other hand, it also means that where a party fails to meet all of his/her obligations the contract is not discharged and this may require the other party to be remedied.

The bare and potentially unjust simplicity of the rule can be seen in the case from which it emerges.

Cutter v Powell (1795)

Cutter was the second mate on a ship, *The Governor Parry*, sailing from Jamaica to Liverpool. The boat set sail on 2nd August and reached Liverpool on 9th October. Cutter died during the voyage on 20th September. When his wages were not paid his wife sued on a '*quantum meruit*' basis (meaning for the amount owed). Her action failed because her husband had signed on for the complete voyage. By dying he had failed to complete his contract and since it was an entire contract there was no obligation on the ship owners to pay.

An entire contract is one where all of the obligations are seen as a single transaction that cannot be broken down in any way. The case illustrates the effect of failing to perform such a contract. It also shows how it can work injustice since Cutter could hardly be said to have defaulted by dying, an event that was beyond his control.

Application of the rule

Application of the strict rule can be commonly seen in sale of goods contracts where the description applied to the contract may mean that all rather than part is essential to completion of the contract.

Arcos Ltd v E.A. Ronaasen & Son (1933)

A buyer of wooden staves (described in the contract as half an inch thick) was allowed to reject the consignment sent to him. Those delivered were a sixteenth of an inch narrower and so did not correspond to the contract description. The rule is shown for its strictness here since the staves could still be used for the purpose for which the buyer wanted them. Lord Atkin commented that 'a ton does not mean about a ton, or a yard about a yard. If a seller wants a margin he must, and in my experience does, stipulate for it'.

The strict rule has been applied even in the case of ancillary obligations such as packaging.

Re Moore & Co. v Landauer & Co. (1921)

Tinned fruit was sold described as being in cases of 30 tins. When delivered, some of the cartons contained 24 tins, although the overall total number of tins ordered was correct. The buyer intended to resell the goods so the difference would have no impact on him. Nevertheless, the Court of Appeal, applying the strict rule, held that packaging could be included in a description and that the buyer was correct in rejecting the goods and repudiating the contract.

Despite that it is of course always possible that a judge in a case may apply the maxim *de minimis non curat lex* (the law will not grant a remedy for something that is too trivial).

Reardon Smith Line Ltd v Hansen-Tangen (1976)

We have already seen in this case, using innominate terms, how the judges were not prepared to accept a repudiation of obligations where the term was a mere technicality describing the shipyard and job number.

This principle that a buyer should not be allowed to reject goods delivered when there is a slight shortfall or excess has now been incorporated in the Sale of Goods Act as s30(2A).

15.1.3 Ways of avoiding the strict rule

The potential injustice of the rule, as seen in *Cutter v Powell*, has led to judges accepting exceptions when the rule does not operate.

a) Divisible contracts

In these the contract can be seen as being made up of various parts. If each part can be discharged separately then it might also be enforced separately, and the strict rule need not apply. The rule here can be particularly appropriate for instance where there is delivery by separate instalments, except where the seller has stipulated for a single payment.

Taylor v Webb (1937)

Premises were leased to a tenant for rent. A term in the lease required the landlord to keep the premises in good repair. In the event the landlord failed to maintain the premises and the tenant then refused to pay the rent. In the landlord's action the court held that the contract had divisible obligations, to lease the premises, and to repair and maintain. The contract was thus not entire and the tenant could not legitimately refuse payment.

b) Acceptance of part-performance

Where one of the parties has performed the contract but not completely if the other side has shown willingness to accept the part performed then the strict rule will usually not apply.

Part-performance may occur where there is a shortfall on delivery of goods or where a service is not fully carried out. This exception to the rule will only apply though when the party who is the victim of the part performance has a genuine choice whether or not to accept.

Sumpter v Hedges (1898)

A builder was hired to build two houses and stables. Some of the work was done when the builder ran out of money and was unable to complete it. The landowner then had the work completed using materials left on the land. The builder was awarded the value of the materials that had been used. His argument, that part-performance had been accepted, was rejected. The landowner had no choice but to complete the work. The alternative was to leave the partly completed buildings as an eyesore on his land.

c) Substantial performance

If a party has done substantially what was required under the contract then the doctrine of substantial performance can apply. That party can then recover the amount appropriate to what has been done under the contract, providing that the contract is not an entire contract.

Dakin & Co. v Lee (1916)

Here, a builder was bound by contract to complete major repair work to a building. He did complete all of the work but some of it was carried out so carelessly that the owner of the building refused to pay on the grounds that performance was in effect incomplete. The builder was able to sue for the price of the work less an amount representing the value of the defective work.

- The price is thus often payable in such circumstances and the sum deducted represents the cost of repairing the defective workmanship.

Hoenig v Isaacs (1952)

A decorator was hired to decorate and furnish a flat for £750. He finished the work. The owner moved into the flat and paid £400 by instalments. Then, because of defects to a bookcase and a wardrobe that would cost about £55 to put right, he refused to pay the remaining £350. The Court of Appeal held that the contract was substantially performed and the balance was payable less the amount representing the defects.

- However, what is deemed to be substantial performance is a question of fact to be decided in each case. It will largely depend on what remains undone and its value in comparison to the contract as a whole.

Bolton v Mahadeva (1972)

An electrical contractor was hired to install central heating. When completed it gave off fumes and did not work properly. When payment was refused as a result, the contractor sued for the price. The Court of Appeal rejected his claim on the ground that there was not substantial performance. Part of the reasoning lay in the fact that there were £174 worth of defects in a system costing £560.

d) Prevention of performance

If the other party prevents a party from carrying out his obligations because of some act or omission then the strict rule cannot apply. In these circumstances the party trying to perform may have an action for damages.

Planche v Colburn (1831)

A publisher hired an author to write one of a series of books on a theme. When the publisher decided to abandon the whole series, the author was prevented from completing the work through no fault of his own. He was entitled to recover a fee for his wasted work.

e) Tender of performance

A similar situation with slightly different consequences occurs where a party has offered to complete his obligations but the other side has unreasonably refused performance. In such a situation the party 'tendering' performance can sue and recover under the contract. He may also consider his own obligations discharged even though there has been no performance.

Startup v Macdonald (1843)

The contract was for 10 tons of linseed oil to be delivered by the end of March. The seller delivered at 8.30 p.m. on 31st March which was a Saturday, and the buyer refused to accept delivery. The seller was able to recover damages. (The answer might be different now under the Sale of Goods Act since delivery should be at a 'reasonable hour'.)

In the case of money owed which is tendered and refused though the debtor is freed from making further offers to pay the debt will still exist.

15.1.4 Stipulations as to time of performance

Traditionally, a failure to perform on time would give only an action for damages but not to repudiate the contract.

While under the common law it was accepted that time could be 'of the essence', this principle was not generally accepted in equity, and this is now the general assumption.

There are three principal occasions when time will be considered to be 'of the essence' and a repudiation of the contract is therefore available as a remedy:
- where the parties have made an express stipulation in the contract that time is of the essence
- where the surrounding circumstances show that time of performance is critical, as would be the case with delivery of perishable goods
- where one party has already failed to perform his obligations under the contract. In this case the other party is able to confirm that unless performance is then complete within a stated period repudiation will occur.

KEY FACTS

- The strict rule on performance is that in an 'entire contract' all obligations must be performed – so there can be no payment for part-performance – *Cutter v Powell*
- There are exceptions to this strict rule:
  - if obligations are 'divisible' then payment should be made for the part performed – *Taylor v Webb*
  - where a party has accepted part performance then this should be paid for – *Sumpter v Hedges*
  - where there has been substantial performance then the full price will be paid less the sum appropriate to what has not been done – *Hoenig v Isaacs*
  - unless too much remains to be done under the contract – *Bolton v Mahadeva*
- A party can sue for damages where his performance has been prevented by the other party – *Planche v Colburn*
- And also where he has offered to perform but this has been refused – *Startup v Macdonald*
- Time of performance is 'of the essence' when (i) it says so in the contract; (ii) the circumstances make it so; (iii) one party has already failed to perform

Activity

Self-assessement questions

1 In what circumstances is a contract considered to be 'entire'?
2 How can the strict rule cause injustice?
3 What is a 'divisible contract'?
4 In what way can the *de minimis* rule be applied to performance?
5 What is the effect of a contract being only partly performed?
6 How is it possible to measure 'substantial performance'?
7 What effect does failing to perform on time have on a contract?

15.2 Discharge by agreement

15.2.1 Introduction

If a contract is formed following an agreement then it seems almost pure logic to suggest that the contract can also be ended by agreement without necessarily having been performed. Inevitably, what is required is mutuality.

There are in fact two ways in which the contract could be discharged by agreement:

- a **bilateral** discharge – here, the assumption is that both parties are to gain a fresh but different benefit from the new agreement;
- a **unilateral** discharge – the benefit is probably only to be gained by one party, who is therefore trying to convince the other party to let him/her off the obligations arising under the original agreement. Lack of consideration is an inevitable problem if one party is merely promising to release the other from existing obligations.

So possibly two problems are immediately apparent where a contract is discharged by agreement:

- absence of consideration for the fresh agreement
- the possible lack of proper form for the new agreement in the case of speciality contracts.

15.2.2 Bilateral discharges

Wholly executory arrangements

If neither side has yet performed any obligations under the contract it is possible that there is no problem at all. Each side can release the other form performance and there is consideration for the new promise in each case – not having to perform the obligations under the original agreement.

A further possibility occurs where the parties wish to continue the contractual arrangement but to substitute new terms for the old ones. In this case it is possible for the parties to 'waive' their rights under the old agreement and to substitute the new agreement.

Arrangements which are partly executory and partly executed

In this situation one of the parties wishes to give less than full performance and it is possible for the other to waive rights. However, the obvious problem with this is the absence of consideration.

Where form is an issue

Traditionally, this would have been dealt with subject to the rule in s40 Law of Property Act 1925 and the doctrine of part-performance. Now, an agreement to vary the terms in a contract requiring specific form may be invalid unless it is evidenced in writing. If a new agreement is to be substituted for an existing agreement then again this change will be unenforceable unless evidenced in writing.

15.2.3 Unilateral discharges

Where the contract is left unperformed by one party despite the willingness to contract of the other party there are a number of possible consequences.

Firstly, the party not in default might release the other from performing, but this would require a deed for validity otherwise it would fail for lack of consideration. However, as we have already seen in consideration, the principle in *Williams v Roffey Bros & Nicholls Contractors* may be sufficient to discharge the other party's obligations in circumstances where there is an extra benefit gained.

It is also possible to discharge the party in default from full performance where there is 'accord and satisfaction'. This could be as indicated in the rule in *Pinnel*, either by adding a new element which would count as consideration, or by making a smaller payment at an earlier time than the full payment is due.

Finally, by the equitable doctrine of promissory estoppel, where the party waiting for performance has agreed to waive rights under the contract, knowing that the other party is relying on this promise to forego performance, then the party making the promise may be prevented from going back on the promise.

KEY FACTS

- Since a contract can be formed by agreement then it can also be discharged without performance by agreement of both parties
- There are two types of discharge by agreement – a bilateral arrangement and a unilateral agreement – the first is where both parties wish to back out of the arrangement, the second is where in effect only one does
- Bilateral discharge is simple where the contract is executory – the waiving of rights is given by the one party in return for the waiving of rights by the other
- Where form is an issue the discharge will need evidence in writing
- Where only one party wants to back out of the contract then that party will need to give some consideration, as in accord and satisfaction, unless estoppel applies

Activity

Self-assessment questions

1 Why should parties to a contract be able to discharge their obligations by agreement without actually performing?

2 What is the difference between a bilateral discharge and a unilateral discharge?

3 In what way is form a problem in discharge by agreement?

4 When is it easiest to discharge a contract by agreement?

5 What is the easiest way of discharging a contract in a unilateral discharge?

6 What exactly is 'accord and satisfaction'?

15.3 Discharge by frustration

15.3.1 Introduction

In the strictest sense, effective discharge of a contract, as we have seen, requires performance of the obligations under the contract. Inevitably, there will be times when the requirement for strict performance will lead to injustice.

This can be particularly the case where there is a factor preventing a party or parties from performing which is beyond the control of either party to the contract. It is because of this potential injustice that the doctrine of frustration developed in the 19th century.

The original common law rule was that a party was bound to perform his/her obligations under the contract regardless of the effect of intervening events making it more difficult or even impossible to perform.

Paradine v Jane (1647)

Paradine sued Jane for rent due under a lease. Jane's defence was that he had been forced off the land by an invading army. The court held that he had a contractual duty to pay the rent due under the lease, which was not discharged by any intervening event. If he had wished to reduce his liability to take account of intervening events preventing his performance then he should have made express provision for that in the lease.

This was the strict rule and it would override any circumstances.

15.3.2 The development of a doctrine of frustration

The clear injustice of the strict rule above led inevitably on to exceptions. In the 19th century a doctrine was developed whereby a party bound by a contractual promises, in circumstances where (s)he was prevented from keeping the promise because of an unforeseeable, intervening event, would be relieved of the strict obligation. As a result, that party would not be liable for a breach of contract.

This is said to be the origin of the doctrine of frustration. The judges achieved the desired result by the fiction of implying a term into the contract.

Taylor v Caldwell (1863)

Caldwell had agreed to rent the Surrey Garden and Music Hall to Taylor for four days for a series of concerts and fêtes. Before the concerts were due to start, the music hall burnt to the ground and performance of the contract was impossible. The contract contained no stipulations as to what should happen in the event of fire. Since Taylor had spent money on advertising the concerts and other general preparations, he sued Caldwell for damages under the principle in *Paradine v Jane*. The court held, however, that the commercial purpose of the contract had ceased to exist, performance was impossible, and so both sides were excused further performance. As Blackburn J. stated:

> 'in contracts in which performance depends on the continued existence of a given person or thing, a condition is implied that the impossibility of performance arising from the perishing of the person or thing shall excuse the performance . . . that excuse is by law implied, because from the nature of the contract it is apparent that the parties contracted on the basis of the continued existence of the particular person or chattel'.

The doctrine then developed to cover those situations where the frustrating event meant that performance as envisaged in the contract was impossible.

Davis Contractors Ltd v Fareham UDC (1956)

A building firm contracted to build houses for a local council for £92,450 over a period of eight months. In fact, due to a shortage of skilled labour, the work took some 22 months to complete and the builders wanted an extra £17,651. The council paid the contract price. The builders claimed that the contract was frustrated in order to claim the extra on a *quantum meruit* basis. The House of Lords held that the contract was not in fact frustrated, but Lord Radcliffe did explain those factors that would justify the doctrine when used: 'without default of either party, a contractual obligation has become incapable of being performed because the circumstances in which performance is called for would render it a thing radically different from that which was undertaken by the contract'.

The immediate consequence of application of the doctrine then is that both parties are relieved of the burden of further performance, and of liability for not performing. This will inevitably not remove all apparent injustice since the one party to the contract is still being denied the performance of the other party through no fault of his, and may have incurred costs in anticipation of the contract being performed.

As a result operation of the doctrine is subject to a number of limitations, and parties may provide in their contracts for what happens if there are intervening frustrating events, the so-called *force majeure* clauses.

15.3.3 Frustrating events

The doctrine has developed largely out of the case law, and will operate in three main types of circumstance:
- where the intervening event makes performance impossible
- where performance of the contract becomes illegal
- where the contract becomes commercially sterilised.

Impossibility

The contract may be frustrated because of the destruction of the subject matter.

Taylor v Caldwell (1863)

Here, the destruction of the music hall was the cause of the impossibility and hence the frustration.

It may alternatively be the case that the subject matter becomes unavailable when the contract is to be performed.

Jackson v Union Marine Insurance Co. Ltd (1874)

A ship was chartered to sail from Liverpool to Newport and from there with a cargo of iron rails to San Francisco. The ship ran aground and could not be loaded for some time. The court accepted that there was an implied term that the ship should be available for loading in a reasonable time and the long delay amounted to a frustration of the contract.

Where a contract is for services the frustrating event may be the unavailability of the party who is to render the service due to illness.

Robinson v Davidson (1871)

A husband, acting as agent for his wife, a celebrated pianist, contracted for her to perform. A few hours before her performance was due she became ill and the husband contacted the claimant to inform that she would be unable to attend. When the claimant sued the court held that the contract was conditional on the woman being well enough to perform and because of her illness she was excused. The contract was frustrated.

This principle of impossibility because of unavailability may apply even where there is only a risk that the party will be unavailable.

Condor v The Baron Knights (1966)

A contract entered into by a pop music group allowed that the group should be available to perform for seven evenings a week if necessary. One member of the group became ill and was advised to rest and work fewer hours. Though he actually ignored this advice, the court still held that the contract was frustrated since it was necessary to have a stand-in musician in case he fell ill.

In fact, any good reason that will mean that a party is unavailable to perform his obligations may lead to a frustration of the contract.

Morgan v Manser (1948)

A music hall artiste was contracted to his manager for a 10-year period commencing in 1938. Between 1940 and 1946 he was in fact conscripted into the forces during the war years. His absence rendered the purpose of the contract undermined and both parties were excused performance.

An excessive but unavoidable delay in performing will often be classed as impossibility and mean that the contract is frustrated.

Pioneer Shipping Ltd v BTP Tioxide Ltd *(The Nema)* (1981)

A time charter of nine months was agreed which anticipated a possible seven voyages. In fact due to strikes at the port where the vessel was loaded this was reduced to two and the contract was held to be frustrated.

Outbreak of war is also a common frustrating event.

Metropolitan Water Board v Dick Kerr & Co. Ltd (1918)

In July 1914 a contract was formed for the construction of a reservoir and a water works. The contract allowed that the work should be completed within a six-year period. In 1916 a government order stopped the work and also requisitioned much of the plant. It was held that the contract was frustrated at the time of the government order.

Subsequent illegality

A contract may be frustrated as the result of a change in the law that makes the contract illegal to perform in the manner anticipated in the contract.

Denny, Mott & Dickson Ltd v James B. Fraser & Co. Ltd (1944)

Lord Macmillan said that a contract to import certain goods to an English port would be frustrated if the law was changed so that importing goods of that kind became illegal.

Outbreak of war is an obvious time when laws may change rapidly and cause a contract to be frustrated.

Re Shipton Anderson & Co. and Harrison Bros & Co. (1915)

A cargo of grain was sold but before it could be delivered war broke out. The government requisitioned the cargo and the contract was frustrated.

Commercial sterility

Even where the contract is not impossible to perform but the commercial purpose of the contract has disappeared as a result of the intervening event then the contract might still be held to be frustrated. This is sometimes also known as frustration of the common venture, and it is commonly claimed when an event that is fundamental to the contract does not occur.

Krell v Henry (1903)

A contract was reached for the hire of a room overlooking the procession route for the coronation of King Edward VII. There was no specific mention of the purpose of the hire in the contract. However, when the coronation did not take place because of the King's illness and the defendant refused to pay for the room, the court, applying the principle from *Taylor v Caldwell*, accepted that the contract was frustrated. Watching the coronation procession was the 'foundation of the contract'; the defendant was relieved further performance.

All commercial purpose must be destroyed, however. If any is left then the contract is not frustrated and obligations under it continue.

Herne Bay Steamboat Co. v Hutton (1903)

This was another case arising from the delayed coronation. The defendant hired a boat from which to see the review of the fleet by the King. His claim that the contract was frustrated failed. One purpose had disappeared, but it was still possible to use the boat and to see the fleet.

15.3.4 Limitations on the doctrine of frustration

Because one party to the contract is still left harmed there are a number of situations where the courts have stated that the doctrine cannot apply.

Self-induced frustration

Frustration demands that the event is beyond the control of either party so the doctrine is unavailable when the event is within the control of one party.

Maritime National Fish Ltd v Ocean Trawlers Ltd (1935)

A fishing company owned two trawlers but wished to run three and so hired one. It required a licence for each vessel but was granted licences only for two. It used its own and, in failing to pay for the hire of the other, claimed frustration. The court rejected its claim. It had chosen not to use the hired vessel rather than was prevented from doing so.

Contract more onerous to perform

There will be no release from obligations merely because the contract has become less beneficial as a result of the intervening event.

Davis Contractors Ltd v Fareham UDC (1956)

Here, merely because the builders were unable to make the same profit was not accepted as justifying declaring the contract frustrated.

Foreseeable risk

If the event claimed as frustrating the contract was in the contemplation of the parties at the time of contracting then the plea will be rejected.

Amalgamated Investment & Property Co. Ltd v John Walker & Sons Ltd (1977)

The defendants contracted to sell a building to the Investment Company who wanted it for redevelopment. Unknown to either party, the Department of the Environment then listed the building, meaning that it could not be used for development, resulting in a drop of £1.5 million from the contract price of £1.71 million. The court rejected a claim of frustration, holding that listing was a risk associated with all old buildings of which the developers should have been aware.

Provisions made in the contract for the frustrating event

If the parties have contemplated the possibility of a frustrating event and catered for that in the contract then there can be no release from obligations.

So that if a *force majeure* clause does not specifically cover the event in question frustration may still be claimed.

Absolute undertaking to perform

Where the contract contains an undertaking that performance should occur in any circumstances then a frustrating event will not affect the obligations. This was the case with the lease in *Paradine v Jane*.

Activity

Quick quiz
Which of the following involve frustrating events and which do not?

1 A famous comedian dies just before he is due to appear on stage.
2 A plumber is contracted to fit central heating in a house. He under-estimates the days needed to complete the work and as a result he will lose profit on the price agreed.
3 A car I had contracted to buy is destroyed when an explosion sets fire to it.
4 As a lecturer, I have contracted personally to take 15 students on a trip to court. An Act is passed requiring teaching and lecturing staff to take no more than 10 students per one member of staff on educational visits.
5 In a contract to supply a Far Eastern state with machinery one clause stipulates what happens in the event of war. In fact, war is declared after the making of the contract.

15.3.5 The common-law effects of frustration

The contract terminates at the point of the frustration. This means that the parties are released from their obligation to perform from that point on. Nevertheless, they would still be bound by obligations arising before the frustrating event occurred.

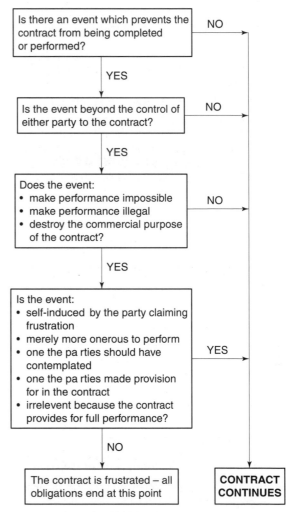

Figure 15.1 *Diagram illustrating when a contract will be considered frustrated*

Chandler v Webster (1904)

This was another case arising from the delayed coronation of Edward VII. Again, a room was hired. However, unlike in *Krell v Henry*, where the room was to be paid for on the day of the procession, in this case it was paid for in advance. Despite the frustration, there could be no recovery of the money.

This is clearly an unsatisfactory situation because it means that the effect on the parties depends entirely on what point in the contract they have reached.

The House of Lords overruled this principle in the *Fibrosa* case and modified the harshness of the rule. It held that a party could recover payments made prior to a frustrating event provided that there was a total failure of consideration. This is an improvement, but of course it still means that one party will lose out and will receive no payment for work done in advance of a contract.

15.3.6 The Law Reform (Frustrated Contracts) Act 1943

Frustration is a common law doctrine originally developed to avoid some of the harshness of existing rules. Nevertheless, as has been shown, it can produce injustice itself. As a result the Act was passed specifically to deal with the consequences of frustrating events.

The Act covers three main areas:
- recovery of money paid in advance of a contract
- recovery for work already completed under the contract
- financial reward where a valuable benefit has been conferred.

In this way s1(2) confirms the principle in the *Fibrosa* case that money already paid over is recoverable despite the apparent lack of consideration. Money due under the contract also ceases to be payable.

Under s1(2) the court also has the discretion to provide some form of reward for a party who has carried out work under the contract, thus mitigating the harshness of the rule in *Fibrosa*. The sum awarded is discretionary and is what the court believes to be fair, not what has actually been incurred in the way of expenses.

Finally, under s1(3), a party is able to recover for a partial performance which has conferred a valuable benefit on the other party. Again application of this principle is at the court's discretion.

BP Exploration Co. (Libya) Ltd v Hunt (No. 2) (1979)

Hunt had a concession to explore for oil in Libya. BP financed him in return for a half share of the concession. Its expenses would be three-eighths of the oil found till it had recovered 120% of its outlay. Oil was discovered but Libya confiscated it. While BP had already spent $87 million it was awarded $35 million by the court.

The Act's effectiveness is limited because it does not apply in some circumstances.

These include:
- contracts for the carriage of goods by sea, except time charter parties
- insurance contracts (which in any case are all about risk)
- perishing of goods under the Sale of Goods Act 1979.

Activity

Self-assessment questions

1 What exactly is a 'frustrating event'?
2 How did *Taylor v Caldwell* help to modify the harshness in the law?
3 What are the differences between 'impossibility' and 'commercial sterility'?
4 In what ways is the doctrine still unfair on at least one party?
5 Is there really a frustrating event where the frustration is self-induced?
6 How does the *Fibrosa* case modify the principle?
7 How does the Law Reform (Frustrated Contracts) Act modify the principle?

KEY FACTS

- A frustrating event is one that prevents performance of the contract but is beyond the control of either party
- The original rule on frustrating events was that a party was still bound by all obligations under the contract – *Paradine v Jane*
- A doctrine was developed in the 19th century so that in such cases obligations finished at the point of the frustrating event – *Taylor v Caldwell*
- Frustrating events include:
  - impossibility – which could be through the destruction of the subject matter (*Taylor v Caldwell*) or the unavailability of the other party (*Robinson v Davidson*) or outbreak of war (*Metropolitan Water Board v Dick Kerr & Co.*)
  - subsequent illegality – *Re Shipton Anderson & Co.*
  - commercial sterilisation – the commercial purpose in the contract is lost –*Krell v Henry*
- The courts will not recognise frustration where it is self-induced – *Maritime National Fish Ltd v Ocean Trawlers Ltd*
  - or the contract is merely more burdensome to perform – *Davis Contractors Ltd v Fareham UDC*
  - or where the risk is foreseeable – *Amalgamated Investment & Property Co. Ltd v John Walker & Sons Ltd*
  - or has been provided for *the Fibrosa case*
- The common-law principle was changed so that payments made before the frustrating event could be recovered – *Fibrosa*
- And now the Law Reform (Frustrated Contracts) Act makes more complex provision

Activity

Answering problem questions

Remember that there are four essential ingredients to answering problem questions:

- Firstly, you must be able to identify which are the key facts in the problem, the ones on which any resolution of the problem will depend.
- Secondly, you will need to identify which is the appropriate law which applies to the particular situation in the problem.
- The third task is to apply the law to the facts.
- Finally, you will need to reach conclusions of some sort. If the question asks you to 'advise', then that is what you need to do. On the other hand, if the problem says 'Discuss the legal consequences of . . .' then you know that you can be less positive in your conclusions.

Consider the following problem:

Darren and Jim are both keen ornithologists (bird watchers). Neither of them has ever seen the Lesser Spotted Scrote. The Taffwillum Wild Bird Reserve in West Wales is home to a variety of rare breeds of wild birds including the Lesser Spotted Scrote. Darren and Jim arrange to rent a cottage for a fortnight from Geraint in Llanfairfiddlybits, a village which is only two miles away from the bird reserve. The rent for the cottage is set at £200 per week and Geraint has asked for £50 in advance as a deposit, the balance to be paid on their arrival at the cottage. Darren, who has informed Geraint that they will make little use of the cottage as it is their intention to spend the whole fortnight birdwatching, pays the deposit, and has also told Geraint how much they are looking forward to seeing the Scrote. Two weeks before Darren and Jim are due to go to Wales, a forest fire spreads to the bird reserve, destroying most of the habitat and killing many birds including all of the Scrotes which are flightless birds and are therefore unable to escape the fire. Darren then informs Geraint that he and Jim will no longer be needing the cottage and asks for return of his £50 deposit. Geraint refuses and demands a further £75 which he says represents costs he has incurred in cleaning and painting the cottage in preparation for Darren's and Jim's arrival.

Advise Darren and Jim.

The facts

It is important to have a clear idea of the principal facts, particular as here where the facts appear to be quite complex and an original contract is subject to changed circumstances. The question is then whether or not it is discharged, and if so what area of discharge is appropriate and with what consequences.

The main facts seem to be:

1 Darren and Jim intend to have a holiday birdwatching, specifically to see the Lesser Spotted Scrote, a rare bird.
2 In consequence, Darren and Jim have rented a nearby cottage from Geraint.
3 They have explained that the sole purpose of hiring the cottage is the proximity to the bird reserve

and that they intend to spend all of their time birdwatching.
4 Darren pays a £50 deposit as required by Geraint – the balance is to be paid on arrival at the cottage.
5 A fire then destroys the bird reserve and kills all of the Scrotes.
6 Darren and Jim try to cancel the cottage rental and ask for return of their £50 deposit.
7 Geraint refuses and demands an extra £75 for decorating and cleaning the cottage.

The appropriate law

It is very important when answering problem questions that you use only the law that is relevant to the precise facts, if for no other reason that you are not getting any marks for using law that is irrelevant, and so you are wasting valuable writing time. By looking at the various facts we can say that the following law may be relevant in our problem here:

1 There are actually a few possible areas of law of relevance even though frustration is the central theme – breach is also possibly relevant, and to a lesser extent remoteness of damage could also be considered.
2 On frustration the first point that could be identified is the original rule in *Paradine v Jane*, demanding payment regardless of any frustrating event.
3 The doctrine of frustration was introduced in *Taylor v Caldwell* – that where the contract becomes impossible to perform through no fault of either party all obligations cease at the point of frustration.
4 There are three types of frustrating events:
   - **impossibility** – whether through the destruction of the subject matter (*Taylor v Caldwell*) or factors such as the unavailability of a party to the contract in a service contract (*Morgan v Manser*)
   - **subsequent illegality** – *Re Shipton Anderson*
   - **commercial sterilisation** of the contract – *Krell v Henry*.
5 There is no further obligation to perform – so only where payment was to be made before the date for performance will a payment be

enforceable – compare *Krell v Henry* with *Chandler v Webster.*

6 If there remains a viable purpose to the contract then the contract continues despite the frustrating event – *Herne Bay Steamboat Co. v Hutton.*

7 The doctrine will not apply, e.g. where:
- there is self-induced frustration – *Maritime National Fish Ltd. v Ocean Trawlers Ltd*
- contract merely more onerous to perform – *Davis Contractors Ltd v Fareham UDC.*

8 Common-law effects of frustration are:
- obligations cease at the point of frustration – *Taylor v Caldwell*
- money is only payable if due before the contract date – *Krell v Henry* and *Chandler v Webster*
- but a party may recover money paid over where there is a failure of consideration – *the Fibrosa case.*

9 Effects of frustration following the Law Reform (Frustrated Contracts) Act 1943:
- money already paid over is recoverable
- money due ceases to be payable
- money is recoverable for work already done under the contract
- a party can recover for any partial performance which confers a valuable benefit on the other party.

10 Repudiatory breach occurs where one party indicates to another party to the contract that he will not carry out his obligations under the contract – *Hochster v De la Tour.*

11 Damages can only be recovered for losses that are a natural consequence of the breach or which are in the contemplation of both parties at the time when the contract was made – *Hadley v Baxendale* – and the latter must be foreseeable loss – *Victoria Laundry v Newman Industries.*

Applying the law to the facts
1 The issue is whether or not the contract between Darren, Jim and Geraint is frustrated.
2 The purpose of the visit to Wales has ceased to be viable because of the destruction of the bird sanctuary and the death of all of the Scrotes.

3 The logical type of frustration would be impossibility.
4 But it is questionable whether the contract for renting the cottage is still viable – this depends on whether or not the sole purpose of hiring the cottage was to birdwatch (*Krell v Henry*) or whether any purpose remains (*Herne Bay Steamboat Co. v Hutton*).
5 Darren and Jim did point out to Geraint that their only reason for hiring the cottage was to visit the bird reserve and to se the Scrote – and also stated that they would hardly use the cottage.
6 If the contract between them is frustrated then Darren and Jim may be able to recover their deposit as there is a complete absence of frustration – *Fibrosa* and s1(2) Law Reform (Frustrated Contracts) Act 1943.
7 If not, then Darren and Jim may be in repudiatory breach – and Geraint would be able to recover for his loss of profit.
8 In respect of the £75 it is unlikely that Geraint could recover this as it is not a natural loss – nor was it specifically or impliedly in the contemplation of both parties at the time the contract was formed.

Conclusions
The law and its application have been clearly shown above. It remains to reach a conclusion and advise based on the analysis above. Just as in real life, there might not be a definite or straightforward answer. The point is to reach a logical conclusion by using the law correctly.

- Because of the pains that Darren and Jim went to explain the sole purpose of the visit it is possible that the doctrine of frustration may apply in a similar way to *Krell v Henry*.
- If this is the case then there is every chance, following the 1943 Act, that they could recover their £50 deposit.
- In any case in the circumstances it is unlikely that Geraint could claim the £75 for decorating, although if the contract is not considered to be frustrated he may claim all of his lost profit from Darren's and Jim's breach of contract in that case.

15.4 Discharge by breach

15.4.1 Introduction

Whenever a party fails to perform an obligation arising under a contract then that party can be said to be in breach of contract.

A breach of the contract can actually though occur in one of two ways:
- by failing to perform obligations – this situation itself can occur in one of two ways: either the contract is not performed at all, or the contract is not performed to the standard required under the contract, e.g. providing goods that are not of satisfactory quality
- by repudiating the contract without justification.

Breach is described as a method of discharge although this seems slightly illogical since by definition a breach means that obligations under the contract have not been discharged.

Lord Diplock explained this position in *Photo Productions Ltd v Securicor Transport Ltd.* He suggested that the terms of a contract, whether express or implied, are primary obligations. If a party fails to perform what (s)he has promised to do then this is a breach of a primary obligation which in consequence is then replaced by a secondary obligation, for instance to pay damages. So breach is not so much a discharge of the contract but a replacing of one set of obligations with a different set.

Lord Diplock also saw there being two basic exceptions to his proposition:
- The doctrine of **fundamental breach** – whereby if a breach of a term deprives the other party of substantially the benefit they were to receive under the contract then the whole contract is said to be breached. (It is unlikely of course that this doctrine has actually survived the *Securicor* cases).
- **Breach of a condition** – where the term is so central to the contract that its breach renders

the contract meaningless and thus entitles the other party to repudiate their obligations under the contract.

The significant difference between the two traditionally would have been that, while exclusion clauses would be rendered ineffective by the first, it would still be possible to successfully rely on an exclusion clause despite a breach of a condition. This is precisely what the *Securicor* cases demonstrate.

15.4.2 The different forms of breach

There are three identifiable forms of breach:

Breach of an ordinary term

Here, in effect the character of a term is unimportant. Regardless of whether it is a condition or a warranty, if a term is breached there will always be available an action for damages.

Breach of a condition

A condition can either be expressed by the parties or indeed it can be implied by law, as in the case of the implied conditions in the Sale of Goods Act. However, if it is identified as being a condition it must of course conform to the nature of a condition to attract the range of remedies associated with a condition.

Schuler (L) AG v Wickman Machine Tools Sales Ltd (1974)

Here, the claimants could not rely on the term regarding the required frequency of visits by the defendants to the motor manufacturers to repudiate their obligations. They had accepted numerous similar breaches in the past. The term obviously did not go to the root of the contract.

A breach of a condition could also in effect include a breach of an innominate term where the effect of the breach was so serious as to justify repudiation by the other party. If the doctrine has survived then it might also include a fundamental breach.

Anticipatory breach

An anticipatory breach can occur whenever one party to a contract gives notice, whether expressly or implied by conduct, that (s)he will not complete his/her obligations under the contract.

Again, this does not necessarily mean that all obligations will remain unperformed. It may of course be that the obligations will be performed but not in the manner described in the contract. An obvious example of the latter would be late performance, as in delivery of goods after the contract date.

The doctrine can probably be more correctly described as a breach by an anticipatory repudiation, as this is in effect what is usually taking place.

Hochster v De la Tour (1853)

The claimant was hired to begin work as a courier two months after the contract date. One month later, the defendants wrote to him cancelling the contract. In answer to his claim they argued that he could not sue unless he could show that on the due date he was ready to perform. The court disagreed. There was no requirement that the victim of a breach of contract should wait until the actual breach to sue.

15.4.3 The effects of breach

The consequences for the party who is the victim of a breach of contract and the remedies available will vary according to the categories of breach that we have already considered.

Breach of an ordinary term

An action for damages is always available for breach of any kind of term. If the term is only a warranty or, in the case of innominate terms the breach is not a serious one justifying repudiation, then only an action for damages is available. Any attempt to repudiate in such circumstances will itself amount to a breach of contract.

Breach of a condition

Where, on the other hand, a condition is breached or the breach is sufficiently serious the party who is the victim of the breach has more choice. (S)he may continue with the contract and sue for damages, or repudiate his/her own obligations under the contract, or indeed both repudiate and sue for damages.

Before repudiating of course a party should be certain that the term is in fact a condition entitling repudiation or the breach by the other party is so serious as to justify repudiation. Otherwise his/her own repudiation might be a breach.

Cehave NV v Bremer Handelsgesellschaft mbH (The Hansa Nord) (1976)

Here, the buyer's refusal to accept the animal feed was an unlawful repudiation. Using innominate terms it could be shown that, since they went on to buy the goods and use them for the same purpose, the effects of the breach could not have been sufficiently serious to justify repudiation.

Anticipatory breach

Here again, the party who is victim of the breach has choices available once having discovered that the contract will be breached.

(S)he might immediately consider the contract at an end and sue for damages.

Frost v Knight (1872)

At one time, a broken promise to marry was actionable. Here the defendant had promised to marry his fiancée when his father died. Before his father did die, he broke off the engagement. The claimant sued successfully for the breach of promise even though the date of the actual beach had not yet arrived since the father was still alive.

As an alternative, it is possible to continue with the contract, wait for the due date of performance and, if the contract is not performed, sue at that point.

Avery v Bowden (1855)

Bowden was contracted to load cargo onto a ship for Avery. When it was clear that Bowden would be unable to meet his obligations Avery could have sued. He waited, however, in the hope that the contract would be completed, and intending to sue if it was not completed. This actually turned out to be a mistaken strategy since the Crimean War then broke out, frustrating the contract, and Avery thus lost out.

It is always a danger for a party to take this latter course of action. The contract remains live and as a result it is always possible for the party not only to lose their remedy but also to become liable for a breach themselves.

Fercometal SARL v Mediterranean Shipping Co. SA (The Simona) (1989)

A charter party contained an 'expected readiness to load' clause, entitling the charterers to repudiate if the ship was not loaded by 9th June. The ship owners asked for an extension on 2nd June and the charterers then chartered another ship. The ship owners, instead of repudiating here for the breach by the charterers, gave notice of readiness to load instead. In fact, this was not the case and the charterers contin-

ued to use the other vessel. The ship owners' action eventually failed in the House of Lords. Since they had elected to affirm the contract they were bound by their own original terms, of which they were in breach for not being ready to load on 9th June.

It is also possible that the fact of the innocent party having the right to affirm the contract can itself cause apparent injustice to the other party.

White and Carter Ltd v McGregor (1962)

Under a contract, one party was to supply litter bins for a local council. The bins were to be paid for from advertising revenue from businesses that would have advertisements placed on the bins for a three-year period. One such business backed out of the arrangement before the bins had been prepared. The supplier of the bins nevertheless prepared the advertising and continued to use it for the whole period of the contract and then sued successfully for the full price.

Where the innocent party decides to accept the repudiatory breach of the other party then (s)he is entitled to recover for the loss of any benefits that would have resulted from performance of the contract. The party in breach cannot then try to reduce damages because of a subsequent act of the innocent party that might have the effect of reducing the overall loss.

Chiemgauer Membrand Und Zeltbau (formerly Koch Hightex GmbH) v New Millenium Experience Co. Ltd (formerly Millenium Central Ltd) (No. 2) (2001)

The claimant was given the contract to build the roof of the Millennium Dome. Under the contract the defendants could terminate provided they paid a sum of compensation identified in the contract as 'direct loss and damage'. The claimants then became insolvent. In their claim against the defendants they argued that 'direct loss' should include their loss of profits and the court, applying the first limb of *Hadley v Baxendale*, agreed. The defendants argued that the claimants would have been unable to complete the contract even without their termination and that their subsequent insolvency meant that they should not be fixed with the claimant's loss of profits. The Court of Appeal disagreed, and considered that the facts could be compared with those cases where an innocent party accepts the other party's repudiatory breach and is still entitled to all benefits arising naturally under the contract.

─ *Activity* ─

Self-assessment questions

1 In what way does a breach of contract discharge the obligations under it?
2 What are Lord Diplock's 'primary obligations' and 'secondary obligations'?
3 How limited are the remedies available to a party who has suffered a breach of warranty?
4 Why is there a difference between the remedies available for a breach of a condition and those available for a breach of a warranty?
5 What effect does breach of an innominate term have?
6 Exactly what is an anticipatory breach?
7 What possible problems are there in waiting till the actual breach when there is an anticipatory breach?

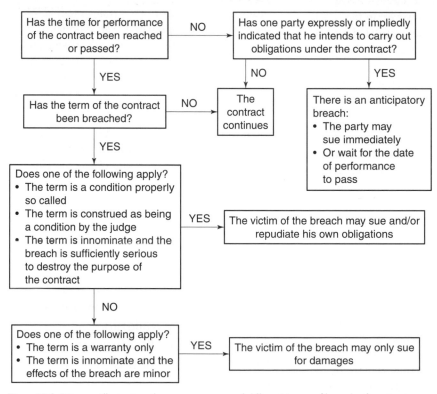

Figure 15.2 Diagram illustrating the consequences of different types of breach of contract

KEY FACTS

- A breach occurs when one party fails to perform at all, or does less than is required under the contract, or does not perform satisfactorily
- It will also be a breach where one party wrongly repudiates
- Breach of a warranty allows only an action for damages
- Breach of a condition allows for action for damages and/or repudiation, but only if the term is really a condition going to the root of the contract – *Schuler v Wickman Machine Tool Sales Ltd*
- The same choice applies where the effect of breach of an innominate term is sufficiently serious – *The Hansa Nord*
- An anticipatory breach occurs where a party makes known before performance is due that the contract will not be performed – *Hochster v De la Tour*
- The victim of an anticipatory breach has the right to treat the contract at an end and sue immediately – *Frost v Knight*
- Or to wait until performance is due and then sue for the breach – *Avery v Bowden*
- The latter course can be unfair to the party in breach – *White & Carter Ltd v McGregor*
- Waiting for the actual breach can also mean losing the remedy – *Fercometal v Mediterranean Shipping Co.*

Chapter 16

REMEDIES IN CONTRACT LAW

16.1 Limitation periods in contract law

16.1.1 The purpose of limitation periods

All actions in contract law, as in tort, are subject to limitation periods out of which an action cannot be brought. There are a variety of reasons why a claimant should be limited in the time that (s)he can wait before bringing an action for the damage suffered. Even in equity we can see the maxim 'delay defeats equity' operating so that a claimant who delays too long in bringing a claim will be prevented from succeeding. See, e.g. *Allcard v Skinner* on undue influence or *Leaf v International Galleries* on misrepresentation and common mistake as to quality.

Firstly, if there is a valid case to be fought then the claimant is to be encouraged to bring the action as soon as possible. If the evidence for the claim can be gathered, there is no purpose in delaying.

Secondly, there is the difficulty of actually preserving evidence intact if a claim is delayed for too long. Certainly the scene will be disturbed over time, forensic evidence may deteriorate, but also the memory of witnesses can only fade.

Finally, it is only fair on a defendant to bring the claim as early as possible if it is indeed actionable. Although many claims are settled out of insurance, a defendant may be damaged by the uncertainty of his/her budget when contemplating the possible costs of a successful action against him/her. This may in turn prevent the potential defendant from planning effectively for the future.

16.1.2 Basic limitation periods

The majority of contract and tort actions are subject to the same basic limitation period of six years from the date on which the action accrues. In the case of tort this is contained in s2 Limitation Act 1980: 'An action founded on tort shall not be brought after the expiration of six years from the date on which the action accrued.' In the case of contract the period is identified in s5: 'An action founded on simple contract shall not be brought after the expiration of six years from the date on which the action accrued.'

There are also a number of different periods applying in more particular instances, for instance in the case of speciality contracts, in respect of defective products under the Consumer Protection Act 1987.

16.2 The purpose of damages in contract

Damages is a sum of money paid by the defendant to the claimant once liability is established in compensation for the harm suffered by the claimant.

In the case of damages awarded for a breach of contract the purpose of the award is to compensate the claimant for the losses suffered as a result of the breach. As Baron Parke put it in *Robinson v Harman* (1848) 'the purpose is to put the victim of the breach, so far as is possible and so far as the law allows, into the same position he would have been in if the contract had not been broken but had been performed in the manner and at the time intended by the parties'. In this way damages in contract law are aimed to put the victim in the position (s)he would have enjoyed if the contract had been properly completed and performed by the defendant.

This contrasts with damages in tort where the purpose of damages is, as far as is possible to do so, to put the claimant in the position (s)he would have been in had the tort never occurred. So tort damages by contrast to contract damages represent a very artificial remedy. Inevitably there is a large measure of speculation involved in awarding damages in tort since it involves predicting what would have happened if the tort had not occurred, whereas in contract damages will represent an actual financial loss, and are rarely speculative.

16.3 The problem of remoteness of damage in contract claims

16.3.1 Introduction

There are in effect two tests used in assessing an award for an unliquidated sum of damages in contract. The first test concerns the loss in respect of which the claimant can recover. The second concerns the quantity of damages available.

The first of these two questions actually concerns causation. There must be a causal link between the defendant's breach of the contract and the damage suffered by the claimant. Moreover, there is a general principle that damages will never be awarded in respect of a loss that it is too remote a consequence of the defendant's breach.

16.3.2 Causation in fact

Causation is a question of fact in each case. The court will decide whether or not the breach is the predominant reason for the loss suffered by the claimant.

> ### London Joint Stock Bank v MacMillan (1918)
>
> A customer of a bank owes a contractual obligation not to draw cheques so that they are easily alterable. Here, a customer who did so was liable when a third party fraudulently altered the cheque, causing a loss to the bank.

If the loss arises partly from the breach and partly as the result of intervening events the party in breach may still be liable provided that the chain of causation is not broken.

> ### Stansbie v Troman (1948)
>
> A decorator was entrusted with keys to the premises in which he was contracted to work. When he left the premises unlocked a thief entered and stole property. The decorator was liable for the loss which was the result of his failure to comply with his contractual duty to secure the premises properly on leaving.

16.3.3 Remoteness of damage

The test of remoteness was originally derived by Alderson B. in the case of *Hadley v Baxendale*:

'Where the parties have made a contract which one of them has broken the damages which the other party ought to receive in respect of such breach of contract should be such as may fairly and reasonably be considered arising either naturally, i.e. according to the usual course of things, for such breach of contract itself, or such as may be reasonably supposed to have been in the contemplation of both parties at the time they made the contract as the probable result of the breach.'

Hadley v Baxendale (1854)

In the case a mill owner contracted with a carrier to deliver a crankshaft for his mill. The mill was actually not operating at the time because the existing crankshaft was broken. The carrier did not know this at the time the contract was formed. The carrier was then late with delivery. The mill owner sued unsuccessfully because the carrier was unaware of the importance of prompt delivery.

So in essence the test is in two parts: one is measured objectively according to what loss is a natural consequence of the breach, the second is subjectively based on specific knowledge of potential losses in the minds of both parties at the time the contract is formed.

The test remains to this day, although it has been modified on occasions.

Victoria Laundry Ltd v Newman Industries Ltd (1949)

Here, the defendants had been contracted to deliver a boiler to the laundry company and failed to deliver until five months after the contract date. The laundry sued for loss of its usual profits of £16 per week from the date of the breach. It succeeded since this was a natural consequence loss. It also sued in respect of lost profits of £262 per week from a government contract that it had been unable to take up without the boiler. It failed in this action since the government contract was unknown to the defendants at the time the contract was formed.

Asquith LJ made a number of vital points on the issue of remoteness:

- to give the claimant a complete indemnity for any loss suffered by the claimant no matter how remote is too harsh a test to apply
- as a result, recoverable loss should be measured against a test of reasonable foreseeability
- foreseeability of loss is itself dependent on knowledge at the time of formation

- knowledge can be of two types: common knowledge and actual knowledge enjoyed by the defendant – the two types identified in *Hadley v Baxendale*
- but knowledge can also be implied on the basis of what a reasonable man may have (rather than must have) contemplated in the circumstances.

Nevertheless the test can cause confusion and be made unnecessarily complex.

Koufos v C. Czarnikow Ltd (The Heron II) (1969)

A vessel was chartered to carry sugar to Basrah, a known sugar market. Owing to the carrier's breach, the vessel arrived nine days late during which time the price of sugar had fallen considerably. The claimant had intended to resell the sugar on its arrival in port, a fact unknown to the defendant carrier. The claimant sued for his reduction in profits following the fall in price of sugar. This was held to be too remote in the Court of Appeal. The House of Lords, however, held that the claimant could recover under the first head of *Hadley v Baxendale*, and suggested that in certain circumstances the reasonable man ought to contemplate that a particular loss was a natural consequence of a breach (although this actually seems more like implied knowledge). It was also suggested that foreseeability differed between contract and tort, although different judges gave different definitions: Lord Reid described it as 'not unlikely . . . considerably less than an even chance but nevertheless not very unusual and easily foreseeable'; Lord Morris as 'not unlikely to occur . . . liable to result'; Lord Hodson as 'liable to result'; and Lords Pearce and Upjohn as 'a real danger . . . a serious possibility'.

However, Lord Scarman has subsequently held that the test of remoteness depends not on contemplation of the level of injury but merely on proof that the loss could have been anticipated.

H. Parsons (Livestock) Ltd v Uttley Ingham (1978)

The contract was for the sale and installation of an animal feed hopper. The ventilation hatch was sealed during transit and the installers then forgot to open it. As a result, the feed became mouldy, the pigs contracted an intestinal disease and 254 died. The judge at first instance considered the loss was too remote and not within the contemplation of the defendants but this was reversed by the Court of Appeal.

16.4 Quantification of damages in contract claims

Once the tests of causation and remoteness have established that there is indeed liability for the loss claimed the court then has to determine how much the claimant can recover.

16.4.1 Nominal damages

If no loss is actually suffered but the breach has been established then it is possible for the court to award 'nominal damages'. Proof of damage has never been an essential of contract law as it is in many areas of tort.

The likely motive of the claimant in suing is to ensure that there is a declaration by the court that the contract is at an end.

Staniforth v Lyall (1830)

Lyall was under a duty to load his cargo onto the claimant's boat by a certain date. He failed and the boat owner sued for breach. He had actually hired his boat out to another party immediately following the breach and for a greater profit than he would have made. He succeeded in having the contract declared terminated and, having suffered no loss, was awarded a nominal sum.

16.4.2 The bases of assessment

There are normally said to be three bases for assessing awards of damages in contract claims.

1. Loss of a bargain

The idea here is to place the claimant in the same financial position as if the contract had been properly performed. This may represent a number of positions:

a) The difference in value between the goods or services of the quality indicated in the contract and those actually delivered where they are of inferior value. This sum can be assessed according to the diminution in value or the cost of bringing them up to the contract quality.

Bence Graphics International Ltd v Fasson UK Ltd (1996)

The defendant supplied vinyl film on which the claimant printed decals to put on bulk containers. In the claimant's contract with the container company there was an implied term that the decals would survive in a readable form for five years. In fact, they lasted only two. The claimant sued for the whole purchase price or an indemnity against its customer's claim. This was rejected at first instance, but the Court of Appeal held that the claimants could recover the actual loss.

b) The difference between the contract price and the price obtained in an 'available market' where there is either a failure to deliver the goods or services and an alternative supply has to be found, or where there is a failure to accept delivery and an alternative market has to be found.

If the claimant's ability to make a profit remains then there is no entitlement to damages.

Charter v Sullivan (1957)

Here, the defendant contracted to buy a car then refused to take delivery. Because demand for the particular model at the time easily outstripped supply there was no interference in the seller's ability to sell the car. In consequence, he recovered only nominal damages.

However, if there is no available market then the claimant can recover the full loss.

W.L. Thompson Ltd v Robinson Gunmakers Ltd (1955)

Similar facts to the last case, but here there was an excess in supply of the type of car ordered. As a result, when the buyer breached the seller could recover full damages.

c) Loss of profit
    A claimant may recover for the profit on contracts that (s)he would have been able to complete but for the breach of contract.
d) Loss of a chance
    In rare circumstances the courts have allowed a claimant to recover a loss that is entirely speculative in the circumstances, although generally in contract law a speculative loss is not recoverable.

Chaplin v Hicks (1911)

An actress had a contractual right to attend an audition. At this audition 12 actresses would be chosen out of the 50 invited to attend. When she was wrongly prevented from attending, the court awarded her £100 in compensation even though she only had a 50:12 chance of gaining work from the audition. The court stated that the mere fact that damages were difficult to calculate should not prevent her recovering.

2. Reliance loss

A claimant is entitled also to recover for expenses (s)he has been required to spend in advance of a contract that has been breached.

Such a claim will normally be made where the any loss of profit is too speculative to be able to calculate effectively.

Anglia Television Ltd v Reed (1972)

Anglia paid out a large sum of money in preparing to make a film, including paying scriptwriters, hiring production and technical staff and other necessary expenses. The actor contracted to make the film then backed out in breach of his contract and the company was forced to abandon the project, since there was no appropriate substitute. Their reliance loss was much easier to account for in the circumstances than any loss of profit.

Generally, it is not possible to claim for both loss of profit and reliance loss since it is said to be compensating twice for the same loss. However it is possible where the claim for lost profit concerns only net rather than gross profit which would include the reliance loss.

Western Web Offset Printers Ltd v Independent Media Ltd (1995)

The defendant wrongly repudiated a contract under which the claimant was to print 48 issues of a weekly newspaper. The claimant sued for £176,903, having deducted the costs of printing such as ink and paper from the contract price. The defendant argued that labour costs and other overheads amounting to £38,245 should also be deducted from the claim. The Court of Appeal held that since the claimant had no alternative work for the workforce the whole claim could be recovered.

But it may also on occasions be possible to recover damages for the loss of a valuable amenity.

Farley v Skinner (2001)

The claimant hired a surveyor before buying a house and asked the surveyor to report specifically on whether the property was affected by aircraft noise. The report stated that it would not be substantially affected by aircraft noise but this was wrong and negligent as the house was near a beacon for stacking aircraft at busy times. The claimant paid £490,000 for the house and spent £125,000 on it before moving in. When he moved in and discovered the noise he decided not to move but sued the surveyor for damages for loss of amenity. The House of Lords held that for loss of amenity to succeed, it was not essential for the contract to be one the object of which was to provide pleasure, relaxation etc. The claimant did not forfeit his right to non-pecuniary damages by not moving and was awarded £10,000.

3. Restitution

This is simply a repayment to the claimant of any money or other benefits passed to the defendant in advance of the contract that has been breached.

Restitution is a massive area of law in its own right and full explanations are only to be found in books dealing specifically with the subject.

Inevitably restitution in contract law has to do with consideration and the presence or absence of consideration may determine the appropriateness of the remedy.

Stocznia Gdanska SA v Latvian Shipping Co. (1998)

Here a shipyard entered into a contract under which it was bound to both design and build a ship for the buyers. The shipyard later rescinded the contract before any ownership in the goods had passed to the buyers. The buyers claimed for return of an installment of the contract price on the basis that there was a failure of consideration. The shipyard successfully resisted this claim. The House of Lords held that the true test of whether there was a failure of consideration was not based on whether the buyer had received nothing under the contract but on whether the seller had done nothing under the contract.

16.4.3 The duty to mitigate

There is a clear principle of English law that the party injured by a breach of contract must take reasonable steps to minimise the effects of the breach, known as the duty to mitigate. The principle is as appropriate to tort as it is to contract law, and a failure to mitigate may be taken into account in awarding damages.

British Westinghouse Electric and Manufacturing Co. Ltd v Underground Electric Railways Co. of London Ltd (1912)

In a contract for the supply of turbines the goods delivered did not match the specifications in the contract. As a result, the buyers had to replace them with turbines bought from another supplier. In the event these turbines were so efficient that they soon paid for the difference in price. As a result, this could not be claimed for but losses sustained before the originals were replaced were recoverable. Lord Haldane LC said that a claimant has 'the duty of taking all reasonable steps to mitigate the loss consequent on the breach [which] debars him from claiming in respect of any part of the damage which is due to his neglect to take such steps.'

However, a claimant is not bound to go to extraordinary lengths to mitigate the loss, only to do what is reasonable in the circumstances.

Pilkington v Wood (1953)

As the result of a solicitor's negligence the claimant bought a house with defective title, and was thus unable to take up residence for some time, and incurred the extra costs of hotel bills and travelling to and from his old house. The solicitor's argument, that the claimant could instead have brought his action against the vendor and thus mitigated the loss in his action against the solicitor, was rejected.

Similarly, in the case of an anticipatory breach, the claimant is not bound to sue immediately (s)he knows of the possibility of the breach.

White and Carter v McGregor (1962)

A firm had contracted to buy advertising space on litter bins to be fitted by the claimants to lamp posts. When it backed out in breach of its agreement the claimants continued to produce the bins. The argument, that the claimants might have mitigated the loss by not continuing to fit the bins, failed.

16.5 Other common-law remedies in contract law

16.5.1 Liquidated damages

A sum of liquidated damages may be available where the parties have fixed the amount in the contract that will be available in the event of a breach. However, the courts will accept this sum and deny the victim of the breach a claim for an unliquidated sum only where the sum identified in the contract represents an accurate and proper assessment of loss. If it is not then this is seen as a 'penalty' and will be unenforceable.

Any clause providing for a greater sum than the actual loss is prima facie void.

Bridge v Campbell Discount Co. (1962)

A depreciation clause in a hire purchase agreement for a car bore no relation to actual depreciation in value. The clause was declared void as a penalty.

The courts have developed rules for determining the difference between genuine liquidated damages and a penalty.

Dunlop Pneumatic Tyre Co v New Garage and Motor Co. (1914)

Under its contract with Dunlop the garage was bound to pay £5 in respect of breaches such as selling under the recommended price. In this case the House of Lords accepted that the sum represented a genuine assessment so was not a penalty. Lord Dunedin's test included a number of points:

- an extravagant sum will always be a penalty
- payment of a large sum for a failure to settle a small debt is probably a penalty
- a single sum operating in respect of a variety of different breaches is likely to be a penalty
- the wording used by the parties is not necessarily conclusive
- it is no bar to recovering a liquidated sum that actual assessment of the loss was impossible before the contract.

16.5.2 *Quantum meruit*

This is merely recovery of an unqualified sum in respect of services already rendered, and we have seen its operation in relation to part-performance.

There are three common circumstances in which such an award is made:

a) where there is a contract for services that is silent on the issue of remuneration

Upton RDC v Powell (1942)

Where a retained fireman provided services with no fixed agreement as to wages the court awarded a reasonable sum in the circumstances.

b) where the circumstances of the case show that a fresh agreement can be implied in place of the original one

Steven v Bromley (1919)

Steven had agreed to carry steel at a specified rate. The steel when delivered to Steven contained extra goods and thus Steven was able to claim extra for carrying them.

c) where a party has elected to consider the contract discharged by the other's breach or where a party has been prevented form performing by the other party, in either case they might claim for work they have already done.

De Barnady v Harding (1853)

A principal wrongly revoked his agent's authority to act on his behalf. The agent was then entitled to claim for the work he had already done and for expenses incurred.

16.6 The effect of speculation in contract

As has already been said, the purpose of awarding damages in contract and tort varies. Where in contract the compensation is financially to recreate the situation that would have been but for the breach of contract, in tort, damages are to put the claimant in the position (s)he would have been in had the tort not occurred. On this basis, in tort damages are frequently of a speculative nature, in other words an attempt to assess what the claimant's position would have been if (s)he had not been wronged by the defendant. This is known as general damages, and a major feature of tort claims, for instance in personal injury, is in calculating future losses.

In contract law, on the other hand, we have already seen that the courts have been careful to avoid granting damages of a speculative nature since damages in contract are awarded in respect of a specific loss. Of course, there have been rare exceptions such as that in *Chaplin v Hicks* (1911) where damages were awarded for the loss of a chance in an audition.

The courts have always been careful to separate contract and tort. This is seen in the reluctance of judges to allow a remedy for a pure economic loss in negligence, which they see as being more appropriate to principles of contract law. They have been equally careful in traditionally avoiding allowing recovery in contract law for a claim seen as being more appropriate to principles in tort.

Addis v The Gramophone Company (1909)

The claimant was wrongly dismissed from his post as manager and replaced even before he left. The House of Lords refused his claim for damages for injury to his reputation and the mental distress caused by the humiliating manner of his dismissal, the proper place for this according to Lord Atkin being the tort of defamation. He recovered only for the loss of salary and commission owed.

However, an exceptional group of cases has developed a principle in contract law in recent times allowing damages of a highly speculative nature in relation to mental distress. The cases are generally known as the 'holiday cases'.

The principle was first accepted in relation to a spoiled holiday.

Jarvis v Swan Tours Ltd (1973)

The claimant contracted for a Tyrolean holiday, advertised as a 'house party'. In fact, he was on his own for the second week, and the holiday was inferior to most aspects advertised in the brochure. The judge at first instance awarded him £31.72 for the difference between the quality of the holiday as described and the actual holiday. However, the Court of Appeal upheld his claim for disappointment and mental distress and awarded him damages of £125.

The courts had actually previously created an exception to the rule in *Addis*.

Cook v Spanish Holidays (1960)

Travel agents failed in their contractual duty when a honeymoon couple were left without a room on their wedding night and they were awarded damages for loss of enjoyment.

The principle has been extended, effectively as an exception to the doctrine of privity where the claimant has recovered not only for his own mental distress but that of his family also in *Jackson v Horizon Holidays* (1975).

The reason for allowing the claims is that in holiday contracts 'the provision of comfort, pleasure and "peace of mind" was a central feature of the contract'.

The principle also appears to have been extended to include certain problems caused by solicitors.

Heywood v Wellers (1976)

The claimant was awarded damages for mental distress where her solicitors, in breach of their contractual obligations, failed to obtain an injunction to prevent her former boyfriend from molesting her.

More recently damages for 'loss of amenity' have been allowed where the sole purpose of the con-

tract was for 'the provision of a pleasurable amenity'.

Ruxley Electronics and Construction Ltd v Forsyth; Laddingford Enclosures Ltd v Forsyth (1995)

A swimming pool was built six inches shallower than stated in the contract. Since this might prevent the purchaser from safely enjoying the pleasure of diving into the pool, damages were awarded.

Nevertheless, the courts are still reluctant to allow the principle to develop too far or to extend into purely commercial territory. In *Hayes v James and Charles Dodd* (1990) Staughten LJ stated that recovery for mental distress should not include 'any case where the object of the contract was not pleasure or comfort or the relief of discomfort, but simply carrying on a commercial contract with a view to profit'. Similarly, the court in *Woodar Investment Development Ltd v Wimpey Construction UK Ltd* (1980) suggested that the principle should be restricted to the holiday cases.

Activity

Self-assessment questions
1 What is a court trying to achieve when it makes an award of damages in contract law?
2 When will it be possible to recover damages even though the injured party has suffered no loss?
3 How does a court decide whether the defendant's breach of contract caused the actual damage suffered?
4 What are the basic differences between the judgments in *Hadley v Baxendale* and *Victoria Laundry v Newman Industries*?
5 In what ways is the judgment in *The Heron* not a sensible one?

6 Why was the case rejected in *Parsons v Utley Ingham*?

7 How does the 'available market' rule affect an award of damages?

8 When is reliance loss awarded rather than loss of a bargain?

9 Is it possible to recover both?

10 What effect does an anticipatory breach have on an award of damages?

11 What restrictions exist in the case of recovering damages for mental distress?

12 In what ways is a penalty different to liquidated damages?

16.7 Equitable remedies in contract law

Equitable remedies are available in both contract and tort, although equity is much more closely associated with contract law. The whole purpose of equitable remedies is that they should operate where an award of damages is an inadequate remedy and justice is not served.

On that basis there are a number of different remedies available to the court, particularly in contract law, which more adequately reflect the need of the claimant. Equitable remedies are at the discretion of the court, unlike an award of damages, which is an automatic consequence of liability being established. Because the remedies are discretionary they are awarded subject to compliance with the various 'maxims of equity' such as 'he who comes to equity must come with clean hands'.

16.7.1 Injunctions in contract law

Again, in contract law injunctions are rarely mandatory and are usually then negative restric-

tions on the defendant. Again, injunctions may be either final or interlocutory.

There are three common instances where an injunction is claimed in respect of contracts:

a) To enforce a contract in restraint of trade.

Such contractual clauses are *prima facie* void, and so an injunction will only be granted if the restraint is reasonable as between the parties and in the public interest, and only if they protect a legitimate interest.

Fitch v Dewes (1921)

Here, a lifelong restraint on a solicitor's clerk from taking up the same employment in a seven-mile radius of Tamworth Town Hall was held to be reasonable.

Fellowes v Fisher (1976)

Here, a five-year restraint on a conveyancing clerk from taking similar employment in Walthamstow was held to be unreasonable by Lord Denning since the clerk was relatively unknown in a densely populated area.

b) To enforce a provision protecting legitimate trade secrets or specialist information.

Faccenda Chicken v Fowler (1986)

The injunction was sought to prevent competition by a former employee who had devised a sales system of fresh chickens from refrigerated vans. The action was unsuccessful because the termination was reasonable and there was no express provision in the contract.

c) To encourage compliance with a contract of personal service.

Since this appears similar to a mandatory injunction it will only be awarded where there is an express negative restriction in the contract and will not be awarded where it amounts in effect to a mandatory award.

Page One Records v Britton (1968)

'The Troggs', a sixties pop group, were tied by contract, indefinitely, to their manager under extremely unfavourable conditions. When they became disillusioned and found a new manager the old manager tried to enforce the contract but failed.

Similarly, it will be unavailable where the clause is unreasonably wide and would prevent the other party from earning a living.

Lumley v Wagner (1852)

An opera singer had a contract with an express stipulation that during its three months' currency she would not take up work with any other theatre. When she did so she was successfully restrained. Bearing in mind the duration of the contract, it in no way interfered with her general ability to earn a living.

16.7.2 Rescission in contract law

This is particularly common in both misrepresentation and mistake and is an order of the court returning the parties to their original pre-contract position. As a result it is only available where to do that is actually possible.

Restitutio in integrum must apply for a successful claim for rescission of a contract. That is it must be possible to return to the actual pre-contract position without the subject matter of the contract having been substantially altered in any way.

Clarke v Dickson (1858)

Clarke was persuaded to buy shares in a partnership as a result of misrepresentations made to him. Later the partnership became a limited company. When it failed Clarke then discov-

ered the misrepresentation. He was unable to rescind because the nature of the shares had changed from partnership shares to company shares. The judge gave the example of a butcher who buys live cattle, slaughters them and then wishes to rescind. It would be impossible.

Other important requirements for rescission include that the party seeking rescission must not have already affirmed the contract

Long v Lloyd (1958)

A lorry was bought which proved defective. The purchaser lost the right to rescind after allowing the seller twice to make repairs to the lorry. He had thus affirmed the contract.

Also that (s)he has not delayed too long in seeking the remedy, as was the case in *Leaf v International Galleries* (1950) where the remedy was lost because the claimant waited five years.

Finally, that no third parties have subsequently gained rights over the subject matter, as occurred in *Oakes v Turquand* (1867).

16.7.3 Specific performance in contract law

This is an order of the court for the party in default to carry out his/her obligations under the contract. It is rarely granted because of the difficulty of overseeing it.

Ryan v Mutual Tontine Westminster Chambers Association (1893)

Under a tenancy agreement the landlord was obliged to provide a hall porter to take care of the common areas. The person employed failed to do the work properly. An order for specific performance was refused because the court could not supervise the work.

This contrasts with *Posner v Scott-Lewis* (1987) which again involves an obligation to provide a hall porter. The court could award the remedy here where the landlord had merely failed to employ one.

Such an order is only usually granted then in the case of transfers of land or where the subject matter of the contract is unique in some way so that it could not be replaced in an 'available market' and an award of damages is thus inadequate. An example would be a valuable work of art, as in *Falcke v Gray* (1859). So it will never be able for instance in a contract of service – *De Francesco v Barnum* (1890), where it was denied in the case of a breach of a contract of apprenticeship.

Since the remedy is discretionary under equity it will not be awarded where the claimant's actions in seeking the order are unconscionable, as would be the case with all equitable remedies.

Webster v Cecil (1861)

The claimant was trying to enforce a written document for the sale and purchase of land that he knew contained an inaccurate statement of price. Since there was evidence to show what the actual price should be his action failed and the document of sale was rectified to accurately reflect the price actually agreed.

16.7.4 Rectification of documents in contract law

This is an order of the court to rectify a mistake in a written contract. Again the remedy is discretionary and will only be granted where the actual agreement and it is unconscionable to allow the existing written document to stand.

Craddock Bros Ltd v Hunt (1923)

Craddock agreed to sell his house to Hunt, not intending an adjoining yard to be included in the sale. By mistake, the yard was included in the conveyance so Craddock immediately sought rectification of the document and succeeded.

Activity

Self-assessment questions

1 What are the common features of property that can be the subject of an order for specific performance?
2 In what circumstances will an order for specific performance be denied?
3 Why are the courts reluctant to award mandatory injunctions?
4 When, if ever, is an injunction possible in a contract of employment?
5 In rescission, why is the rule relating to *restitutio in integrum* necessary?
6 What other bars to rescission are there?
7 What has gone wrong when rectification of a document is ordered?

Chapter 17

CONSUMER PROTECTION

17.1 General

'Consumer protection' is a general term and covers not only areas of contract law but of tort also. Product liability under the principle in *Donoghue v Stevenson* is as important to the consumer as are the Sale of Goods Act 1979 and the Supply of Goods and Services Act 1982.

Of course, while the consumer can use both contract and tort in his action the remedies are likely to be different and this has to be borne in mind when choosing which action to bring.

Contract actions under the two Acts are better for the person who has purchased goods or services because they are in effect strict liability and the full range of loss can be recovered. However, they do depend on being a party to the contract and for other parties a tort action may be the only way.

Besides providing civil law remedies, consumer protection is achieved through the **criminal** law, through Acts that provide criminal sanctions, mainly through fines. Trading Standards officers generally police these and keep a watch on unscrupulous traders and tradesmen. Two specific Acts which deal with product safety and misleading descriptions applied to goods respectively are the Consumer Protection Act 1987 and the Trade Descriptions Act 1968.

It is interesting to note, finally, the important impact that EU law has had on the whole area of consumer protection, as we have already seen in other chapters.

17.2 Sale of goods and supply of goods and services

The most significant aspect of both the Sale of Goods Act 1979 and the Supply of Goods and Services Act 1982 is the implied terms that they insert into any contract covered by each Act respectively. These terms are already covered in detail in Chapter 8 as well as in Chapter 9 on exclusion clauses.

Another important feature of the Sale of Goods Act 1979 is the rules relating to the passing of property.

Goods can be specific or unascertained. If they are unascertained, meaning, e.g. that they have yet to come into existence or the exact portion of a larger consignment is yet to be identified, then property (ownership) in the goods does not pass to the buyer. Any loss is still the responsibility of the seller.

In the case of specific goods, property (and the risk of loss) generally passes when the parties decide that it should.

Under s18 there are also some specific rules as to when property passes:
- rule 1 – where goods are in a deliverable state, property passes when the contract is made
- rule 2 – where the seller is bound to do something to the goods to put them in a deliverable state then property passes when it has been done
- rule 3 – is similar to rule 2 but applies where the seller must weigh, measure or test in order to ascertain the price – property will not pass until this is done
- rule 4 – concerns goods sold on sale or return (approval) – property only passes on acceptance by the buyer

One important point to make about the Supply of Goods and Services Act 1982 is that its provisions apply also to contracts for the hire of goods.

There is also some very specific additional legislation which applies to contracts for goods or services.

The Package Travel, Package Holidays and Package Tours Regulations 1992 create liability on the part of sellers or organisers of package holidays. They must ensure that the holidaymaker is not subjected to any misleading information and are responsible for the proper performance of the contract even though they are not the actual suppliers. As such, they supplement rights under the Contracts (Rights of Third Parties) Act 1999 and the common-law protection in *Jackson v Horizon Holidays* in respect of third-party rights.

The Unsolicited Goods and Services Act 1971 was introduced to protect consumers against aggressive selling techniques. Where goods are sent to a person who has not requested them, if they then send written notice that they are unwanted, if they are not collected within 30 days they can be claimed free.

17.3 The Consumer Protection Act 1987

The Consumer Protection Act was the UK's response to the EC Directive on Product Liability Directive 85/374 that required the harmonisation of law of member states on the issue of product liability.

The Act is both criminal and civil in content, and in its regulatory sense has since been supplemented by the Product Safety Regulations 1994 (which again is a response to EC law). It is at least arguable that the criminal sanctions under the Act provide ultimately a more effective control of defective products than common law product liability.

The civil liability in the Act is contained in s2(1): 'where any damage is caused wholly or partly by a defect in a product, every person to whom subsection (2) applies shall be liable for the damage'.

Those who can be sued

Potential defendants under the Act are listed in s2(2) :

- **Producers** – these are defined in s1(2) and include:
  - the manufacturer – who can be the manufacturer of the final product, but also manufacturers and assemblers of component parts, and also producers of raw materials
  - a person who 'wins' or 'abstracts' products – e.g. someone who extracts minerals from the ground
  - a person carrying out an industrial or other process which adds to the essential characteristic of the product – e.g. freezing vegetables.
- **Importers, suppliers and 'own-branders'** are also defined in s2(2), and can be liable to the consumer in certain circumstances:
  - importers – under s2(2)(c) will include anybody who in the course of a business imports a product from outside of the EU
  - suppliers – these are obviously retailers or equivalent persons – ordinarily they will be liable only in contract law – but under s2(3), where it is impossible to identify either a 'producer' or an importer, the supplier can be liable if the consumer has asked the supplier to identify the producer, within a reasonable time of the damage suffered, because it is impractical for the consumer to identify the producer, and the supplier has failed to identify or refuses to identify the producer (this means businesses must keep records of their suppliers)
  - own-branders – under s2(2)(b) would be, e.g., supermarket chains who, while not producers, effectively hold themselves out as producers by declaring a product to be their own brand – they must indicate that someone else is producing the goods for them in order to avoid liability under the Act.

So, three important points can be made:
- any person in the chain of manufacture and distribution is potentially liable
- liability is both 'joint and several' – meaning that the consumer can sue the person with the most money or best insurance cover
- and liability is 'strict' – meaning that fault need not be proved.

Products covered by the Act

'Product' is defined in s2(1) as 'any goods or electricity and (subject to subsection (3)) includes a product which is comprised in another product, whether by virtue of being a component part, raw material or otherwise'.

'Goods' are defined in s45(1) as 'substances, growing crops, and things comprised in land by virtue of being attached to it and any ship, aircraft or vehicle'.

A number of things are specifically **exempted** from the scope of the Act:
- buildings – because they are immovable – though building materials are included
- nuclear power
- agricultural produce which has not undergone an industrial process – the problem here is in defining what is an industrial process, e.g. would butchery be in the light of the BSE and CJD problems?

Defects covered by the Act

'Defect' is defined in s3(1) as 'if the safety of the product is not such as persons generally are entitled to expect, taking into account all the circumstances'.

The courts can take into account a number of circumstances in defining safety:
- the manner in which and purposes for which the product has been marketed, its get-up, the use of any mark in relation to the product and any instructions for, or warnings with respect

to, doing or refraining from doing anything in relation to the product
- what might reasonably be expected to be done with or in relation to the product
- the time when the product was supplied by its producer to another.

Market can be important, e.g. toys and children. But the use of warnings can be, too. In that case, the way that a consumer uses products can relieve liability, e.g. fireworks not to be used indoors.

Defects in production or design, which render the product unsafe, will result in liability under the Act. However, the consumer may cause the damage by improper use, e.g. drying wet pets in microwaves.

Another important factor is time, because knowledge is always increasing – so the question is: once knowledge has changed, should a producer recall all products sold however long ago in the past?

Damage to which the Act applies

The Act covers death, personal injury, and loss or damage to property caused by unsafe products.

Some limitations are placed on this:
- no damages will be given in respect of small property damage under £275 – a consumer here would need to use basic contract law instead
- no damages will be awarded in respect of business property – so the property must have been intended for private use, occupation or consumption
- no damages are recoverable for loss or damage to the defective product itself.

Limitation

The claimant must begin proceedings within three years of becoming aware of the defect, the damage or the identity of the defendant, or If the damage is latent the date of knowledge of the plaintiff provided that is within the 10-year period.

The court has discretion to override the three-year period in the case of personal injury.

In all cases there is an absolute cut-off point for claims of 10 years from the date that the product was supplied.

Defences

All defences are contained in s4 of the Act.

They include:
- that the product complies with statutory or EU obligations – and so the defect was an inevitable consequence of complying with that requirement, e.g. a chemical required to be in a product by law which then turns out to be dangerous
- the defect did not exist at the time it was supplied by the defendant – this might include, e.g., animal rights campaigners 'doctoring' baby food, but also the case where the defect arises in the subsequent product but not in the component
- the product was not supplied in the course of a business
- where the defendant can show that it was not him/her who actually supplied the product
- where the state of technical or scientific knowledge at the relevant time was not such that the defendant could be expected to have discovered the defect – *Roe v Minister of Health* (1954) (precedes the Act but makes the same point) – this is highly controversial and out of step with many other EU countries, which follow the Directive's wording of when the product was put into circulation.

Some criticisms of the Act

The Act was a step forward in a few ways:
- it has put producers on their guard, and knowledge of the need for appropriate checking and quality control

- as a result, there is a greater likelihood of product recall
- it also allows the consumer more chance of an action because (s)he has a greater range of potential defendants to choose from.

However, the Act has shortcomings also:
- it does not apply to all products, nor to all defects, nor to all damage
- the limitation period is very strict
- the Act in any case does not apply to products supplied before 1988
- there are probably too many defences, making it difficult for a claimant to succeed
- causation is still a requirement and the standard of care is very similar to negligence, making it too similar to negligence and not enough like the strict liability it is supposed to be.

Activity

Self-assessment questions
1 Why was contract law inadequate on its own to deal with consumer problems?
2 What was the purpose in passing the Consumer Protection Act?
3 Which consumers does it protect?
4 How does a civil action under the Act differ from one in tort?
5 What injustices could arise from the fact that agricultural products not undergoing an industrial process are not covered in the Act?
6 How does the defence of state of technical or scientific knowledge cause problems for the consumer?

Activity

Problem solving

Consider the following:

Derek buys a pocket electronic calculator, an electric paint stripper, and a speaking teddy bear from Cheapbits electrical goods discount warehouse. The calculator is manufactured by Supelec plc, an English company. The paint stripper is from Taiwan but has no manufacturer's address. Supelec's manager bought it for cash in a consignment of 100 from a travelling salesman. The teddy bear has no identified producer and is in sealed packaging marked 'Supelec Talking Ted'.

Derek gives the calculator to his nephew Trevor as a birthday present. Trevor uses it in an exam. The calculator fails to perform certain mathematical functions properly, as a result of which Trevor fails his exam.

Derek's wife, Wendy, uses the paint stripper to dry her hair and it burns her scalp very badly.

Derek's little daughter, Natalie, is given the bear. The talking mechanism fails after only a few days. Derek intends to return it to Cheapbits but is busy at work. Natalie takes the bear to bed with her every night. She develops a bad asthma condition and dies in an attack. A year later, scientists discover a connection between artificial fur and asthma.

Decide whether any party has a right to sue for compensation under the Consumer Protection Act 1987.

17.4 The Trade Descriptions Act 1968 and applying false descriptions to goods or services

Introduction

The Act was created to deal with false statements made in a business context. The mere fact that the seller is a trader is insufficient on its own. The transaction in question must be one that is a regular occurrence in that particular business.

The Act produces criminal liability for making false ands misleading statements and any action would usually be by Trading Standards in the Magistrates' Court.

It therefore complements civil law actions in contract law for misrepresentation or for breach of the implied term relating to description under s13 Sale of Goods Act. The Act applies both to goods and services

False description of goods

By s1(1):

'Any person who, in the course of a trade or business:

a) *applies a false trade description to any goods; or*

b) *supplies or offers to supply any goods to which a false trade description is applied;*

shall, subject to the provisions of this Act, be guilty of an offence.'

S1(1)(a) would apply where the seller has personally made the false description.

S1(1)(b) would apply where the seller is offering goods to which a false description has been applied by another person e.g. a label in a garment.

By s2 a trade description is any direct or indirect indication relating to:
a) quantity, size, gauge
b) method of manufacture, production, processing, recondition
c) composition
d) fitness for purpose, strength, performance, behaviour, accuracy
e) any other physical characteristics
f) testing by any person and the results of such tests
g) approval by anyone or conformity with a type of approval
h) place or date of manufacture, production, processing or reconditioning
i) the person who manufactured, produced, processed, or reconditioned
j) any other history, including previous ownership.

A number of further points can be made:
- the false trade description may be applied verbally, in writing, pictorially or even by conduct
- to be an offence under the Act the false trade description must be false or misleading to a material degree
- an offence under s1 may be committed by any person not just the seller
- a person may be guilty under s1(1)(b) even if he does not know that the description is false, provided that he knows that the description has been applied to the goods by another person
- under s23 a person who is not in the course of a trade or business may still be convicted if it was because of his default or omission that the false description was applied to the goods.

False statements concerning provision of services, accommodation or facilities

By s14(1):

'It shall be an offence for any person in the course of any trade or business:

a) to make statements which he knows to be false; or

b) recklessly to make statements which he knows to be false; as to any of the following matters:

(i) *the provision of any services, accommodation or facilities;*

(ii) *the nature of any services, accommodation or facilities;*

(iii) *the time at which, the manner in which or persons by whom any services, accommodation or facilities are provided;*

(iv) *the examination, approval or evaluation by any person of any services accommodation or facilities;*

(v) *the location or amenities of any accommodation.'*

For a conviction the prosecution must show that the defendant actually knew the statement was false at the time he made it or was reckless whether it was true or not.

The statement must actually be false at the time it is made – it is not sufficient that it becomes false at a later stage

Defences

By s24 a defence is available if the defendant can show both:

a) that the commission of the offence was due to a mistake or to reliance on information supplied to him or to the act or default of another person, an accident or some other cause beyond his control; and

b) that he took all reasonable precautions and exercised all due diligence to avoid the commission of such an offence by himself or any other person under his control.

Under s25 a defence is also available for, e.g. newspapers that merely innocently publish a misleading advertisement.

Where a dealer is unsure as to the accuracy of descriptions applied by other people he may apply a notice of disclaimer for the accuracy of the trade description provided that the disclaimer is 'as bold, precise and compelling as the trade description itself'. This will then provide an effective defence

Activity

Self-assessment questions

1 What is a false description?
2 To what range of descriptions does the Act apply?
3 How is the Act administered?
4 To whom can the Act be applied?
5 Does the Act cover services as well as goods?
6 In what circumstances is a trader entitled to a defence under the Act?

Activity

Multiple choice question
Consider which of the following answers applies to the scenario below:

Electrical Retailers make and supply an Astral Telescope described in all materials as being capable of '455x magnification'. In fact, evidence shows that actual useful magnification amounts to at most 120x, although scientifically the telescope is capable of 455 magnification but of blurred images only.

1 The retailers can be charged under s14 Trade Descriptions Act 1968.
2 The retailers can be charged successfully under s1(1)(b) Trade Descriptions Act 1968.
3 The retailers can be charged successfully under s1(1)(a) Trade Descriptions Act 1968.
4 The retailers can be charged under s1(1)(a) Trade Descriptions Act 1968 but have a defence under s24(b).

Chapter 18

THE SYNOPTIC ELEMENT

18.1 The nature and purpose of synoptic assessment

The synoptic element on A Level Law papers was introduced with Curriculum 2000 for first possible sitting in January 2002. In fact, initially it was intended that the synoptic element should only be sat as the final A Level examination, as a result of which effective first assessment should have been in June 2002. However, QCA subsequently relaxed the rules and it can now be taken at either sitting in the A2 year.

The synoptic element was an inclusion to all A Levels insisted upon by the Dearing Report which preceded Curriculum 2000.

The general principle behind it is that candidates should be assessed in a form that demonstrates both a good overall understanding of the different components of their course, i.e. the legal system, as well as the substantive area studied, and also of the ways in which the individual components connect or affect each other. So it is a general overview of the course.

Candidates choosing criminal law as an option on A2 would be expected to show an understanding of the way that the criminal law operates within the legal system. The individual examination boards chose different styles of papers for the synoptic element, mirroring the different emphases in their individual specifications.

AQA chose a model of synoptic assessment, mirroring interest previously shown in abstract conceptual aspects of law such as justice, principles of fault, morality etc., illustrated by use of contract law examples (or other substantive law areas chosen as a course of study in Units 4 and 5).

OCR chose a narrower focus, basing its synoptic assessment on a previously selected theme for both legal system and substantive law elements. The theme for legal system is common for all substantive law options. A specific theme for each option is then illustrative of the central legal system theme. Building on the style of the existing Sources of Law paper, candidates also have the support of pre-released resource materials in the exam.

WJEC chose a modular structure based on style of assessment rather than on content. For the synoptic element, a model of assessment based on a single compulsory synoptic question drawn from the AS content and an Option content was chosen.

18.2 OCR synoptic element

OCR Law examiners who prepared the draft specification for Curriculum 2000 chose to base the synoptic element, termed the 'Special Study', on a theme, and on use of pre-released source materials, building on use of source materials in Sources of Law.

Each theme lasts for two years or four papers.

The original theme, which lasted through the original sample materials and the January and June 2002 papers and the January 2003 papers, is 'The Law Commission and Law Reform'. Each option then has its own specific theme to go with the central theme. In the case of Contract Law this included both elements of consideration and privity of contract.

From June 2003 until January 2005, inclusive, the theme will be precedent and the development of law. *The theme specific to the Contract Law option is consideration, but only adequacy and sufficiency, past consideration, and performance of existing duties.*

Centres are provided with booklets of source materials with which candidates can familiarise themselves during the course of their A2 year. Teachers also will be able to use the materials and the past papers to prepare candidates for the style of exam.

Candidates cannot take their original copy into the exam, but have the benefit of a clean copy of these materials in the exam room at the time of sitting the paper.

These materials are available from OCR and are usually on its website also. They include extracts from judgments of leading cases, extracts from articles in legal journals, and extracts from better-quality text books. The questions are designed to draw on material found in these sources.

Each paper has four questions, and these are of distinct types:

Question 1
This is always a discussion of the area of the central theme (up to and including January 2003 – The Law Commission; from June 2003 – precedent).

Questions are likely to be based on the first source in the Special Study materials, but answers should include illustration from substantive law.

Question 2
This is always a question about a case that appears in the source materials, e.g. in June 2002, for the Contract Law option, the theme was based on both consideration and privity, with the case being *Jackson v Horizon Holidays.*

With the new theme of specific aspects of consideration the materials include reference to cases such as *Thomas v Thomas, Chappell v Nestlé, Lampleigh v Braithwaite, Williams v Roffey, Stilk v Myrick, Pao On v Lau Yiu Long, Glassbrook Bros v Glamorgan CC*, and with less detail *Roscorla v Thomas, Re McArdle, Shadwell v Shadwell, Scotson v Pegg*, and *New Zealand Shipping v Satterthwaite (The Eurymedon)*. Inevitably, on any paper Question 2 will be taken from one of these cases.

Questions will ask candidates to discuss the case in the light of the overall theme of precedent. So they may demand an understanding of how the case changed or developed the law, whether the case has restricted the law, whether the case remedies or produces injustice etc.

Question 3
This is always the major discussion question about the substantive law theme (up to and including January 2003 – consideration and privity; from June 2003 – specific aspects of consideration).

Discussions under the previous theme focused on areas such as the effects of the Contracts (Rights of Third Parties) Act and criticisms of the rules on adequacy and sufficiency.

It is easy to see areas of discussion that could be asked for in relation to the new theme. There is obvious disparity between *Williams v Roffey* and *Stilk v Myrick*. Definitions of adequacy and sufficiency are strained, and past consideration and its exceptions is an odd rule.

Question 4
Always involves pure application of the area of law in the theme. This can come in the form of a small problem or as three individual scenarios. In either case, what

is required is application of the principles of law appropriate to the problem. It is not the same as answering traditional problems on Paper 1 or Paper 2 of the options.

These four types of questions have specific demands in what is required in the exam:

Question 1
- Will always require a discussion – and may well be based on a quote from the first source.
- Candidates should be encouraged to use the source materials and illustrate by reference to them.
- Better candidates will also be supplementing information offered them in the materials by showing a wider knowledge and understanding.
- In any discussion question a balanced debate, and one that answers the question set produces the best marks.

Question 2
- Always requires a response to a case actually to be found in the materials.
- So merely reciting the facts of the case is insufficient – it requires some critical awareness of the significance of the case to the theme.
- In relation to the Law Commission theme, what was required was inevitably to do with how the case contributed to reform of the law.
- In relation to the precedent theme from June 2003, what is required is reference back to the precedent context in which the question will be set.

Question 3
- Always requires a discussion about the substantive area – but candidates should not forget the overall theme of precedent and the development of law.

- Again, the source material will be relevant and should be used.
- The question will ask for a criticism of some aspect of consideration.
- Or may refer to a quote from a source from either an article or a judgment and then require comment on the quote.

Question 4
- This always calls for pure application of law to be found in the source materials.
- Again, it is the understanding of the principles through application that is important rather than regurgitating facts.
- Candidates have already scored high marks on this question by employing the skills learned on the sources of law paper.

Below are examples of these types of questions taken from past papers or from the specimen paper submitted to QCA. They refer to the previous Law Commission/consideration, privity theme, but the style of question could be applied to the precedent/consideration theme to get an idea of what is required:

Example question 1:
Discuss the extent to which the creation of the Law Commission in the Law Commissions Act 1965 has shifted the emphasis 'from reliance on judicial law-making to reliance on legislation to reform the law'. [January 2002]

Example question 2:
Consider the effect of the judgment in the case of *Jackson v Horizon Holidays* on the principles of both consideration and privity of contract. [June 2002]

Example question 3:
What criticisms can be made of judicial developments in the rule that 'consideration need not be adequate but it must be sufficient'? [January 2002]

Example question 4:

Consider whether or not good consideration will be found in the following three transactions so that the agreements involved are enforceable:

1) Martin's car has broken down and he must get from Birmingham to an important interview in London. He asks Pat to give him a lift there. She does so. After they have returned from London, Martin says that he is so grateful that he will pay her £500.

2) Lynda, a teacher, is due to present an A Level law revision conference for 400 pupils organised by Stella, the principal at the college where Lynda works. When two more centres totalling another 75 pupils book to attend the conference Stella offers to pay Lynda an extra £100. However, she never does so.

3) Kath is under contract to type a 50,000-word manuscript for Elaine for £500. When this money is due, Elaine explains to Kath that she is unable to pay the full £500 but asks if she can pay £300 and give Kath a box of ink cartridges worth £100. Kath agrees. [January 2002]

18.3 AQA synoptic element

For the synoptic unit, candidates sitting AQA Unit 6: Concepts of Law are expected to use material in illustration of their answers from anywhere in the other five units.

In order to demonstrate a synthesis of their understanding of legal processes and institutions as well as the substantive areas of law studied, candidates are asked to answer questions on a number of conceptual areas.

These concepts of law are:
- the law and morals
- the law and justice
- the balancing of conflicting interests
- the principle of fault
- judicial creativity.

Even a very brief examination of these broad headings can hint at fairly obvious areas of interest in a study of contract law:

- contract law involves moral judgments even if less so than in crime
- contract inevitably seeks justice for the victim by the provision of compensation
- contract law is all about balancing competing interests of the two parties to the contract and even third parties
- fault is a means of identifying liability for a breach of contract
- judges say that they only declare the law, not make it. However, the part played by 'policy' in the development of much contract law seems to suggest that judges can be quite creative.

In answering questions on these concepts, candidates will need to demonstrate understanding of the concepts themselves:

In the case of law and morality:

- Questions here will involve exploring the distinction between the two, e.g. that morals depend on voluntary codes while legal rules are enforceable in the courts; that morality can have a social context and develops over time, where legal rules can be introduced instantly without reference to popular views, that things included in a moral code do not always appear in legal rules, and that some things that are accepted in law may still offend some people's sense of morality, e.g. abortion.
- It will inevitably involve exploring the Hart/Devlin debate, i.e. between the views that morality is a private concept and that the law should not intervene in a person's private morality, and the view that judges have an

inherent right to protect the public from moral lapses.

- Some context will be introduced to illustrate whether law and morals do coincide. In the case of contracts declared illegal by common law they include contracts for immoral purposes (*Pearce v Brooks*) or corruption in public office (*Parkinson v College of Ambulance*).

In the case of law and justice:

- Questions will involve some discussion of individual theories of justice and explanations of the theories of natural lawyers, positivists, the utilitarian theories of Bentham and John Stuart Mill, as well as Marxist theorists, could all be explored.
- Problems that surface here obviously include the fact that what is just for society as a whole may be unjust to the individual and *vice versa*.
- The fact that unjust laws are possible can also be considered, e.g. the privity rule, the number of judicial exceptions and the eventual move to legislate.
- Ways of achieving justice should also be considered, e.g. the development of controls on exclusion clauses for the protection of consumers.

In the case of balancing conflicting interests:

- Again, questions here will focus on the extent to which individual rights can be protected as against the interests of the state or indeed competing interests.
- Contract law, in essence, should be seeking to remedy the party whose contractual rights have been infringed.
- However, the use of commercial arbitration is an indication of the law and the parties reaching compromises.
- A good example of balancing competing interests is the rules on minors' contracts where the minor is protected against unscrupulous businessmen who would take advantage of them (*De Francesco v Barnum*) but the person dealing with a minor is also protected against their

unjust enrichment (s3(1) Minors' Contracts Act 1987).

In the case of the principle of liability based on fault:

- Questions here would demand an understanding of fault, i.e. that liability should depend on culpability and responsibility.
- Fault appears in contract law mainly through the principle of remoteness of damage in deciding whether to award damages – *Hadley v Baxendale.*
- But fault is also an issue in contracts resulting from fraudulent misrepresentation – even though this is in effect an action in the tort of deceit.

In the case of judicial creativity:

- Questions will inevitably involve an explanation of the restrictions on judicial creativity, i.e. Parliament is the supreme law-maker, judges adhere to a declaratory theory of law, a rigid doctrine of precedent.
- Means of avoiding this would also be considered, e.g. any flexibility within the doctrine of precedent including the Practice Statement 1966, the impact that judges can have on legislation through statutory interpretation, and processes like judicial review.
- In illustration reference could be made to the fact that contract law is still in the main a common law area – major areas such as consideration and mistake having no statutory intervention.

Example question 1:

Discuss the meaning of 'justice'. Consider the extent to which justice is achieved in the application of legal rules. Relate your answer to examples drawn from civil law, criminal law or both.

Example question 2:

Discuss the relationship between law and morals. Consider how far the law seeks to uphold and promote moral values.

[Both June 2002]

INDEX